COUNSELLING SUPERVISION

Titles in the *Counsellor Trainer and Supervisor* series

COUNSELLING SUPERVISION

THEORY, SKILLS AND PRACTICE

Michael Carroll

SAGE Publications
Los Angeles • London • New Delhi • Singapore

© Michael Carroll 1996

First published 1996
Reprinted 1996, 1998, 2001, 2003

Reprinted by Sage Publications in 2004, 2006, 2007 (twice)

SAGE Publications Ltd
1 Oliver's Yard
55 City Road
London EC1Y 1SP

SAGE Publications Inc
2455 Teller Road
Thousand Oaks, California 91320

SAGE Publications India Pvt Ltd.
B1/I 1 Mohan Cooperative Industrial Area
Mathura Road, New Delhi 110 044
India

SAGE Publications Asia-Pacific Pte Ltd
33 Pekin Street #02-01
Far East Square
Singapore 048763

British Library Cataloguing in Publication data
A catalogue record for this book is available from the British Library

ISBN: 978-1-4129-0210-6 (pbk)

Library of Congress catalog record available

Typeset by York House Typographic Ltd.
Printed and bound in Great Britain by
Athenaeum Press Ltd., Gateshead, Tyne & Wear

Contents

Acknowledgements

I would like to thank Pat Grant, Francesca Inskipp, Brigid Proctor and Margaret Thorlstrup for reading and commenting on chapters in this book: their feedback was extremely helpful. Elizabeth Mann read the first draft of the full book and her comments and editorial assistance on the content raised the quality of the book immensely. Windy Dryden (the series editor) and Naomi Roth at Cassells gave very valuable assistance throughout.

Over the last few years I have had the joy of meeting and working with a number of supervisors (researchers and practitioners) from the USA. Their generosity has been impressive and I cannot begin to measure the debt I owe them. In particular I want to mention Mary and Puncky Heppner, Elizabeth Holloway and Bruce Wampold. Not only had I access to vast stores of knowledge and wisdom but I discovered friendships that have become very dear to me and will remain long after my interest in supervision has waned.

I would also like to thank Roehampton Institute, London, for its generosity in granting me study leave during which this book was written. Without this time the book would not have seen the light of day.

And finally, to Cathy, to whom I dedicate this book. This is only a very small token to thank you for the riches you have brought to our relationship. Without you the book would have been completed, but I would have been so much the less.

Foreword

I first trained as a counsellor in 1975. Since that time interest in counselling in Britain has mushroomed. For example, membership of the British Association for Counselling (BAC) continues to grow and training courses in counselling are cropping up everywhere. Fortunately, this growth in the development of counselling in Britain has been paralleled by an increasing concern that counsellors need to be properly trained and their work professionally supervised. The Counsellor Trainer and Supervisor series is designed to reflect this developing interest in the training and supervision of counsellors. It is the first series in Britain devoted to these two important and related professional activities and seeks to provide a forum for leading counsellor trainers and supervisors to share their experience with their novice and experienced colleagues.

Together with continuing professional education, supervision is the major way that trained counsellors ensure that they are providing their clients with an effective professional service. On training courses, supervision is the place where trainees' attempts to marry theory and skills with their clients can be monitored. Thus counselling supervision occupies a central place in counsellors' professional growth and development.

Michael Carroll has carried out doctoral-level research on the supervision of counsellors and has brought his knowledge of the research literature to this volume. The result is a book that integrates practical ways to approach counselling supervision with a scholarly consideration of the relevant issues.

Windy Dryden

Preface

At the very least, one comes away from this material with a sense of
humility about the complexity, subtlety, and depth of human
relationships. One is struck by the multifaced nature of what on the
surface seems to be a simple and even limited relationship. Having
discovered this order of complexity in a seemingly limited relationship,
one wonders about the complexities that must infuse other human
affairs. (Doehrman, 1976, p. 82)

Two individuals sit in a room, talking. An ordinary counselling
session. They are not alone. Pathways trampled by hundreds of other
people move through the counselling room. The air buzzes with
unseen voices.

Some are subtle entrances – invited and uninvited guests. Some
break in, some intrude, some are dragged in. By both. And their
presence affects the talking pair. The counselling room is filled with
people, from the past, and from the present, with the embryos of those
born to the future.

Two individuals face one another. Each has her own history, his
own family, a past/present/and future, ways of thinking, feeling and
behaving. Each perceives life differently.

Two individuals relate to one another. Their relationship creates the
space between them. What kind of relationship is it? How does it
affect them as a couple? As individuals?

And this room where two individuals relate to one another is part of
a larger environment. Someone owns the room. How do the room and
the context influence the relationship and the individuals?

And who will talk to whom about what when the counselling talk is
over? Will the client share with another, a talk about a talk? Maybe the
'talk about a talk' will result in the client not returning, or two
returning.

And the counsellor? The counsellor will talk to another, the
supervisor. How will the client be presented, or re-presented? How
will the counsellor bring self, and the relationship, into the supervision

room? Another room, peopled with even more people, all of whom share in some way in the lives of the counselling room. Another talk about a talk, another room within a room.

Maybe tapes will be used to present the counselling talk, or notes.

Maybe a report. Will these truly portray the relationship and the individuals? Will they distort, intrude upon, invigorate, trivialize?

And will 'the talk about a talk' influence the counselling talk when the couple next meet? Even more people in the counselling room. Supervisors will join the throng and bring their significant people with them.

And a simple chat turns out to be a complicated set of pathways (like motorway crossovers) where two unique individuals meet, where they bring their lives and their people, where they are influenced by the context, from where they move out to their own lives bringing their counselling relationship, and to which they will return for the next conversation.

Is it any wonder that supervision is complicated and complex?

Books, chapters, and journal articles abound on aspects of the above scenes covering personality, communications, social psychology, family life, developmental psychology, counselling psychology. Each area is a major field of study in its own right.

This book will 'zone-in' on one of the people to whom the counsellor talks after the counselling session – the supervisor – and review the processes involved in the interpersonal interaction between supervisor and supervisee. It will concentrate on the talking session that focuses on the counselling session, which we call supervision, for supervision is a conversation about a conversation, supervisor/supervisee talking about supervisee/client. By pinpointing one point on a line, or one segment of the whole, we lose perspective. We can de-contextualize, with the result that supervision could take on a life of its own rather than be seen as part of the human relationship process. It can be magnified out of proportion to its neighbouring factors. Or it can be isolated so that the whole process becomes a series of interactions rather than a single journey.

We are dealing with a complex interpersonal transaction that is part of a communication process involving clients, counsellors and supervisors in a network of intertwining relationships. That is supervision.

Introduction

Psychotherapy supervisors serve as the keepers of the faith, and the mentors of the young. Theirs is a quiet profession that combines the discipline of science with the aesthetic creativity of art. They teach, inspire, cajole, and shape their students toward their own standard of professional excellence. It is a curious paradox that at their best they are the least visible. (Alonso, 1985, p. 3)

My interest in counselling supervision began in the late 1970s when, two years after finishing my counselling training, I was asked to supervise the client work of a couples and family therapist. Flattered by a request, which in my view placed me firmly amongst the ranks of the experienced counselling fraternity, I moved eagerly to engage in the work, and discovered that I was supervising as I had been supervised, not very well. In my experience supervision had been haphazard, leaving the initiative up to me and, when supervision did take place, it did so in a laissez-faire manner, the supervisor insisting I was doing fine and would only need him when emergencies arose. There was no time spent on contracting, no attempt to look at my learning objectives, no ability on the part of the supervisor to adapt teaching methods to my learning needs. Reports consisted of a few scrawled lines (when absolutely needed). Supervision was viewed as a legal requirement that both of us 'got through' with a minimum of suffering on both parts. As I look back I realize my appointed supervisor did not have supervision high on his agenda and I did not know enough to ask for what I needed. We colluded, he to get away with as little supervision as possible, me not to face too rigorous an evaluation and to pass my counselling placement without much difficulty. What a pity we both missed such a valuable opportunity for learning.

My first excursions into being a supervisor made me realize how much I had missed. Counselling training and experience were not enough on their own. I needed an underlying philosophy of supervision, a model to guide me, structures to inform the supervisory work and formats that made supervision interventions sensible and systematic rather than accidental.

There was little to read on counselling supervision in the late 1970s and early 1980s, and what was there was almost entirely within the psychoanalytic tradition. Several questions emerged for me:

- What exactly is supervision? What are its purposes, its functions and its tasks/roles?
- What knowledge and skills do I need to be a good supervisor?
- What is the difference between counselling and supervision?
- What will my supervisees and I focus on during our supervisory time together?
- Is it possible to work out a training curriculum for counselling supervisors?

My interest in supervision led me to do a short project on it for a training in Adult Learning, and for the first time I realized that supervision was more solidly an educational activity than it was a counselling one. I knew then that experienced counsellors are not automatically good supervisors, though good supervisors will probably need to be good counsellors. Different skills are needed for two quite different activities. It was at this same time that a question emerged for me that has fascinated me since. It has been articulated well by Hess (1987a, p. 251): 'Is psychotherapy supervision a domain that calls for a theoretical understanding in its own right, or is it sufficient to adopt theories from psychotherapy, tinkering with a concept here or a process there, in order to elucidate the dynamics of supervision?' My experience has encouraged me to think that 'a theoretical understanding in its own right' is appropriate, though I think we are some way from being able to formulate this.

My research interests continued and in 1988 I formulated a proposal for an M.Phil/Ph.D. in Psychology on counselling supervision.

My first research goal was to get 'inside' supervision, to see how it helped the supervisee, and consequently helped the supervisee work with clients, and finally how it helped clients. I wanted to tape client sessions and the following supervision session over an extended period of time to consider the impact of supervision on client work. For a number of reasons I found it impossible to set up such a project. My interest next focused on the supervisory relationship and what effect it had on counselling work, and indeed on both parties to that relationship. I read the literature on supervision. A new surge of interesting reports, articles and books had emerged on different aspects of counselling supervision. Again, I was disappointed in my ability to investigate the supervisory relationship without having to fragment it. Furthermore, I had been involved in my first training in counselling supervision, with time to reflect on what it meant, on how I involved myself as a supervisor with supervisees, and for the first time began to look at counselling supervision models.

My lack of knowledge gave way to confusion: I was suddenly aware that there was a lot of counselling supervision material around without co-ordinating factors, with few strands to link models, approaches and/or roles. And hence my next interest: are there generic tasks involved in supervision? There is no doubt that this question was linked to my work in counselling psychology, since by this stage I was director of an M.Sc. in Psychological Counselling, and beginning to investigate common factors across counselling orientations. Was it possible that there might be common factors (in this case tasks) across supervision models? If there were, and these could be researched, the results would make for a firm foundation for training in counselling supervision. After all, theorists like Rogers had begun this way, looking for the necessary and sufficient conditions needed for personality change. Not that my aim was so grandiose – it was simply to isolate the supervisory tasks (with research evidence) and formulate them into training packages.

I re-read the literature (especially on the social role models of supervision which clearly outlined the tasks), and slowly, as from the mists, an impression began to form. I isolated five tasks in which supervisors involved themselves with supervisees, then there were six, and suddenly seven. It seemed to stop there. I called these tasks 'generic' to indicate that they were summative tasks, foundation tasks to which other sub-tasks related. They were tasks (behaviours) that pertained across supervisory models and, if the developmental models of supervision had contributions to make, then these tasks would probably change as supervisees became more experienced. Chapter 4 presents findings on these generic tasks from interviews with BAC-accredited supervisors.

This book is a result of that journey. In writing it I have become aware that supervision is much more complex than I at first imagined. I have also moved to seeing it as more separate from counselling theories and models than I had originally expected. I have been surprised by the amount of interesting material around on counselling supervision, which only began to come to the surface when I started excavations. The first International Conference on Counselling Supervision (held in London in 1990) indicated that while most of the models and research in supervision come from the USA, there is much training in and practice of supervision in Britain. This book has been written at an exciting time for counselling supervision in both the United States and in Britain, when attempts are being made to co-ordinate the material available into understandable units before new models are created.

Above all, my interest and reading in supervision has taught me that supervisors, like counsellors, are mostly made, not born. This book is about the 'making' of supervisors, and the 'making' of supervisees. My hope is that it will be of assistance to a number of people. First of all it is aimed at those who see themselves as supervisors or who are beginning their journey towards becoming supervisors, to supervise either trainee or qualified counsellors. The main focus of the book is on the supervision of counsellors in training. Since supervision is largely an 'inherited role' and one for which most supervisors have no training, this book is aimed to help them understand what supervision is, and how to set up supervisory arrangements. Though not primarily a 'training manual', it will provide working knowledge of supervision and will isolate the purposes, functions and tasks of supervision in a clear and systematic way. It will offer a model for understanding supervision.

Second, the book, being based on the up-to-date literature on supervision (both research and models), will help those who are already experienced supervisors but who have not kept up to date with reading or training. It represents an attempt to move individuals away from counselling-bound models of supervision (i.e. in which supervision is closely allied to the counselling orientation of the supervisor) to developmental and social role models of supervision (which start with the learning situation of the supervisee). It could be used by experienced supervisors as a way of monitoring their work and as a help in updating their knowledge.

And third, although not primarily written for supervisees, it can be of help to them. Supervision has been recognized as an essential ingredient of counselling training and ongoing counselling support. However, there is little to help the supervisee understand what supervision is about, how to use it most effectively, how to find a supervisor who will be of best service, and how to prepare for and utilize supervision time. There is some evidence that even after two years of being supervised regularly supervisees are still uncertain about what to expect from supervision (Carroll, 1995a). This book may help them articulate their supervisory needs and put them in a stronger position when they go in search of a supervisor who will negotiate with them.

Above all, the book is a series of 'frameworks' for use by both supervisors and supervisees, little models that can help at different times. I like frameworks, and collect them. They help me make sense of realities in a visual way. And I find, in supervision, that I offer lots of frameworks: supervisees seem to find them helpful too.

Chapter 1 is a brief overview of the history of supervision and its importance in initial and ongoing counselling training. Of particular interest in this chapter is the up-to-date review of the British and American literature on counselling supervision. Chapter 2, an exciting chapter to write, tries to bring together contemporary themes and debates within supervision. Chapter 3 presents my own linear model of supervision, connecting goals, functions and tasks, and makes a brief comparison of this model with two others. Chapter 4 presents the seven tasks of supervision and moves through each of them individually. I chose to do this through the presentation of the results of my interviews with BAC-recognized supervisors. The richness of this material, and its aliveness, speaks for itself. After a brief introduction to each task, the interviewees' material is presented, by theme, in brief quotations. Chapter 5 provides the second model in the book, that of managing the supervisory process. Here I offer a five-stage chronology of the steps through which a supervisory relationship travels. Several frameworks are referenced without evaluation. One of the pioneering aspects of this chapter is its section on terminating supervision, about which little has been published. Chapter 6 offers insights into another little discussed area: the supervision of counsellors employed by organizations. Chapter 7 moves through a number of supervisory formats (individual, group, peer, team), evaluating the strengths and weaknesses of each. It does the same for modes of presentation within supervision. Chapter 8 is not just the customary chapter on 'ethics' in supervision but is an attempt to offer a model of ethical decision-making applicable to both counselling and supervision. It reviews, in some detail, the various responsibilities of supervisors. Finally, the Appendix includes the revised *BAC Code of Ethics and Practice for Supervisors of Counsellors* (1995).

ONE

Understanding supervision

Supervision provides an opportunity for the student to capture the essence of the psychotherapeutic process as it is articulated and modeled by the supervisor, and to recreate it in the counseling relationship. (Holloway, 1992)

Supervision is that part of the overall training of mental health professionals that deals with modifying their actual in-therapy behaviours. (Lambert, 1980)

WHAT IS SUPERVISION?

The word 'supervision' has many meanings. In common usage it means 'to oversee' with connotations of authority and line-management. Generally, this is not how it is seen within counselling supervision. Still, there is no agreed definition. Some authors have played with the word 'supervision' and given valuable insights into understanding how it works within counselling training. Houston (1990) talks about SUPER-vision while Inskipp and Proctor (1993) use the word EXTRA-vision to identify what supervisors bring to the supervisory process. Hawkins and Shohet (1989) have applied the Winnicottian notions of 'good-enough' and 'play' to explain how supervisors and supervisees can be co-creators of a learning atmosphere which emphasizes new ways of thinking and learning. On the other hand, Crowley (1984) has suggested abandoning the word 'supervision' totally because of the superhuman qualities demanded of supervisors and has offered substitute words such as consultancy as more benign representatives of what actually happens. Zinkin (1989), in a refreshing paper entitled, 'Supervision: the impossible profession', uses the word 'torment' to describe supervisory happenings and argues that if we, as supervisors, think we are supervising what *actually happens* between clients and counsellors, we are deluding ourselves. He too dislikes the 'super' part of supervision which gives the impression that supervisors monitor supervisees from a superior position.

Besides different understandings of the actual term 'supervision', there are a number of controversies within supervision which make it difficult to arrive at a common definition. There is still some disagreement on how far, if ever, counselling should be part of supervision and where the interface between the two begins and ends. We are still some way from agreement in how far formal evaluation 'ought to be' an essential element in supervision, with some seeing it as destroying the supervisory relationship and others refusing to acknowledge supervision that makes no formal judgements on the effectiveness of trainees. A modern struggle within supervision tries to wean it away from counselling and create a profession of supervision in its own right. Opponents of this view refuse to allow clear water to appear between the two professions and argue that coherence in counselling orientation between supervisors and supervisees is the best basis for learning within supervision. To date there is little common ground on the development of the supervisory process: some apply it equally to trainees and experienced practitioners, others demand different terms to clarify roles within each relationship. How far should organizational aspects of counselling be allowed to intrude into supervision? Should formal teaching be part of supervision? What modes of presentation (process notes, audio-tapes, verbal reports) should characterize effective supervision, and how far have supervisors the right to demand counselling tapes as requirements for supervision?

These are a few of the complexities that surround supervision and make it difficult to conceptualize and define. My aim is to look at these, and other controversial areas, not because final definitions are possible, but to enable us to continue the discussions, face the dilemmas and work towards an understanding of supervision in which at least we all talk the same language.

In general, supervision can be viewed as either training supervision or consultative supervision. Training supervision is part of the ongoing educational training of a student into one of the helping professions, e.g. social work, counselling, clinical psychology, psychiatry. This book will concentrate almost exclusively on training supervision. Consultative super-vision, on the other hand, is an arrangement between two qualified person-nel where one offers to help the other reflect on a case or cases (Brown, 1985; Ekstein and Wallerstein, 1972; Gallessich, 1982, 1985). The latter is generally characterized by mutuality, less formal evaluation, and more of an ad hoc nature than training supervision. To date, very little has been written specifically for consultative supervisors.

For the moment, despite the many reservations about it, it appears we are stuck with the term 'supervision'. Rather than opt for a definitive definition and align with one aspect of supervision, I take counselling supervision, as outlined in the literature, to include:

a) a student who is training in counselling/psychotherapy/counselling psychology and is a member of an organized training course;

b) a supervisor who is an experienced counsellor/psychotherapist/counselling psychologist and who, hopefully, has had some training in becoming a supervisor; and

c) an arrangement whereby they meet, either as a dyad, or with other supervisees, to review and reflect on the therapeutic work of the trainee/s.

The main purposes of this relationship are the professional development of the supervisee and the welfare of the client.

Supervision seems to me to be a combination of different elements – goals, functions, tasks, roles, strategies, foci, process elements, personalities, beginnings, middles and endings – and this book will attempt a model that connects these different aspects. The working definition above contains a number of assumptions and hypotheses that will be dealt with more fully throughout the book (and stated rather bluntly below). They arise from my experiences of being supervised and of supervising, from my reading of the supervision literature, and from the exciting exchanges that have taken place on the training courses, conferences, workshops on supervision of which I have been a part.

1. Supervision is now an essential requirement of counsellor training and no longer an optional extra.
2. Supervision is a formal, professional relationship between supervisee and supervisor.
3. The purposes of supervision are the professional development of supervisees and the welfare of clients.
4. Supervision is not counselling or psychotherapy.
5. Supervision is primarily an educational process focused on the learning of the supervisee.
6. Good counsellors do not necessarily make good supervisors.
7. Supervisors require training in supervision.
8. Supervision is moving towards being a profession in its own right.
9. Supervisors enable supervisees find *their* way of being counsellors.
10. Evaluation (formal and informal) is a crucial part of supervision.
11. Contracting and negotiating in supervision is essential.
12. The roles and responsibilities of supervisors and supervisees ought to be clear to all participants in supervision.
13. Bad/poor supervision exists.
14. There are a number of forms of supervision; all have strengths and weaknesses.

15. The relationship in supervision is made up of a number of roles, not one, and good supervisors are able to provide a multiplicity of roles with supervisees.
16. Issues of gender, race/culture, and power play large parts in supervision and need to be addressed.
17. Supervision is a life-long commitment for individuals seeing clients for counselling.
18. Ideally, supervisors should have a forum where they can discuss their supervision.
19. Supervisors and supervisees ought to be aware of the ethical codes for supervision.
20. Supervisees have a right to expect help in taking on the role of supervisee, and be assisted in preparing for supervision.
21. Supervision works best when both parties in supervision are allowed the choice to work together and supervisees are not always best served by being assigned to a supervisor, either individually or in groups.
22. The learning process in supervision emerges from the counselling work of supervisees. Supervision is not about formal teaching, skills training in counselling, learning ethical codes, dealing with personal issues, that are unconnected to the work being done with clients.

SUPERVISION FORMS, STYLES, MODELS

Given the extent and range of supervision models, relationships and styles, as well as the difficulties in generating workable definitions, there is little wonder that confusion is generated – principally confusion over the purposes of supervision and in the lack of agreed meaning of terminology within supervision. The impact of this confusion results in supervisees being unclear about the meaning of supervision and how best to use it (Inskipp and Proctor, 1993; Proctor, 1986). Clarification and agreement on terms, recognition of common tasks and roles, and agreed-upon procedures within supervision would go a long way in helping both supervisors and supervisees prepare for supervision. It would facilitate training supervisors, and would help inter-professionally where supervisors interact with other professionals and/or amongst themselves.

Whereas there is a richness and variety within supervision with its many models, there is a paucity of research to show whether there are common elements within these models, how models compare with one another, and whether or not different contexts demand different supervisory approaches. Furthermore, there is no current research to show how transferable are the conclusions of supervisory research, and whether the supervisory models developed within the USA are applicable to other countries. My own research (Carroll, 1994c), while not specifically set up to gauge this transfer, indicates that some caution needs to be exercised when we take conclusions from the research in the USA and apply them to Britain.

Supervision is a complex process encompassing not only various styles and models but also a variety of forms. The list below shows the rich, though not always apparent, variety in these forms of supervision, i.e., the setting which determines the relationship between supervisor and supervisee:

- *managerial* (Falvey, 1987), where counselling supervisors are also line managers to supervisees;
- *administrative* (Falvey, 1987), in which supervisors are responsible for leadership;
- *training* (Hess, 1980), where supervisees are part of training courses in counselling;
- *groupwork* (Houston, 1985, 1990), where supervision is focused on supervisees' work with groups;
- *consultative* (Gallessich, 1985), in which supervisees are qualified counsellors;
- *non-managerial* (McKay, 1986), in which supervisors have no managerial responsibilities for supervisees;
- *self-supervision* (Bernstein, Hofmann and Wade, 1986; Casement, 1985; Langs, 1980; Meyer, 1978; Yager and Park, 1986), in which supervisees monitor their own work;
- *organizational* (Hawkins and Shohet, 1989), during which the focus is on the organization rather than the individual client;
- *individual* (Hess, 1980), which is an arrangement between one supervisor and one supervisee;
- *individual supervision in a group setting* (Virgo, 1982), where supervision is conducted on a one-to-one basis within a group;
- *group* (Hays, 1989; Holloway and Johnson, 1985), where one supervisor meets with a number of supervisees;
- *peer group* (Borders, 1989a; Fizdale, 1958; Nobler, 1980), which is usually a small leaderless group of supervisees who monitor each others' counselling work.
- *staff* (Jennison, 1982), where the composition of the group is also the team or staff within a particular organization (the supervisor usually coming from outside the organization);
- *dual* (Davis and Arvey, 1978), where two supervisors monitor the work of a supervisee.

Cherniss and Egnatios (1977) have pinpointed five supervisory styles, i.e. the approach adopted by a supervisor vis-à-vis supervisees. These five are probably a good indication of the extent of supervisory styles:

- the didactic–consultative;
- the insight-oriented;

- the feelings-oriented;
- the laissez-faire;
- the authoritative.

An interesting array of supervisee modes of presentation from live supervision to verbal reports have been outlined (Borders and Leddick, 1987). Within supervision there are different focus points (DeBell, 1963; Hawkins and Shohet, 1989) depending on the emphasis of the supervisory work: client-centred, helper-centred, process-centred.

Supervision models abound, many emerging from counselling/psychotherapy backgrounds, some integrative, and some distinct from counselling approaches. Supervision models focus upon the conceptual and theoretical underpinnings that direct the supervision. Included in these models are:

- Psychodynamic (Bordin, 1983; DeBell, 1963; Moldawsky, 1980)
- Behavioural (Delaney, 1972; Linehan, 1980)
- Cognitive–Behavioural (Schmidt, 1979)
- Integrative (Boyd, 1978)
- Systems (Boyd, 1978; Ryan, 1978)
- Systemic (Liddle, 1988)
- Developmental (Loganbill, Hardy and Delworth, 1982; Stoltenberg and Delworth, 1987)
- Multimodal (Ponterotto and Zander, 1984)
- Social influence model (Dixon and Clairborn, 1987)
- Humanistic (Hawkins, 1985; Hawkins and Shohet, 1989)
- Working alliance model (Bordin, 1983)
- Family therapy (Tucker, Hart and Liddle, 1976)
- Person-centred (Patterson, 1982; Villas-Boas Bowen, 1986)
- Rational-emotive (Wessler and Ellis, 1980)
- Gestalt (Harmon and Tarleton, 1983; Mintz, 1983)
- Discrimination model (Bernard, 1979)
- Cognitive–developmental (Blocher, 1983)
- Social learning (Hosford and Barmann, 1983)
- Social role models of supervision (Carroll, 1995a; Holloway, 1995)
- A systems approach (Holloway, 1995)
- Cyclical model (Page and Wosket, 1994)

As with counselling/psychotherapy approaches there is a quota of more esoteric types such as:

- Spinal-ecological supervision (Cooper, 1984)
- Rehabilitation supervision (Beardsley, Riggar and Hafer, 1984)

- Supervision in communications analytic therapy (Beier and Young, 1980)

THE IMPORTANCE OF SUPERVISION

An increasingly important role is being given to supervision as part of the overall training of students in counselling. Pruitt, McColgan, Pugh and Kiser (1986) conducted research with psychiatrists who had trained at the Menninger Foundation between 1946 and 1954 around the training experiences which meant the most to them in later years and most affected their functioning. They discovered that supervision was rated as more influential than lectures, case conferences and personal reading.

There seems little doubt that counselling professionals are being asked to spend an increasing amount of time supervising. Robiner and Schofield (1990), speaking from the USA, have pointed out that 'more than two thirds of counseling psychologists provide clinical supervision' (p. 297). Hess (1987a) found that 55 per cent of clinicians spend between 10 and 29 per cent of their time in supervision and another 7 per cent claim to spend over 30 per cent of their time in this way. Hess and Hess (1983) discovered that supervisory staff spend an average of 3.76 hours per week supervising. There is no similar research in the British context to indicate how much importance is attached to or how much time is spent in supervision by supervisors and supervisees. However, the British Association for Counselling in its Code of Ethics and Practice for Counsellors (1990) demands that counsellors, both in training and qualified, should be supervised for their client work. And the British Psychological Society is even more particular in demanding that supervisees spend one hour in supervision for every five hours of client work (BPS 1995: *Regulations and Syllabus for the Diploma in Counselling Psychology*). If the increasing number of courses in training supervisors can be taken as a guideline of the importance of supervision, and if the impression is that there is a dearth of supervisors around, then there is every reason to believe that the demand for supervision is increasing rapidly.

It is not just its 'obligatory' nature that makes supervision more in demand. Supervisees indicate that they find both their supervision and supervisors effective. Carroll (1994c) reports that trainees, over two years of their courses, rate their supervision and their supervisors very positively (giving supervision a six out of ten in year 1 and a seven out of ten in year 2; and giving their supervisors a six and a half in year one and a seven in year 2).

In short, it is clear from the literature, and especially from ethical codes for supervisors (British Association for Counselling, 1988; Association for Counselor Education and Supervision, 1993) that supervision is being viewed as an increasingly important part of counselling training. Within the therapeutic profession it is now seen as an essential, rather than an optional feature of effective counselling work, being 'mandated' in almost all training in counselling.

HISTORICAL DEVELOPMENT OF SUPERVISION

There are three phases in the history of counselling/psychotherapy supervision, as outlined below:

Phase 1	Phase 2	Phase 3
Psychoanalytic model	Counselling models	Developmental and social role models

Phase 1: Psychoanalytic model

Supervision, in the early days with Freud, was informal, with small groups gathering to train, discuss and review each others' client work. Max Eitingon is cited as the first to make supervision a formal requirement in the Berlin curriculum in the 1920s (Lewin, 1972). With the advent of formal training in psychoanalysis (around 1922 when standards were set by the International Psychoanalytic Society) came the requisite 'personal analysis' as the cornerstone, i.e. the main focus of training was the analysis of the trainee. However, with the development of further training establishments a distinction gradually began to occur between 'personal analysis' and 'supervisory or control analysis' (Ekstein and Wallerstein, 1972). At this juncture (in the early 1930s) a division occurred. The Hungarian school integrated the personal and supervisory analysis by having the analyst fulfil both tasks. The Institute in Vienna did not agree that the same person should fulfil both roles and, since in their view the supervisory analysis was more akin to teaching than therapy, they considered that the two functions should be carried out by different people (Bibring, 1937). The supervisor's task was to teach: personal problems, even those arising from work with clients, were to be referred to the personal analyst. Thus began a controversy that has stayed with us, and remained unresolved: the distinction (or not) between therapy and supervision.

Even at this early stage of supervision development there were noticeable critical issues which are still present in the modern literature on supervision:

a) Where is the interface between therapy and supervision? Is supervision a teaching or a therapy modality?

b) What is the place of administration in supervision? Is it the task of supervision to monitor the 'environment' in which client work takes place?

Supervision, in this era of its existence, was tied rigidly to its parent psychotherapy orientation, i.e. psychoanalysis.

Phase 2: Counselling models

The second phase of supervision arrived in the 1950s with the advent of other counselling orientations besides the psychodynamic. It was largely characterized by being counselling-bound, i.e. supervision models were linked closely to their counselling roots and took on the counselling name, e.g. person-centred supervision, rational-emotive supervision. The philosophy and approach within supervision was based almost exclusively on the supervisor's counselling theory (Bernard and Goodyear, 1992; Holloway, 1992).

Several factors characterized supervision during this period:

a) With the arrival of methods of taping therapy sessions came the opportunity to observe what was actually happening rather than what was being reported by the supervisee to be happening.

b) Other forms of supervision began to emerge besides individual supervision: e.g. supervision in small groups and peer group supervision. Even though Freud had set up small groups to discuss client work, these modern groups were characterized by the use of the group process as a learning process.

c) An emphasis on skills approaches to counselling and psychotherapy (e.g., Traux and Carkhuff, 1967) influenced supervisory practice, making the supervisor somewhat responsible for the skills development of the supervisee. A stronger didactic framework saw its way into some supervisory approaches.

As in the first phase in supervision history, the supervisor remained firmly allied to his/her parent counselling orientation, even though a greater repertoire of methods for accessing counselling sessions was available. Also supervisor roles increased to include a more skills-based teaching mode.

Phase 3: Developmental and social role models

The advent of developmental and social role models of supervision may well be seen as the beginning of the third era in the history of supervision. In this era (from 1970s onwards) there is a movement away from clinical models of supervision tied to counselling orientations to more educational, psychosocial models emphasizing the roles/tasks of supervisors and the learning stages of supervisees. While this trend took place in the USA, principally because supervision was tied into university training, in Britain there was still the tendency to stay with the counselling-bound models of supervision.

DEVELOPMENTAL MODELS OF SUPERVISION

Overall, developmental models of supervision work on premises similar to models of developmental psychology. In the latter people are seen as moving through distinct stages of life, each stage characterized by its own tasks and demands which have to be fulfilled before the individual is ready and able to move to the next stage. Developmental models of supervision describe similar movements. The supervisee, the supervisor and the supervisory relationship all move through discernible and somewhat predictable stages, each stage characterized by its own tasks and issues.

In 1989 Borders (1989b) pointed out that there were twenty-five developmental models of supervision in existence (an increase from twelve in 1984) and pleaded for a moratorium on new developmental models with a redirection of research energy towards what she called 'instructional approaches that would lead to a technology of supervision interventions' (p. 6). Both points have been heeded to some degree. Certainly there has been an upsurge in attempts to isolate interventions, tasks and functions within supervision (Hawkins and Shohet, 1989; Holloway, 1995). Also, a serious approach to integrating research into new developmental models has taken place. Skovholt and Ronnestad (1992) are the latest to outline a developmental model of supervision, but unlike many of the others, theirs is based on their own research. Using a qualitative approach (interviews and a grounded theory analysis), they interviewed 100 counsellors at different stages of training and post-training (five groups in all), and emerged with an eight-stage paradigm of counsellor development.

Worthington (1987) presented a summary of eighteen different developmental models of supervision and related research, and Holloway (1987) critiqued five major models. The conclusions from both were similar; they considered there was 'marginal support' (Holloway, 1987, p.214) and 'some support' (Worthington, 1987, p.18) for developmental models. From their work and from a review of developmental models a number of questions can be raised about which we know little at present. For example:

Are supervisees merely satisfied with their perceived improvement or does it affect their work with clients? How do supervision developmental models relate to counselling orientations? What can hinder supervisee development? How do transitions from one stage to the next take place, and what facilitates (or obstructs) that movement? What is the role of the supervisory relationship in supervisee development? What influence does culture, age, location, training and/or gender have on supervisee development?

A number of issues arise regarding developmental models. It is difficult to see these models as truly developmental in the sense in which psychosocial theories are developmental. There is no evidence to suggest that the stages outlined are fixed or sequential. Individual counsellors may have their own pace for development, and at present there is insufficient evidence to connect the roles adopted by supervisors, or their supervisory styles, or theoretical opinions, to developmental stages. Worthington (1984) discovered geographical location affected trainee development and the theoretical orientation of the supervisor seems to have some effect (Reisling and Daniels, 1983). This raises questions of how developmental models of supervision apply in countries other than the USA where they have been created. Carroll's (1994c) research has addressed this to some degree showing that developmental models, while accepted theoretically by supervisors, do not seem to have found their way into practice in Britain in a significant manner.

Furthermore, developmental models do not indicate how change takes place but merely state the stages through which supervisees move. How are such models connected to supervisors, to the supervisory relationship, to the personality of the supervisee? All these are unanswered questions within the supervisory literature.

There is little consideration given to how supervisors change as a result of being engaged in supervision. Hess (1986) has outlined a three-stage model of supervision development and Alonso (1983) has focused on a career model of supervisor change. However, neither of these models has been researched. More research is needed as the number of training courses in supervision grows, to isolate changes over time for supervisors, if indeed such change takes place at all.

Perhaps the most telling criticism questions the connectedness between the changes that take place within supervisees as they move through training and the assertion that they are taking part in a developmental process. There is little longitudinal data to investigate developmental change; the cultural and historical development of the supervisee have not been assessed; how personality structure enters this process continues to be unclear and there is a lack of knowledge on the changes taking place within individuals across training courses.

In short, although the introduction of developmental models increased sophistication within supervision, at present there are a number of unanswered questions about how trainees 'develop' over time. Furthermore, while developmental models of supervision have an attractiveness and appeal to supervisors, perhaps that appeal attracts supervisor weaknesses rather than their strengths, i.e. providing them with a source of reference to direct their supervision rather than help them struggle with the learning environment in which both they and the supervisee are engaged. At this moment it is still unclear how developmental models affect supervision, and though worked out in some detail, they still lack sufficient evidence to validate their claims. They remain at a strong theoretical level rather than an empirical one. One of the main strengths of developmental models is that they offer supervisors possible categories in which they can anchor their observations around supervisory interventions. This assumes that supervisors are both able, and willing, to change their supervisory interventions. As yet we do not know that they can. The small amount of evidence that supervisors adapt their strategies to meet the learning needs of supervisees is still inconclusive (Worthington, 1987). The only British research in the area (Carroll, 1994c) used a longitudinal design to code supervisory tapes over the course of a year: there was no significant change in the use of the tasks by supervisors over that time.

SOCIAL ROLE MODELS OF SUPERVISION

The second strand in the third phase of the history of supervision emerged with the social role models. These models have their roots in early understandings of supervision, where supervisor and supervisee adopt certain relationships towards one another. The social role models attempt to tell us what supervisors and supervisees *do* within supervision, what tasks are performed and by whom.

Tasks are the behavioural side of roles. A role is person-centred (teacher/pupil): the task is action-centred (to teach/to learn). Even though a strong notional distinction is made between roles and tasks, in reality they combine.

A number of social role models of supervision have been outlined specifically addressing the roles of supervisors (Bernard, 1979; Boyd 1978; Ekstein, 1964; Ekstein and Wallerstein, 1972; Hess, 1980; Holloway, 1984, 1995; Kadushin, 1985; Litrell, Lee-Borden and Lorenz, 1979). Five in particular summarize the trends within supervision over the stages of its history: Bernard's (1979) discrimination model is a pioneering study in roles; Ekstein's (1964) and Ekstein and Wallerstein's (1972) are the earliest to isolate supervisor roles; Hess's relationship model offers a different vantage point with its concentration on the supervisory relationship; Litrell, Lee-Borden and Lorenz (1979) attempt to combine a developmental model with supervisor roles; and Holloway's work is the most recent and the most detailed role approach. Using these as a basis Carroll (1994c) has utilized 'grounded theory' (Strauss and Corbin, 1990) to name the 'generic tasks of counselling supervision' and has isolated seven. They are:

to create the learning relationship
to teach
to counsel
to consult
to evaluate

to monitor professional/ethical issues

to work with the administrative/organizational aspects of client work

These tasks will be considered individually in Chapter 4.

SUPERVISION LITERATURE IN BRITAIN AND THE USA

In recent years there has been a significant increase in the research and theoretical publications on counselling supervision. I will survey these in both US and Britain before drawing out some contemporary trends and debates within supervision (Chapter 2). There seem to be two separate strands in the history and understanding of supervision, one emerging from the USA and the other from Britain. What distinguishes them is the location of counselling training. In the USA counselling training has largely taken place in, and been controlled by, the universities; in Britain counselling training has existed almost exclusively within the private domain and only in the past ten years have universities and colleges of higher and further education become involved. As a result, the USA has concentrated largely on the conceptual and intellectual pursuit of supervision, while Britain has stressed the practice of supervision, the training of supervisors, and the supervision of supervision.

Britain

Although counselling supervision has been practised in Britain for some time, it was only in the 1980s that any significant published material found its way onto the market. In the 1970s there were some publications in supervision, mostly in the areas of social work and, interestingly enough, youth work. Joan Mattison's work on the reflective process in supervision was published in 1975, and remains a classic in the field of social work. Tash's book *Supervision in Youth Work*, initially published in the 1970s, was the overall accepted textbook on supervision in youth work.

It was the arrival of the 1980s, and the work of Brigid Proctor and Francesca Inskipp, that began what has become a formidable array of publications specifically in counselling supervision. Proctor formulated her 'functions of supervision' in the early 1980s and wrote these up in an article in 1986. This, in my view, besides the ongoing supervision material in psychotherapy from a psychoanalytic perspective, was the first significant contribution to counselling supervision in Britain. It was the first clear articulation of a way of thinking about supervision as a practice modality. Using an apprenticeship model and seeing supervision as containing the formative, normative and restorative functions, Proctor's model of supervision became an inspiration for some research (Simms, 1991), and found its way into a number of training courses in supervision. At the same time as outlining her model, Brigid Proctor was engaged in supervision training at South West London College. Later in the 1980s she and Francesca Inskipp published a small booklet (plus tapes) called *Skills for Supervising and Being Supervised* (1988). Noticeable in this publication was the emphasis on helping supervisees use their time most effectively in supervision, and for perhaps the first time there was a creative attempt to focus on supervisees' use of skills in using supervision. But the publication was more than that: it also defined and outlined the tasks of supervision.

The year 1988 also saw the emergence of the *Code of Ethics and Practice for the Supervision of Counsellors* (BAC), a key publication in the history of counselling supervision in Britain. Though lacking in some dimensions (e.g. it has nothing to say about sexual contact between supervisors and supervisees), it is still a strong document on the essentials of supervision. It looks at the nature of supervision, the responsibilities of supervisors, issues of competence in its ethics section, and under practice issues considers the management of the supervision work and confidentiality. It contains a brief section in the Appendix describing different models of supervision. This code is presently being reviewed and the revised code is expected to be presented in 1995. (See Appendix, page 167.)

Close on the heels of Proctor's work came Hawkins and Shohet's, *Supervision in the Helping Professions*, published in 1989. This was to become the main textbook in supervisory training for a number of years. The core of this book was its process model of supervision with six foci for supervisors. Like Proctor's work, it was eminently practical, born from the authors' experience of being supervisors, and containing very helpful frameworks and maps for practising supervisors. It summarized theory and had sound theoretical bases, and its main purpose was to help the busy practitioner. The latter part of the book was innovative in looking at supervision within organizational settings, and even today is one of the few publications that has tackled this aspect.

The years from 1990 to 1995 were characterized principally by the number of counselling supervision courses/conferences that emerged in Britain. And with these courses, which fed into the British Association for Counselling's Recognition procedure for counsellor supervisors, came further literature. Gaie Houston's small book entitled *Supervision and Counselling* (1990) was not the least concerned with theory or speculation, but vividly and practically outlined how supervision works, how supervisees can best use it and how supervisors can be most effective. Soon after Houston's book came the publication of *Training and Supervision for Counselling in Action* (edited by Dryden and Thorne, 1991), a series of chapters written by different people containing a number of ideas: the supervisory relationship, approaches to the supervision of counsellors, on being a supervisor, on being a supervisee, training counsellor trainers and supervisors. Again eminently practical, it is a book mainly for counselling supervisors and those involved in the training of counsellors, and was timely in articulating current issues in both training and supervision.

Three major contributions to the counselling supervision literature occurred in 1993 and 1994. First of all, Inskipp and Proctor (1993) updated and professionalized their 1988 *Skills for Supervising and Being Supervised*. In the first of the new edition's two parts, *Making the Most of Supervision*, they combined insights from their considerable expertise as counsellors and supervisors with numerous taped interviews of both counsellors and supervisors to produce a very strong and readable contribution to counselling supervision. Usable both by supervisees and supervisors and as a training manual, it contains a multitude of frameworks within which counselling supervision can be viewed. It is organized into five units:

1. Supervisor: For what purpose, in what way?
2. You as a developing counsellor
3. Setting up the working alliance
4. Making the most of the session
5. Reviewing

Each unit is subdivided in sections, with accompanying audiotapes that discuss relevant aspects. It is undoubtedly the first systematic and coherent account of counselling supervision in Britain. What characterizes this publication, and what remains original, is its 'supervisee' focus. It is unique, on either side of the Atlantic, in making supervisees, and their preparation for supervision, the key element. Part 2, *Becoming a Supervisor*, is currently under way.

Two other major contributions follow the same trend and produce systematic, practical approaches to the doing of supervision. Feltham and Dryden brought out *Developing Counsellor Supervision* in 1994, with the intention of presenting 'a variety of practical approaches to supervision culled from different models of counselling, which readers may consider and use eclectically, as befits their own situation' (p. ix). They speak directly to supervisors and offer a series of short directives to help them create a supervisory alliance, use a variety of supervisory foci and methods, foster and use the supervisory relationship, use the developmental opportunities of supervision, highlight supervisees' strengths and weaknesses, and protect the client and the counsellor. As with Inskipp and Proctor, their work emerges from experience and contains many examples and conclusions from their own practice. They are also aware of the literature and research in counselling supervision and support their remarks with critical references.

The most recent 'systematic' account of supervision is the book by Page and Wosket (1994) entitled *Supervising the Counsellor: A Cyclical Model*. And systematic it certainly is. While acknowledging the contribution of others before them in the British context they suggest that theirs is the first 'comprehensive supervision model of a systematic, flexible framework and a pragmatic working methodology' (p. 31) applicable to both trainees and experienced counsellors. Since they do not quote either of the other two previously discussed systematic approaches, presumably neither was available to them when they were writing their book.

Nonetheless theirs is indeed a systematic, flexible model. Five circles (contact, focus, space, bridge, review) contain five sub-circles each (e.g. *contact* contains ground-rules, boundaries, accountability, expectations, relationships). The book is an excellent blend of practice, theory, literature and skills. While the need to have five subsections within each circle results in some strain, there is no doubt that this is a fine book for training supervisors and represents a down-to-earth approach to monitoring supervision work. It also contains sections on ethical issues in supervision, and training for supervisors.

Sharpe (1995) has edited a supervision book specifically on analytic groups. It picks up various themes within group analytic supervision and reviews supervision in specific courses. It has three chapters at the end that look in some detail at the impact of institutional dynamics and the organizational context on supervision, and offers an outline curriculum for training supervisors. Its strength is its clear application to groups within a psychodynamic framework.

It would seem that British supervision literature is in a healthy, forward-moving state, characterized by rootedness in practice. There can be little doubt about the richness of supervision work taking place within counselling training as well as in the supervision of seasoned counsellors. Furthermore, British supervision is well on its way to providing excellent training for supervisors. The books mentioned all contain awareness of what is happening in supervision, directives that are clear and helpful and training methodologies for learning the art of supervision. By and large, these helpful contributions to supervision in Britain are not confined to particular counselling orientations but see supervision as a profession in its own right. They recognize and use elements from across counselling orientations to devise outlines that best facilitate the learning of supervisees.

There are a few persistent gaps. For example, none of the books have sections on termination of supervision. There are suggestions on how long supervision between the same supervisory dyad ought to continue, and on changing supervisor, but no detailed examination of termination as part of the supervisory process. Furthermore, there is still the tendency to concentrate on supervision as a one-to-one process, with definite acknowledgement of group supervision but little in the way of publications on group, peer, staff, team and organizational supervision. While the literature discussed above struggles with the differences between supervision and counselling there are no clear stances on this. There is still a sense that, even though distinctions are acknowledged to exist between counselling and supervision, counselling models of supervision pertain and hold sway, even when steps are taken to see supervision as distinct from counselling (Page and Wosket, p. ix). Furthermore, the British literature on supervision is extremely weak on cross-cultural (multicultural) aspects of supervision.

Though I have concentrated on the literature on counselling supervision there are some helpful materials on supervision from professions other than counselling. Prichard (1995) has edited a very interesting book on supervision from a social work perspective, and Gardiner (1989) used his research into social work supervision as the basis of his book. A recent book on supervision in nursing, Butterworth and Faugier (1992), is explicit on the need for the introduction of supervision within nursing practice. Faugier, in *Clinical Supervision: A Position Paper* (undated), suggests that supervision in nursing can best be served by regular one-to-one supervision with a supervisor from nursing and regular one-to-one supervision with a supervisor from a different discipline. Verity (1991) has applied supervision to probation officers and the probation service, and supervision training has been introduced for treatment managers in the prison service who oversee tutors on the sex-offenders programme. Materials from so many different sources can only enrich understanding the many facets of supervision within counselling.

United States and supervision

In contrast to the British literature on supervision, the literature in the USA is very theory- and research-based. Its associations with universities mean that it is replete with models, many of which remain unresearched.

This short review will look in particular at a number of publications representative of the counselling supervision literature. For a more detailed and organized literature review of supervision in the USA up to 1990, readers are referred to Robiner and Shofield's (1990) article, 'References on supervision in clinical and counseling psychology'.

Hess's (1980) *Psychotherapy Supervision* remains one of the major textbooks on supervision. A vast book, it summarizes research and theory under a number of headings, and whereas it is by no means the first book on supervision, it is probably the first to summarize the trends and apply supervision to a number of settings. A second edition is presently in preparation and an updated version would add significantly to the supervision field.

Borders and Leddick published their short *Handbook of Counseling Supervision* in 1987, and it continues to be the shortest overall review of supervision in the field. Allied to no particular model or framework, it summarizes what is happening in the field of supervision concisely and in a very readable manner. It uses a number of frameworks to help supervisors assess, evaluate and understand the competencies of supervisors and supervisees.

Bradley's (1989) edited book is an update on an earlier publication by Boyd (1978). It has reviewed a number of supervision approaches and is one of the first books to look in some detail at training for supervisors.

Stoltenberg and Delworth (1987) is the first book to take a particular developmental model and apply it systematically. With three domains (autonomy, motivation, self- and other-awareness) and eight areas they apply this model across four levels of development. Each level is described in some detail and there are numerous suggestions for supervisors on how to match their teaching to the developmental level of supervisees.

Holloway has been at the forefront of both research and theory in counselling supervision since early 1980. Her 1992 publication reviews the research literature in supervision from 1984 to 1992 and along with Russell, Crimmings and Lent (1984), who survey research in supervision up to 1984, is undoubtedly the main text in this area.

Holloway's recent book (1995) *Clinical Supervision: A Systems Approach* is one of the most comprehensive overviews of the many factors in supervision, looking in turn at six areas of supervision:

supervision tasks
supervision functions
client factors
supervisee factors
supervisor factors
institutional factors in supervision

Her tasks/functions matrix is possibly the best model on how to dissect supervision and can be used as either a training method for supervisors, or as a monitor for supervisory sessions.

In 1992 Bernard and Goodyear produced what is probably the best textbook in clinical supervision. They widen the considerations of Borders and Leddick (1987), and apply findings to different contexts. Not allied to a particular approach nor presenting a particular model, they offer a very valuable overview of supervision. They state the complexities of supervision and indicate the dilemmas, as well as offering helpful frameworks for evaluating supervision.

The Association for Counselor Education and Supervision published *Standards for Counseling Supervisors* in 1989 and *Ethical Guidelines for Counseling Supervisors* in 1993. Because of its strong base in university settings this code reflects that context.

In 1994 DiAnne Borders edited an ERIC/CASS digest on supervision. In brief, focused articles various authors present up-to-date summaries of the effective components of supervision, e.g.; Models of Clinical Supervision, Strategies and Methods of Effective Supervision, Gender Issues in Supervision, Multicultural Issues in Supervision, Peer Supervision, Use of Technology in counselor supervision. This digest is a comprehensive overview of counselling supervision factors. While not covering all aspects it contains the main features of supervision today.

From this overview of supervision, what it means, its history, and a short review of literature in both Britain and the USA, supervision can be seen in its historical perspective. What is noticeable, despite the limitations, is that supervision contains rich strands of theory and practice. Combining the two histories of supervision in Britain and the USA provides a valuable menu for understanding and practising counselling supervision.

TWO

Counselling supervision: trends and debates

Clinical supervision is in its adolescence developmentally.
J.M. Bernard

Throughout its brief history counselling supervision has been attended by disagreements, some of which remain unresolved and many of which have generated much discussion. This chapter will isolate the trends within supervision today, and review its current debates and controversies.

FROM COUNSELLING TO EDUCATIONAL MODELS OF SUPERVISION

Perhaps the main trend within counselling supervision is its gradual but steady movement from a therapeutic stance to a more educational position. Historically, supervision has been tied very closely to counselling, with supervisors handing on the profession to future generations through the instillation of relevant knowledge, skills and attitudes. Usually, this has meant practising within a particular counselling orientation. Hence arose, understandably, the models that have been tied to counselling orientations: what Holloway has called 'counselling-bound models', Bernard and Goodyear have called 'psychotherapy-bound models', and Leddick has named 'orientation-specific models'.

Counselling-and/or psychotherapy-bound models of supervision emerged for a number of reasons, but mainly because counselling adopted an apprenticeship model in its training. The apprentice was overseen by an experienced practitioner who guided the fledgling novice through the difficult maze of client work towards becoming an independent professional. Formal training in counselling took place elsewhere, in a classroom, while supervision facilitated the 'doing' side of the counselling work. The apprenticeship model, though it has many strengths, also contributes to a narrowness of learning confined to the experience and the skills of the apprentice-master. Because it is based on 'handing down' what has been inherited, there is little time for reflection on what has been handed down, or indeed on the individuality of the apprentice.

A second feature of counselling-bound models of supervision is their tendency to appoint rather than train those who oversee the apprentices. Supervision becomes an inherited role rather than a role into which one is trained. This reinforces the supervisor as an expert in the profession who hands on the craft as it has been handed to him/her rather than adapting it to the individual learning of an apprentice. This approach is understandable in professions where physical skills are all-important (e.g. carpentry, joinery) and where such skills can be defined and clarified, with a right/wrong way of practising. Expectations that the apprentice should 'imitate' the master make sense when the major skills and competencies revolve around doing. But in professions where the main tool used is the person of the individual, rather than simply the skills he/she has, and where the focus of the training is to enable the beginner to practise in his/her own way, the apprenticeship model is limited.

Counselling-bound models of supervision use the same foci in supervision as they do in counselling. Digging out the often implicit 'educational theory' underlying a particular counselling model reveals its understanding of the learning process. This process is then related to supervisees. So, for example, in person–centred approaches, where educational understanding was made explicit and applied by Carl Rogers (e.g. in *Freedom to Learn for the 80s*, 1983), learning was seen to take place when the core relationship qualities were offered by therapists. Formal teaching, the transfer of knowledge, the role of the expert, all became secondary to the learning relationship set up between counsellor and client. This relationship became the mainstay of supervision, as it was of counselling. Likewise, the educational theories underlying psychodynamic and cognitive-behavioural approaches were applied to the supervisory process. Whereas this procedure ensures congruency in what could be a conflictual field, it represents a narrow (what Holloway calls a parochial) approach to methods of teaching and to research. Rigid counselling models have excluded methods of teaching that did not fit their stringent dictates. Some (psychodynamic approaches in particular) have ignored the value of skills training, roleplaying and other experiential methods of learning. Other models have relegated formal teaching to the sidelines and made the individual learning process the centre of learning (humanistic approaches in particular). Some, especially cognitive-behavioural models, have concentrated on the intellectual side of learning and left the emotional and unconscious learning processes aside. Not all counselling orientations are as rigid as this, and many practitioners are able to integrate educational methods from other professions into their teaching philosophies.

There is some argument for continuing to ally supervision to a particular counselling orientation. Feltham and Dryden (1994) argue for congruence between the counselling orientations of supervisee and supervisor as most trainees are learning counselling from a core theoretical model, there are incompatible areas within different counselling orientations, and especially at the beginning it can be very confusing for trainees to have to digest different approaches. While accepting these arguments, and realizing that at the beginning of training it makes sense to have congruence between supervisor and supervisee, there is no reason for narrowing the educational stance of particular counselling orientations. It is all too easy to sustain a narrowness of approach. Educational models of supervision try to widen the methods of learning used within supervision. They concentrate on how adults learn and on the particular stage of learning that has been reached by an individual or a group. How does this person learn most effectively? How can I adapt my teaching to the learning needs of this individual, at this time in his/her development, with his/her particular learning style, in this context? Asking questions such as these, they assume that supervisees want to learn in their own way, that resistance is not automatic when learning is at stake, and that various forms of the teaching/learning relationship – collegial, trial and error, learning by doing – are all likely to lead to learning.

It sounds a terrible choice, but given the option between a good counsellor who was a poor educator, or a poor counsellor who was a good educator, I would choose the latter as supervisor. Life, fortunately, is not as clear-cut as that, but the point is that education is more at the heart of supervision than is counselling. This is by no means an agreed-upon position. Page and Wosket (1994), state quite clearly that supervision is 'primarily a containing and enabling process, rather than an educational or therapeutic process' (p. 39), placing themselves firmly in the camp that there is little place for the pupil–teacher relationship in supervision (p. 52). Yet they suggest that supervisors give information, recommend articles and books, and set up role-plays (p. 121).

Perhaps the discrepancy here indicates different concepts of education and training. It is easy to construct a continuum of education foci with totally didactic teaching at one end and totally self-directed learning at the other:

Totally didactic teaching	Totally self-directed learning
Supervisor-centred	Supervisee-centred
Authoritative	Collegial
Information/facts-based	Awareness-based
Deductive	Inductive

In my view, what characterizes good supervisors is their ability to move between these extremes and their skill to work at either end of the continuum when appropriate. Good teachers are able to integrate a number of learning formats – they know when to move from the teacher–pupil relationship to the mentor relationship, to the experiential learning stance, to the authoritative stance.

In summary, what will characterize effective supervisors of the future will be their ability to offer a range of educational methods and to be aware of which learning processes suit which individuals; they will be skilled teachers and counsellors who stress the learning of supervisees and the welfare of clients.

TOWARDS SUPERVISION AS A PROFESSION IN ITS OWN RIGHT

Supervision is becoming a profession in its own right. This is shown in a number of ways: ethical codes for supervisors (BAC, 1988; ACES, 1993) and training programmes for supervisors (ACES, 1989; Boyd, 1978; Carroll, 1995a; Inskipp and Proctor, 1993; Page and Wosket, 1994). Supervision is at the adolescent stage of development (Bernard, undated; Carroll, 1988) – which presumably means it is poised for independence. What could this independence mean?

First of all, it is possible that supervisors could be effective across professions (at the moment I supervise two managers of companies, a teacher, counsellors from a number of orientations and in a variety of settings, and a small group of outplacement counsellors). From the INITA Conference on Supervision (September, 1994) it was obvious that supervision in Germany was seen in a wider context than that merely of counselling: it is common for supervisors to work with teams comprised of counsellors, social workers and managers. They understand supervision as being more generic than we do in Britain or USA. And in some ways there are contradictions in having supervisors who focus narrowly on counselling. Counsellors can be closed to other ways of learning, can be very poor on educational theory and methods, and can be trained to work so specifically within one kind of relationship that they are unable to vary roles with the same person. One of the major skills of supervisors is their ability to be flexible across roles: they can teach when needed, they can counsel when required, they can be consultants, evaluators, monitors, models, they can vary style to fit in with the learning of supervisees.

Second, if supervision is moving towards becoming an independent profession there is need to isolate the characteristics of effective supervisors. What will be the features of good, and bad, supervisors of the future? The list below provides an overview of possible differences.

Effective supervisors	Ineffective supervisors
Structure supervision appropriately	Over- or under-structure supervision
Use the counselling role	Substitute counselling for supervision

Help trainees find *their* way of being counsellors	Insist their way of counselling is the only way
Are good teachers	Are poor teachers
Are flexible across roles	Lock into specific roles
Contract clearly	Are poor negotiators
Evaluate fairly and according to agreed criteria	Have few clear criteria for evaluation
Adapt to individual differences in supervisees	Supervise all supervisees in exactly the same way
Train as supervisors	See no reason why they should train as supervisors
Have access to a variety of supervisory interventions	Have a limited number of supervisory interventions
Give feedback clearly, directly, and constructively	Give no feedback, vague feedback, or come across as punitive with feedback

At a recent training day, treatment managers of the Prison Service Sex Offenders Programme offered a number of extra practice features of effective and ineffective supervisors. Ineffective supervisors do not see supervision as a priority, allow interruptions and distractions within the supervisory time, are reluctant to be supervisors, see supervision as applicable only to crisis situations, are punitive in their feedback, have no models or frameworks to guide them, continually tell supervisors what they 'should' do and think they themselves should know everything. Effective supervisors, on the other hand, have professional respect for supervisees, prepare for supervision, encourage self-solving problems, have clear, negotiated goals, are comfortable with the supervisory relationship, are realistic, and have clear boundaries.

Clearly, it is supervisors who make supervision good or bad, not supervisees, nor contexts. Good supervisors engage in the following activities.

Structuring supervision

Good supervisors structure supervision according to the learning of supervisees. The 'understructuring' supervisor allows supervision to happen without any structure, almost by default. I was assigned a supervisor at an early stage of my counselling training who saw no reason for organizing our supervision time together. A delightful person, exceedingly busy, he let supervision take place by chance, when we happened to meet. It amounted to a damage limitation dialogue, with him asking if there were emergencies, danger-points or red-flag moments with which I needed help. Assured there were not (I am not sure what he would have done if I had raised some difficulties), he disappeared back to his work. He insisted he was available for me, offered to meet should I need it, and wrote me a very complimentary supervision report at the end. Perhaps he mistakingly thought he was being supervisee-centred, leaving initiatives to me, or saw himself as non-intrusive in my practice, or maybe justified what he did by a philosophy of allowing me to 'sink or swim'. His lack of structure may well have suited an experienced practitioner who sought help when help was needed, but was poor for a beginner who needed time to reflect and think through the interesting issues emerging from client work. Even more seriously, what he failed to consider were the rights of supervisees and it never seemed to cross his mind that his behaviour was quite oppressive.

Understructuring by supervisors can take place in numerous ways: lack of contracting, unclarity around roles and responsibilities, poor and unidentified evaluation procedures.

The opposite of understructuring, but still bad practice in supervision, is overstructuring. Overstructuring supervisors are obsessive about every detail and leave nothing to chance. Their lack of relaxation, letting go, spontaneity, takes the comfortableness out of supervision, and makes it into a mechanical process rather than a relationship endeavour. I never had such a supervisor but I think I know one. There are lengthy discussions on every aspect of supervision, negotiation and re-negotiations, discussions about discussions, meetings about meetings, supervision on supervision on supervision. And what is definitely missing is any humour. Laughter is rarely around when obsessions are present.

Separating counselling and supervision

The most disagreeable stance for supervisees is when their supervisor takes on the role of counsellor/therapist with them. Good supervisors know when to introduce and use a 'counselling role' when appropriate, when to help supervisees deal with their personal reactions to work with clients, and when to suggest they move into personal counselling as a way of working with blocks to their work. Bad supervisors either overuse the counselling role, and supervision edges towards becoming counselling, or underuse the counselling role when they never allow supervisees to deal with what happens within them, or is evoked, by client work.

Counselling clients through supervisees

Poor supervisors use supervision as a method for counselling clients indirectly. Called 'vicarious' counselling, using supervisees as conduits for their own work, some supervisors see the clients as their total responsibility, and end up telling supervisees what they must do and even how they must do it. They do not trust trainees to do a good enough job, and intervene directly, and sometimes aggressively, to monitor what is happening, and to direct it to their way of working. This comes, like the overstructuring supervisor, from their own anxiety, or from their inability to trust others to work well, or from a sense of responsibility towards clients.

There are supervisors who find it difficult to allow supervisees to find their own way of being a counsellor. Some do so for theoretical reasons, i.e. they believe there is a way of counselling that must be followed by all, and individual personality is not allowed to enter the training field. Others do it for personality reasons, considering themselves the norm for effective counselling and demanding that others take this as the standard. The result is that they interfere too much in the supervisee's life and work.

Good supervisors realize their accountability for monitoring what happens to clients, but trust their supervisees and believe they can find their own way of being good counsellors. It is that respect for supervisee interventions, and for their ability to integrate theory and practice into an individual style, that characterize their monitoring and their trusting.

Supervisors as teachers

Good supervisors are good teachers, poor supervisors are poor teachers. Good teachers have access to a range of teaching/learning methods, can adapt these to individual supervisees, and can provide clear and focused feedback to facilitate learning. They are flexible in their relationships with supervisees, moving easily between roles of teacher, monitor, evaluator, model, mentor, counsellor. Good teachers understand individual differences and adapt accordingly. Borders (1994) summarizes it well: 'One joy and challenge of being a supervisor is the necessity of using skills from a variety of professional roles and knowing when to use each one. I must draw on my teaching, counseling, and consultation background, but integrate them in a unique way' (p. 24).

Poor teachers are limited in their teaching methods, see all individuals as learning in the same way, and have rigid and narrow foci for their teaching. They maintain inflexible roles and are incapable of moving, when needed, between roles.

Carifio and Hess (1987) reviewed research on objectionable supervisory styles through analysis of students' accounts. They elaborated on the four styles most frequently cited as objectionable by supervisees:

- *constrictive* (overly restrictive in that a student's use of certain techniques in psychotherapy is dogmatically limited);
- *amorphous* (students are not provided with sufficient levels of guidance or direction);
- *unsupportive* (observed when the supervisor is seen as cold, aloof, uncaring, or generally hostile);

- *therapeutic*, the most objectionable to supervisees (the focus is on the student as the patient and on his or her personality structure during supervisory interaction).

Good supervisors are characterized by: respect, empathy, genuineness, honesty, non-sexist and non-authoritarian attitudes, are able to share their own work in a facilitative manner, are open to negotiation, flexible in working, and create clear boundaries.

In brief, supervision is crossing professional boundaries and using insights from education, sociology, human delivery services, to formulate a profession in its own right.

MOVING TOWARDS PROFESSIONAL TRAINING FOR SUPERVISORS

We have moved past the era when counselling supervision is an inherited task that comes with counselling experience. Training in supervision is no longer an option that may or may not be accepted. Supervisors should see such training as an ethical requirement for the job. The 1993 *Ethical Guidelines for Counseling Supervisors* from the Association for Counselor Education and Supervision (USA) is in no doubt about its importance:

> Supervisors should have had training in supervision prior to initiating their role as supervisors. Supervisors should pursue professional and personal continuing education activities such as advanced courses, seminars and professional conferences, on a regular and on-going basis. These activities should include both counseling and supervision topics and skills. (Section 2.01/2.02)

The BAC *Code of Ethics and Practice* is no less demanding. In the section 'Issues of Competence' it stresses the requirement for supervisors to engage in 'specific training in the development of supervision skills . . . monitoring their supervision work . . . monitoring the limits of their competence . . . evaluating their supervision work' (Section B.3).

A number of sources have outlined curricula for training supervisors (Bernard, 1981; Bradley, 1989; Carroll, 1995b; Clarkson and Gilbert, 1991; American Association for Counseling and Development, 1989: Hawkins and Shohet, 1989; Page and Wosket, 1994; Sharpe, 1995).

A model curriculum for counselling supervision training would include, in my view, six domains:

1. Knowledge about supervision, understanding different models, review of ethical and professional issues, and knowing how different professions can interface with supervision.
2. Reviewing issues within supervision such as: power, gender, cross-cultural counselling and supervision.

3. Isolating and practising the skills involved in being a supervisor. These skills would range from setting up supervisory contracts to effective evaluation.
4. Understanding and implementing the tasks of supervision. Training here would include the ability to move between different supervisory roles: teacher, counsellor, consultant, evaluator etc.
5. Being supervised for the supervision work taking place. This is best carried out in group supervision and allows supervisors to review their own work and learn from their experience and that of others.
6. Knowledge of the stages that supervisors go through. Although little research has been conducted on the stages supervisors go through as they move from beginners to experienced workers, there are two models that can help supervisors anticipate the stages that lie ahead. Knowledge of such stages can help supervisors monitor their own work. It can also help them anticipate the future and be somewhat prepared for what is to come.

This is an all-too-brief agenda for training in counselling supervision. What is clear is that as more and more supervision training comes on-line, the more sophisticated will the curriculum become.

TOWARDS DIFFERENT FORMS OF SUPERVISION

Chapter 8 will review different forms of supervision in more detail. Here they will be looked at as a trend within supervision. Supervisor forms include how supervision takes place (e.g. individual or group) and the ways in which supervisees present in supervision (e.g. verbal reports or tapes).

Much of the writing in supervision has been geared towards individual supervision, i.e. an arrangement where there is one supervisee and one supervisor. Authors apply these theories, almost by default, to group supervision. And yet, it could be a valid assumption that more supervision takes place in small groups than individually. Holloway and Johnson (1985) recognized this when they entitled their article, 'Group supervision: widely practised but poorly understood'. Unfortunately no-one seems to have risen to the challenge and as yet there are few texts that look in detail at group supervision, its characteristics and its foci. The same applies to peer supervision, to team and staff supervision. Even though there has been an increase in the practice of these forms of supervision there has not been a corresponding increase in theory and literature on them.

We are still not agreed generally on whether the use of audio/videotapes are suitable and effective supervisory foci. As yet there is only a passing glance towards the use of technology in supervision. A recent article by Casey, Bloom and Moan (1994), titled 'Use of technology in counselor supervision', introduced the idea of networked computers into live super-vision where the supervisor may not even be in the same city, and where the results of diagnostic tests can be transmitted during live sessions. They have suggested also that the use of Personal Digital Assistance machines (PDAs), which recognize handwritten communication, could be an effective and non-intrusive communication network between supervisees and supervisors, again with physical distance between them being no obstacle. Advances in the use of VCRs can allow supervisees to use dual track recording (with the session and their comments side by side – a kind of electronic Interpersonal Process Recall). Split screen use can monitor the actual counselling session and at the same time record and display psychophysiological readings such as skin temperature monitoring or reporting emotional states from electromyographs. They also suggest that 'electronic portfolios' could be generated to demonstrate work with clients, comments on that work, examples of skills, etc. Electronic connectivity can also facilitate the use of group supervision where members of the group are in several locations, and video telephone conferences can be used to connect participants.

These are early and challenging days for the use of advanced technology in supervision, and raise a number of ethical issues which are still unresolved (e.g. the difficulty of guaranteeing confidentiality on the airwaves). However, there is room for contact with the electronic experts to see how their advances can be adapted in helpful ways to the use of supervision.

TOWARDS MULTICULTURAL SUPERVISION

A greater awareness has arisen in supervision on issues of individuality and the role they play within supervision. *Standards for Counseling Supervisors* (ACES, 1989) is explicit on these: 'The counseling supervisor demonstrates knowledge of individual differences with respect to gender, race, ethnicity, culture, and age and understands the importance of these characteristics in supervisory relationships' (Section 4.1). It does not mention areas of sexual orientation, and/or disability as areas also requiring consideration.

We will look at two of these in particular: gender and culture.

Gender

Two influences have propelled 'gender' issues to the forefront of supervision. One is the small body of research in this area, and the second is the awareness of sexual contact between supervisors and supervisees. Nelson and Holloway (1990) looked at the connection between gender and issues of power and involvement in supervision. Significant findings indicated that there were major differences in the way male and female supervisees presented themselves to male and female supervisors. Male and female supervisors reinforced male and female messages differently. Possible explanations for this could be: the power differential between men and women, and the 'potential for bias in expectations and/or actions' (Paisley,

1994, p. 13). Besides having the responsibility of creating awareness of how gender issues affect counselling work, supervisors need to model and work with gender issues within the supervision relationship.

A second study (Simms, 1991), has researched supervisees in a psychiatric nursing context in Britain. She used the normative, formative and restorative tasks outlined by Proctor (1986) as the basis of her research. Though there were no significant differences between men and women on the restorative function of supervision, men rated the normative function more highly than women. Simms (1991) concluded that the supervisory relationship was perceived as more important for women while administrative issues and professional and organizational tasks were perceived as more important for men. Such results could have major impact on supervisory relationships and evaluative factors.

Culture

Corey, Corey and Callanan (1993, p. 197) place the cultural dimensions of supervision firmly within the ethical field and are in no doubt about its important and centrality,

> The ACES Guidelines (1990) call for the counseling supervisor to demonstrate knowledge of individual differences with respect to gender, race, ethnicity, culture, and age and to understand the importance of these characteristics in supervisory relationships . . . supervisors have an ethical responsibility to become aware of the complexities of a multicultural society.

Dealing with cross-cultural (multicultural) issues within counselling supervision is a bit like being caught in the 'chicken-and-egg' dilemma. No longer can we ignore cross-cultural issues in supervision on the one hand, and on the other hand there is so little empirical data to guide pioneers in this field. In their up-to-date and comprehensive review of the theoretical and research literature on cultural issues in supervision, Leong and Wagner (1994) found only three empirical articles addressing cross-cultural counselling supervision, one for each of the last decades: Vander Kolk (1974), Cook and Helms (1988) and Hilton, Russell and Salmi (in press). Their answer to the question, 'What do we know about cross-cultural issues in counselling supervision?' is 'very little' (p. 128). It is difficult to know where to begin in this multi-faceted field, and a number of issues emerge to confront us.

1. What language can we use to discuss the field? Leong and Wagner opt for the term 'cross-cultural counselling supervision' while Bernard (1994b) prefers the term 'multicultural'. In using either set of terms, as Bernard points out, it is essential that the term 'cultural' is seen as an umbrella term covering not only ethnicity and race, but 'socioeconomic status, sexual orientation, religion, gender, age, and so forth' (Bernard, 1994; p. 167).

2. Where is training in cultural awareness best situated if cultural awareness is developmental, i.e. if individuals move from lack of awareness of cultural issues in counselling to a deep understanding of how cultural aspects underlie all dimensions of counselling and supervision? Obviously, supervision is not the place to train supervisees in cultural issues, and yet creating awareness of cultural aspects of counselling will emerge within supervision.

3. What should such training include – given that it needs to include the cultural dimension both of counselling and of supervision itself? As yet there is little to guide us in what such training could include. Thompson (1991) is unique in highlighting cross-cultural/cross-racial dimension of supervision within a British context, and rightly points out that racial issues in supervision are missing from most supervision training in Britain. She makes a plea for its formal introduction. She canvassed thoughts from four training courses in supervision, interviewing nine tutors and receiving 38 replies from students to her questionnaire. Of all respondents 83 per cent considered culture and ethnicity as important factors in supervision, and yet indicated that they are included only rarely in supervision training and even then they are included informally rather than formally. All subjects felt that supervisors had an ethical responsibility to explore issues of race and culture within supervision. Thompson's conclusions are well reflected in the most recent British books on supervision (Feltham and Dryden, 1994; Hawkins and Shohet, 1989; Houston, 1990; Page and Wosket, 1994). All almost totally ignore the cultural dimensions of supervision, spending together approximately three pages on the topic. This meagre contribution consists mainly of admonitions not to impose values on people from other cultures, and does not deal with cultural issues in supervision.

4. What should be the responsibilities of supervisors vis-à-vis cross-cultural counselling issues within supervision? Is it their task to see such issues as one amongst many and deal with them should they arise within the counselling and/or supervision domain? Or ought they to highlight certain cross-cultural issues and work towards solutions within supervision? Or finally, ought they have integrative models to make sense of cultural aspects of counselling and supervision? The latter is obviously the view of Leong and Wagner, who helpfully dissect the literature on cross-cultural counselling supervision into three camps: a) those that mention cross-cultural issues alongside other factors in supervision; b) those that deal with particular problems and potential solutions within cross-cultural counselling supervision and; c) those that propose integrative models from which cross-cultural counselling supervision issues can be observed, predicted and explored.

5. *Regard for the welfare of clients needs to be high on the agenda.* Cross-cultural supervision can never exist without reference to cross-cultural counselling. Clients are at the heart of supervision. Understanding cross-cultural aspects of counselling work is imperative for both supervisees and supervisors if supervision is going to be effective.

Multicultural issues in supervision: supervisees

A number of authors have suggested stage models for the development of cross-cultural awareness in trainees (Bernard and Goodyear, 1992; Cook, 1994; Peterson, 1991; Vasquez and McKinley, 1982; Carney and Kahn, 1984, Gardner, 1980). Table 2.1 is a model that integrates dimensions of these, and is offered as a synthesis of the various ideas outlined by Leong and Wagner (1994). Briefly, it looks at the stage of development of the supervisee, and how the supervisor can intervene to help further awareness and action in cross-cultural counselling work. It does not go into detail on how supervisors can actually further these responses, some of which (because of the supervisory arrangements) may be difficult to implement, e.g. facilitating contact with culturally different groups.

This model can be used by supervisors to ascertain at what stage of multicultural development supervisees are, and then fit their responses to that level. However, problems can be multiplied where there is group supervision with trainees at different stages of cross-cultural development.

Multicultural issues in supervision: supervisors

Supervisors will see no need for working with cultural aspects of counselling if they, themselves, are insensitive to the underlying cultural dynamics in all human interactions. Supervisors are not born with automatic multicultural awareness, they need education and training in cross-cultural counselling and supervision work. Priest (1994) has research data that seems to indicate that supervisors may well go through a number of stages in working with cultural issues in supervision (see below). His is the only model I have come across that connects supervisor with stages in cultural awareness and offers a potential training base for training (see Table 2.2).

Those running training courses in supervision, as well as supervisors themselves, can use this model to monitor multicultural development – that of others or that of themselves. However, it is best not to assume, particularly in Britain where cross-cultural training in counselling is still in its infancy, that supervisors are at stage five or six of Priest's model. Many are not. Few supervisors have had in-depth training in multicultural counselling, never mind multicultural supervision.

Table 2.1 *Development of cross-cultural awareness in supervisees*

Supervisee stage	Supervisor responses
1. Unawareness Awareness of multicultural dimensions is minimal. Focuses on 'common humanity' and sees counselling as applying equally to all individuals.	Promotes growth and awareness; encourages exploration of culture in self and others; helps supervisees become aware of limited knowledge and cultural attitudes; provides consciousness-raising experiences; facilitates contact with culturally different groups.
2. Beginning awareness Has a growing awareness of discrepancies between cultures. However, awareness is mostly around demographic or descriptive characteristics. May even see cultural differences as forms of 'resistance' to counselling.	Encourages expressions of feeling around cultural differences; allows confrontation with supervisor; suggests readings and experiments; challenges supervisees to deepen personal exploration; helps expand knowledge of personal attitudes and beliefs.
3. Conscious awareness Supervisee has conflicting emotions around cultural issues. Caught between seeing own culture as the 'norm', and struggles with applying theoretical orientations to other cultures.	Helps supervisee look at the impact of beliefs on clients; promotes cultural competence; helps supervisee resolve interpersonal dissonance.
4. Consolidated awareness Supervisee has developed a multicultural identity	Encourages autonomous decisions; provides cross-cultural counselling experiences; helps supervisees own their own part in culture.
5. Transcendent awareness Supervisee integrates personal cultural values with counselling and supervision values. Negotiates culturally sensitive approaches to supervision and counselling.	Is alert to supervisee taking social action to promote equality and cultural pluralism.

Working with cross-cultural issues in supervision

Several authors have suggestions for supervisors on how to work with cross-cultural issues within supervision (Bernard, 1994b; Fukuyama, 1994; Peterson, 1991). The following is a summary of recommendations:

1. Supervisors need to confront racial/ethic variables early on in the process of supervision.
2. Supervisors ought to be proactive in creating racial awareness and promotion within the various institutions of which they are a part.
3. Supervisors need to be proactive in initiating discussion of multi-cultural issues in supervision regardless of the cultural background of supervisees or clients.

Table 2.2 *Priest's (1994) stages of supervisor multicultural development*

Stage	Supervisor response
1.	Denying that there are appreciable cultural differences that influence supervision ('I treat all my supervisees the same').
2.	A recognition of cultural differences without knowing what to do with the information. At this stage supervisors may feel overwhelmed with the thought of learning about cultural aspects of supervision.
3.	Attempts on the part of the supervisor to identify differences, and try to understand how they impact on supervision.
4.	The supervisor tries to understand how he/she fits within the cultural dimension, creating a cultural identity.
5.	The supervisor begins to appreciate cultural distinctiveness and identifies thought-process and communication patterns that facilitate supervision and assist the supervisee in learning counselling.
6.	The supervisor is able to formulate multiple supervisory methodologies that are respectful of the supervisee's culture and interactive style.

4. More training for supervisors in working with multicultural issues needs to be set up. Supervisors can use their own supervision to work with their multicultural development.
5. Supervisors need to be made aware of not overemphasizing cultural diversity, i.e. trying to be 'politically correct'.
6. Supervisors need to be trained to be sensitive to when supervisees are ready for certain types of counselling experiences working with multicultural processes.
7. Supervisors need to both support and challenge when helping supervisees deal with multicultural issues.

There is no doubt that this whole domain is fraught with difficulty. How do cultural elements affect working within a group supervision setting where there is a range of men/women, different ages, different races, different counselling orientations, different sexual orientations? The mind 'boggles' in trying to unravel some of the issues and some of the dynamics that could arise.

RESEARCH IN SUPERVISION

There is no doubt that research projects in supervision have proliferated over the past ten years. Russell, Crimmings and Lent (1984) reviewed the research up to 1984 and in the second edition of the *Handbook of Counseling Psychology* (1992), Holloway extended their work up to 1990. Both of these, combined with other reviews (Bernard and Goodyear, 1992; Lambert and Arnold, 1987, Worthington, 1987), provide excellent summaries and critiques of research findings in supervision.

While the proliferation of research projects will no doubt continue, there are a few gaps that deserve consideration. Longitudinal data is needed to monitor supervisee developments over time. C. Carroll (1994) used an 'Expectations of Supervision' questionnaire to survey trainee perceptions of the tasks of supervision over the two years of their training courses. Conclusions indicate that there were almost no changes in expectations over time. One possible explanation for this is that supervisees are very ignorant of what supervision means and even after two years of counselling training remain unclear about what to expect from supervision. It is also possible that they see themselves as so powerless within the supervisory relationship that they leave supervision to supervisors and fit in with supervisor ways of working. Future research here could look at particular courses and locations, and how different understandings of supervision affect supervisees.

More access to actual supervision sessions would allow for data about what *actually happens* in supervision rather than what either supervisor/supervisee perceive what happens, and more investigations into the value of supervisory interventions, especially the role of counselling orientation on supervision, would help.

There is also need for considering the needs of experienced counsellors/ supervisees as against those who are in training, with regard to whom most of the research has taken place.

There has been an increase in research in supervision in Britain in the past eight years (Arundale, 1993; C. Carroll, 1994; Frankham, 1987; Kaberry, 1995; Kevlin, 1988; Parker, 1990; Simms, 1991; Thompson, 1991; Waite, 1992). All researchers have used quantitative research methodologies with the exception of Thompson. The subjects of their research have covered a wide domain from supervisee expectations to the place of cultural training in supervision courses. The hope is that the range will continue to expand.

SUPERVISION AS A LIFE-LONG PROFESSIONAL COMMITMENT

A further trend within supervision is its consideration as a life-long commitment. Awareness is growing, somewhat due to negative aspects of counselling, that experienced counsellors need a forum in which they can review their work. And not just counsellors, but professionals from the helping professions such as social workers, nurses, probation officers, teachers, personnel officers, human resource development workers, etc. I was pleasantly surprised recently to be asked by quite an experienced psychiatrist to supervise her work. There is no doubt that counselling has a valuable lesson for other professions with its insistence that supervision be part of professional life. BAC has built this provision into its ethical code, and the *Ethical Guidelines for Counseling Supervisors* (ACES, 1993) has adopted a similar stance (this seems to be the first time such a provision is included in the American setting). The preamble to the *Guidelines* states:

> One overriding assumption underlying this document is that supervision should be ongoing throughout a counselor's career and not stop when a particular level of education, certification, or membership in a professional organisation is attained.

However, we are still at an early stage in deciphering the specifics of consultative supervision, i.e. supervision with qualified counsellors.

CLIENT-CENTRED AND SUPERVISEE-CENTRED SUPERVISION

In supervision the focus of attention is turning from what supervisors can offer to what supervisees need, and a realization that supervision is ultimately for clients. Supervisees see supervisors so that clients can use counselling more effectively. It is not enough that supervisors have clients 'in the corner of their eyes' as they work with supervisees. Rather clients must be between them and their supervisees, as a child is between its parents. The 'nursing triad' has been interpreted too linearly, as if father, mother and child were in a straight line. A more helpful image is that of father caring for mother with child between them.

Some supervision models are good at holding clients at the centre of supervision. Developmental and social role models can concentrate so much on the learning stages of supervisees, or the tasks of supervisors, that clients get lost. Counselling-bound models of supervision can often stress aspects of the counselling work that ignore the client and concentrate on what is happening to the supervisee. Supervision is above all a balancing act, where client and supervisee are held at both ends of the see-saw. Concentrate on one and the other disappears.

The shift in focus of supervision on to the supervisee *as he/she works with clients* has forced supervision to look intently at the supervisee in all his/her dimensions: developmental stage, learning style, ability to use supervision. The emphasis is on the supervisor adapting to the supervisee, not – as has been the basis of past models of supervision, especially the apprenticeship and counselling models – the other way round. Many models of counselling have remained solid in a kind of 'timewarp' since they were founded and take little consideration of modern concepts of informed consent, data protection, consumer rights, nor of legal and ethical dimensions of contemporary relationships. (For instance, is it justifiable today not to provide external evaluation of the work of supervisees as has been the tradition of person-centred counselling, or not to provide detailed explanations of how counsellors work as has been the history of psychodynamic approaches?) Supervision is in a strong position to force counselling to review its tenets and to update them in the light of modern demands. These trends certainly indicate it is a force to be reckoned with in its own right.

The eight trends outlined above summarize some of the 'movement' within counselling supervision today. These are the areas of current debate that will, presumably, characterize the field of supervision in the immediate future. These eight are by no means the only issues of interest to supervisors, but they are the overall focal points of supervision at the moment. Nor are there 'final words' on any of the above: as debating points they have their adversaries as well as their proponents. Such makes for aliveness within a profession.

THREE

A generic integrative model of supervision

Peter had allowed each supervisee to role-cast him in their own way. For the first he was a manager, for the second a case-work tutor and for the third a reassuring counsellor. He sensed that somehow he was colluding with their own defensive patterns; and that to gain more from supervision, perhaps each supervisee needed him to play other roles than those they had seduced him into playing for them. However, he had no model or framework with which to make active choices about his own supervision style. (Hawkins and Shohet, 1991, p. 99)

The task of the supervisor is to organize materials, facilities, conditions and people so that student learning takes place. (Tousley and Kobberger, 1984, p. 134)

There are a number of supervision models available, most of which concentrate on one aspect of supervision. This chapter will present two models as a prelude to my own linear model of supervision.

Holloway in *Clinical Supervision: A Systems Approach* (1995) has elaborated a way of understanding what tasks and roles are being used at any given time within the supervision process. Using a matrix of supervisory tasks and supervisory functions, it is possible to place supervision interventions in one of twenty-five boxes (see Table 3.1). With the matrix she provides an overall model (Figure 3.1) connecting the various factors in supervision.

Holloway's book combines these two models into a very comprehensive method of understanding and applying supervision, usable by either supervisors or supervisees to monitor which tasks and functions are being used.

Table 3.1 *A matrix of supervisory tasks and functions*

	Supervision tasks				
Functions	**Counselling skills**	**Case concept**	**Professional role**	**Emotional awareness**	**Evaluation**
Monitoring					
Instructing					
Modelling					
Supporting					
Consulting					

Source: E.L. Holloway, *Clinical Supervision: A Systems Approach* (1995), p. 59.
Copyright © E.L. Holloway. Reprinted by permission of Sage Publications, Inc.

Page and Wosket's book (1994) contains a systematic model leading the supervisor through the various stages of supervision, stopping at each to look in some depth at what is needed, at the potential pitfalls, and at how best to implement each stage (see Figure 3.2). Though it is difficult at times to find one's bearings within the five subsections of the five sections, their work is valuable for being a practical and comprehensive supervisory guide. It can be used creatively with the models presented in this chapter.

My own model will offer a generic and integrative outline connecting the goals and purposes of supervision to the functions and tasks/roles of supervision. Like Holloway's model (1995) it will try to connect tasks and functions; like Page and Wosket (1994) it will stress understanding the flow of supervision. The characteristics of the model are:

- It is atheoretical: it applies across counselling orientations.
- It is a process model: it allows the practitioner to follow supervision as an underlying dynamic movement between supervisor and supervisee.
- It is a competency-based model insofar as supervisors are provided with a skills base against which they can measure themselves and their array of skills.
- It is compatible with developmental models of supervision, allowing the opportunity for changing interventions and strategies according to the developmental needs of the supervisee.
- It is grounded in the literature on developmental and social role models of supervision.

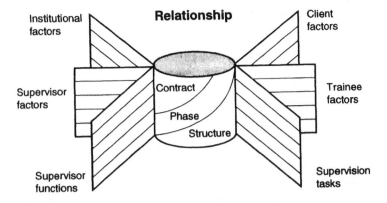

Figure 3.1 *Holloway's systems approach to supervision.*
Source: E.L. Holloway, *Clinical Supervision: A Systems Approach* (1995), p. 58.
Copyright © E.L. Holloway. Reprinted by permission of Sage Publications, Inc.

- It integrates the strengths of different models into a systemic framework.

THE PURPOSES OF SUPERVISION

A purpose is defined as 'that which is set before as a general goal to be attained' (Bradley, 1989, p. 8). What is the overall goal or purpose of supervision? Bradley (1989) has put forward three purposes for counselling supervision:

1. Facilitation of the personal and professional development of the counsellor.
2. Development of counsellor competencies.
3. Promotion of accountable counselling and guidance services and programmes.

Even though the above does not mention the client by name there is little doubt that supervision includes the welfare of the client under its 'accountability' clause. In fact the BAC *Code of Ethics and Practice for the Supervision of Counsellors* (BAC, 1988) places this as the main focus of supervision: 'The primary purpose of supervision is to ensure that the counsellor is addressing the needs of the client' (p. 1). My own conclusions from experience and reading the supervision literature is that there are two overarching purposes to supervision: the welfare of the client and the development of the supervisee.

The welfare of the client

Since in many instances supervisees are trainee counsellors, it is imperative that their work is 'overseen' by competent and experienced practitioners. This provides some guarantee that clients are not being harmed and that counsellors are working within their competencies. In some instances (e.g. in the USA) a supervisor has 'vicarious responsibility' for clients. Cormier and Bernard (1982) define this term as, 'the doctrine, (where) someone in a position of authority or responsibility, such as a supervisor, is responsible for acts of his or her trainees or assistants. Stated another way, supervisors are ultimately responsible for the welfare of clients counselled by their supervisees' (p. 488). The British legal system is different from the American system in that in Britain all actors are deemed responsible for their own actions (Carroll, 1988). However, whether legal responsibility is the order of the day or not, moral responsibility rests with the supervisor to

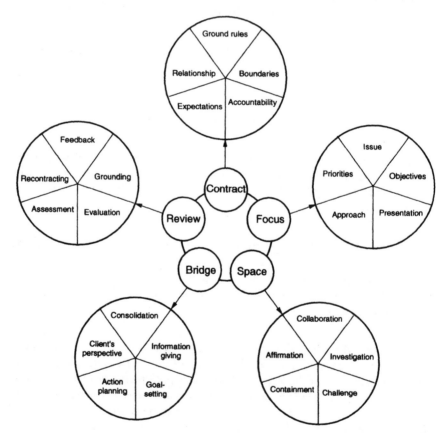

Figure 3.2 *A cyclical model of supervision. Adapted from S. Page and V. Wosket, Supervising the Counsellor: A Cyclical Model (London: Routledge, 1994). Used with permission.*

ascertain that, at worst, clients are not being harmed, and at best they are receiving the best service from this counsellor.

The welfare of the client means that supervisors monitor the work of supervisees in ways that assure them, and can assure others, that clients are not being harmed as trainees work with them. Obviously, different supervisors have different methods of monitoring their work with supervisees. Some use live supervision, observing the counselling session as it takes place, and can intervene in the actual session should that be necessary. Other supervisors require audio- or videotapes of actual counselling sessions as a way of monitoring the counselling work. Others rely solely on reports from supervisees and/or their own relationship with supervisees as the central feature of accountability. Whatever method is used to monitor client work, what is important is that the client is cared for, looked after, and is getting a good service. Counselling work is not about experimenting with clients for the learning of trainees, but about supervisees beginning to work with clients and using that work as a way of learning how to become better counsellors. It is the task of supervisors to ensure that supervisees are not working beyond their capabilities, and are being referred clients who are appropriate for them to see (Carroll, 1993).

The professional development of the supervisee

The second overall purpose of supervision is the personal and professional development of the supervisee, which facilitates the process whereby supervisees move from being novices towards what Stoltenberg and Delworth (1987) call 'master-practitioners'. They offer three areas where this movement takes place:

a) *autonomy*: the counsellor experiences a progressive awareness of being able to function as a professional in an increasingly independent way;

b) *motivation*: the counsellor moves towards more realistic reasons for working with clients and a realization of the hazards involved;

c) *self and other awareness*: counsellors become more alert to themselves, their clients, and the relationships involved.

However, there is no overall agreement on what the professional development of counsellors means. This confusion is seen most clearly in the array of training courses for counsellors, between which there may be some agreement at the early levels of training (Diploma) but almost none at later levels. At higher degree level (Masters courses in counselling, counselling psychology, psychotherapy) there is very little agreement on what constitutes a basic curriculum. Some recent attempts have been made to standardize counselling training (British Psychological Society, 1995; Connor, 1994).

Whatever the operationalized aspects of both goals, the overall aim of supervision is generally accepted as being twofold: the welfare of the client and the professional development of the supervisee. Sometimes these twin general goals are placed chronologically with the emphasis on the welfare of the client assured through the development of the supervisee. Some supervision works on the principle that the best insurance for clients' welfare is the learning of supervisees.

THE FUNCTIONS OF SUPERVISION

The connections between the functions and the purposes of supervision are displayed below.

Functions	Purposes
Educative (formative)	Welfare of the client
Supportive (restorative)	Professional development of the supervisee
Administrative (normative)	

Functions are the first step in making purposes concrete. There is strong overall agreement that the functions of supervision are educative, supportive and administrative (Kadushin, 1985; Proctor, 1986).

The educative function of supervision ensures that supervision maintains an educational involvement with the supervisee and that the personal and professional development of supervisees involves ongoing education. There is some controversy over the responsibilities of the training course and the educational responsibilities of supervisors. Most supervisors consider the training course as having responsibility for formal teaching, i.e. skills training, knowledge and information, personal development, research and research skills. Supervision is the learning-by-doing, allowing supervisees to reflect on their work with clients in the presence of an experienced other who enables that reflection. Supervisors inevitably fill in gaps in knowledge, increase skills, make practical what was once head-knowledge and must now become working-knowledge. They share, with supervisees, responsibility for monitoring learning as trainees work with clients. Proctor (1986) has called this function of supervision the 'formative' task.

The supportive function involves offering supervisees a forum where they are encouraged to look at their own issues and ask for/be given the encouragement they need to explore their way of working with clients. It is this function that provides the 'containment' side of supervision. Supporting supervisees as they struggle to find their own way of being counsellors, as they deal with their own and their clients' difficulties, as they engage emotionally with clients, takes place throughout all aspects of supervision. Proctor (1986) has called this function of supervision the 'restorative' task.

The administrative function has an eye to all aspects of the work that contains accountability and responsibility of the supervisee, and for the welfare of the client. Called the 'normative' tasks of supervision by Proctor (1986), it pays heed to the ethical and professional aspects of client work, the organizational dimensions that affect client contact, and enables supervisees to monitor their own work as professionals. It is here that supervisors become advocates of clients and of the counselling profession making sure that quality service is rendered and that the ethical and professional dimensions are maintained to a high level.

THE ROLES AND TASKS OF SUPERVISION

The connections between tasks, functions and purposes of supervision are shown in Table 3.2.

From the functions and purposes we can understand the tasks involved in supervision. Tasks are the behavioural side of functions and roles. The role is person-centred: the task is action-centred: the function is a combination of both roles and tasks. If the function is education, then the role is teacher/pupil, and the task teaching/learning. Even though a strong notional distinction is made between roles and tasks, in reality they combine, 'Roles are made up of sets of behaviours that create certain

Table 3.2

Tasks	Functions	Purposes
Relating	Supportive	Welfare of client
Counselling		
Monitoring	Educative	Personal and professional development of supervisee
Consulting		
Administrating	Administrative	
Professional/ethical		
Teaching		

expectancies of performance for the actor and the receiver in the encounter' (Holloway and Acker, 1989, p. 3).

There is no agreement on what constitutes the tasks of supervision. Bernard (1979) was the first to concentrate on supervisory roles and created her Discrimination model with three tasks: supervisor as teacher, as counsellor and as consultant. Other role-related models of supervision followed with Holloway's (1995) systems approach to supervision being the most recent. Carroll (1994c) has surveyed a number of social role models of supervision, and concluded that there are seven generic tasks of supervision (Figure 4.1). While these will be considered individually in greater detail in Chapter 4, it is worth making some comments on supervisory tasks in general.

The generic tasks/roles outlined here may not be acceptable in all models of supervision, e.g. some supervisory arrangements refuse to 'evaluate' the supervisee on the basis that it affects adversely the supervisory relationship. Furthermore, there may be different models of supervision that stress different roles/tasks: some (e.g. rational behaviour emotive supervision), are more teaching-based, others more counselling-based (person-centred supervision), others more relationship-based (psychodynamically oriented supervision). Designating generic tasks does not mean that all are found within all supervision models.

Despite the fact that the literature is quite extensive on the tasks involved in supervision, there is little explanation for the conditions or criteria supervisors use for choosing particular roles (Kurpius and Baker, 1977). Agreement on the importance of a task or a role in no way indicates that the individuals or groups who agree actually operationalize the task/role in similar ways, e.g. few would disagree with the 'teaching' task of supervision, but there is wide variation in the way the teaching task is implemented by different supervisors. Some refuse to give 'information' to the supervisee and believe information-giving should take place on the training course. Furthermore, it may well be that the tasks designated by supervisors and supervisees as the ones in which they engage differ from what they actually do.

From his research in the British context Carroll (1994c) found that supervisors and supervisees seem to take responsibility for different super-visory tasks. Using six supervisory dyads, he coded supervision tapes over the course of approximately one year using the seven tasks of supervision as a basis. In all the supervisory dyads, initiation of the relating, teaching and evaluation tasks had higher frequency for supervisors than for supervisees. However, in four of the dyads, consultation and counselling tasks had higher frequencies for supervisees than for supervisors. There were equal frequencies for supervisors and supervisees in two dyads for counselling, professional/ethical and administrative tasks. This seems to indicate that supervisors take responsibility for the relationship, the teaching and the evaluation tasks of supervision, supervisees take responsibility for fulfilling the consultation and counselling tasks. The other two tasks, monitoring professional/ethical issues and the administrative task, are shared. However, because of the small number of dyads and the narrowness of counselling orientations from which they come, some caution is advised in generalizing these findings.

Although there is reasonable agreement across supervisory models and, indeed across professions (psychiatry, social work, counselling psychology, teacher training) about the main supervisory tasks, there is little to help us understand the conditions for performing certain behaviours. Developmental models of supervision locate these in the stages through which supervisees move. Other variables influencing the choice of task may be the orientation of the supervisor, the supervisor's limited choice of task due to his/her skills, allegiance to a particular counselling orientation, the needs of the supervisee or the relationship between the participants.

This chapter has suggested a model of supervision that connects purposes, functions and roles/tasks. In particular it has isolated the main social role models of supervision and named the collection of tasks shown to be pertinent in the literature. There is widespread agreement on the teaching, counselling and consultative tasks of supervision. The evaluating and monitoring professional ethical tasks feature strongly in the literature. The administrative task comes more from a social work background. The relationship in supervision, while not always designated a task, is considered essential to outcome. With this review of the literature and from initial interviews with supervisors, the following generic tasks of supervision were named:

1. Creating the learning relationship
2. The teaching task
3. The counselling task
4. Monitoring professional/ethical issues
5. The evaluating task
6. The consultative task
7. The administrative task

These will be discussed in more detail in the next chapter.

FOUR

The seven tasks of supervision

> Both supervisor and supervisee begin supervision with expectations regarding the appropriate behaviour for the roles in the supervisory relationship. (Holloway, 1992, p. 193)

Chapter 3 outlined a generic model of counselling supervision in which seven tasks were considered. Carroll (1994c) has suggested that these generic or overall tasks underlie all supervision approaches with individual supervisors performing various mixtures of tasks. Some supervisors 'lock into' particular tasks and restrict supervision to performing these. Often the decision about which tasks to employ in supervision, made either conscientiously or unconsciously, accords with theoretical orientation, and/or is due to the limited training and competencies of supervisors. The idea mooted here is that effective supervisors choose from the range of supervisory tasks, as appropriate for the supervisee's learning. This chapter will look in more detail at each of these tasks before offering a model (Chapter 5) which integrates them into a supervisory process. Figure 4.1 presents an overview of the seven generic tasks of supervision.

The material in this chapter is taken largely from my research in supervision (Carroll, 1994c), in which twenty-three supervisors recognized by the British Association for Counselling (BAC) were interviewed on their views of supervision (85 per cent of all BAC-recognized supervisors took part) and, in particular, on how they saw and implemented the seven generic tasks. A semi-structured interview was used and the material analysed using grounded theory. In this section quotations from the interview, grouped by theme, will illustrate how supervisors conceptualize supervision tasks. Quotations given in italic are direct excerpts from the interviews with supervisors.

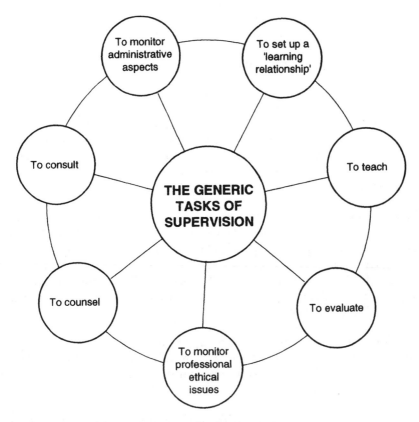

Figure 4.1 *Overview of the seven tasks of supervision*

TASK 1: CREATING THE LEARNING RELATIONSHIP

Throughout the history of supervision the relationship between supervisor and supervisee has been given prominence. Even though it has received relatively little research attention, it has been recognized as a key element of supervision (Doehrman, 1976; Efstation *et al.*, 1990; Markowitz, 1958; Kinder, 1981).

Despite this centrality, there remains a lack of clarity about the kind of relationship involved. Cohen (1980, p. 79) stated the confusion from the perspective of the supervisee: 'To begin with, the nature of the relationship the student therapist is entering is unclear. Will I be an apprentice? Peer? Student? Friend? Lover? Some combination of the above?'

From interviews with BAC-recognized supervisors (Carroll, 1994c) six categories for the supervisory relationship emerged:

1. There was little agreement among interviewees on a clear definition of relationship that makes up supervision:

it's not a teacher/pupil, it's not a counsellor/client, it's not an apprenticeship . . . it's a little bit like a mentor

2. A number of metaphors are used to describe the relationship:

grandmother/mother/baby is like the supervisor/counsellor/client

apprenticeship/mentor/elder sister/junior colleague/almost parental/ tutorial/facilitative/a working relationship/teacher–pupil relationship/a partnership/almost like a young adolescent who wants to go off and have his/her first social experience and then come back and very excitedly, part adult and part adolescent, tells me what happens as a result

None seems adequate to capture the exact flavour of the relationship involved and each image has its deficiency. The apprenticeship model is too dependent on the 'guru' image of the master; the mentor metaphor creates too much of a power mentality. Overall most opt for a 'hybrid sort of relationship' which combines a number of roles. The 'triangular' aspect of supervision involving supervisor, supervisee and client makes it a difficult relationship to conceptualize.

3. Almost all supervisors saw the supervisory relationship changing as supervision progressed. The term 'working alliance' was used several times to combine both the kind of relationship involved and how it changes over time.

The relationship changes over time. At the beginning it may be more like a teacher/pupil relationship but as it progresses it becomes more colleague/ colleague.

[The relationship] changes in all kinds of ways . . . the supervisee can begin to challenge much more . . . the supervisee may become much more critical.

I think you move from the preceptor to the mentor to the sponsor to the colleague.

4. Supervisors generally feel capable of combining other roles with that of supervisor.

I socialize with them [supervisees] insofar as we socialize in semi-formal contexts. Like we may meet at conferences or have parties . . . but I don't socialize with them as I would with friends.

Even though other roles are combined with the roles of supervision there was general agreement that these complicate the relationship and ideally it is better if no other roles exist between supervisor and supervisee. Having stated that, supervisors see themselves as flexible and creative in combining roles, e.g. combining counselling and supervisory roles, changing from a supervisory relationship to a counselling relationship.

> *I would never dream of giving a client a cup of tea but I will sometimes have a cup of tea or coffee with somebody whilst we're supervising.*

Sometimes the stage of the relationship makes a difference, as does the evaluation that takes place. Both can have an impact on the kind of relationship involved.

5. The issue of power in the supervisory relationship is considered.

> *The relationship has elements of judgement and containment ... I don't think it is a symmetrical relationship.*

> *There are a lot of people who see it as a peer relationship. I don't see it that way ... I have a function here as someone who is perceived as being more knowledgeable than the person I'm supervising.*

6. Implications for supervision of the kind of relationship involved are outlined. Several areas were suggested by interviewees as directly related to the supervisory relationship:

- that supervisees should have a choice regarding their supervisor;
- that supervisors self-disclose to supervisees more than to clients;
- that the relationship between counsellor and client is played out in the supervisory relationship (being able to understand the transference/countertransference issues of this is very important – the relationship between supervisor and supervisee will be a key factor in the effectiveness of counselling);
- that the 'supervisory contract' is very important to the relationship.

Summary

There is agreement amongst supervisors that supervision comprises a professional relationship characterized by certain boundaries. The relationship is defined by its roles which are numerous and flexible. A major element is the changing relationship that takes place as supervision moves from a beginning stage, which is characterized by teacher/pupil features, towards a colleague/colleague relationship. Supervisors are aware of the importance of the relationship within supervision and realize that learning only takes place where the environment is safe for the supervisee. This safety is provided by both support and challenge.

The relationship is an area in supervision that requires clear contracting and negotiation. It is also the area where transference, countertransference and parallel process need to be monitored carefully.

There is some evidence that the relationship in supervision is characterized along theoretical orientation lines, with some marked differences between psychodynamic supervisors and those who designate themselves humanistic.

The impact of these various definitions results in more confusion than clarity. Since supervision is made up of a number of roles, inevitably it will be difficult to define. It would be more beneficial for both research and practice to view supervision as a collection of possible roles between trainee and supervisor, rather than search for one term or image that encompasses all aspects of it.

Establishing a supervisory relationship is seen as an essential element in good supervisory practice. This means supervisors and supervisees engage in a variety of roles suitable to enhancing the learning of supervisees. This is a tall order for many supervisors who have been taught, quite stringently at times, that mixing roles creates poor boundaries, and that the essence of the therapeutic relationship is that the counsellor has a single role with clients. Shifting from single to multiple-role relationships is fraught with difficulty and often forces supervisors into counselling-bound models of supervision where they remain within a single role. This book suggests that effective supervision is characterized by flexibility across roles. It also recommends training for supervisors to help them use different roles when appropriate.

TASK 2: THE TEACHING TASK OF SUPERVISION

The responses of BAC-recognized supervisors on the place of teaching in supervision can be divided into eight themes:

1. All respondents saw teaching as an essential aspect of supervision:

> *So I see myself as being a teacher in offering frameworks for understanding. I do that a tremendous amount.*

2. The teaching role in supervision allows for the translation of theory into practice, and for an individualized programme:

> *This part is more personalized ... the trainees bring particular problems that they are focusing on ... they get a lot more individual attention ... and the skills are discussed in terms of their appropriateness in a particular context with a particular person.*

This complements the more formal and general teaching that characterizes the training course.

3. Interviewees were wary of seeing their teaching in supervision in a formal way:

Teaching with a small 't' rather than a capital 'T' ... it's almost a sense of play where the counsellor tells me about it, and I say something, chuck it back to them, and they chuck it back to me, it's almost like we've got a piece of plasticine ... we each try and shape it.

I can be the enabler, the facilitator, the catalyst. I like the word catalyst.

4. Modelling by the supervisor is seen as implicit in supervision:

I think there is the learning by modelling which they pick up by the process itself. I think that is pretty important actually.

5. The teaching task receded as the supervisee became more experienced. There were indications that sometimes the content of the teaching changed.

At the beginning stage people really need confidence building and basic teaching of techniques and sharpening of techniques and once they've got that then they really need slightly more sophisticated treatment planning and sharpening on techniques and checking back on theory and checking back on hypothesis and so on. And the next stage is when they do differential treatment planning and then they are needing more sophisticated input on different treatment plans and why does this perhaps not work, and why does that work better.

6. A number of teaching methodologies are used in supervision. Giving formal information is one:

I see myself as being a teacher in offering frameworks for understanding ... I always have a flip chart around ... I will tell supervisees that I have at my disposal millions of little frameworks that I really am enamoured of and I think are tremendously useful to people and will it be O.K. if I show them.

I wouldn't give a little lecture, but I would give a mini little lecture.

Books, articles, reading are often recommended, and there is some attempt to fit teaching to the learning frames of the supervisee.

7. Some react to this formal didactic side of supervision:

I think I would only do that [formal teaching] to a pretty limited degree because I would see that as moving too far away from the client ... I don't ever give people little lectures. I don't approve of that as a teaching method ... if people discover things for themselves then they retain them: whereas if you tell them they are more likely to forget.

There was one supervisor who questioned the need for information in supervision. Asked how he would respond if a supervisee asked for some informational help on bulimia he responded,

> *No, I would never do that [give the supervisee information on bulimia] . . . I'd say, What is making you take on that person when you know you can't cope, handle it. What are you really into? What's that doing to you? . . . Either go and refer them to an expert or go and get the expertise yourself.*

8. A large number of supervisors use role play as an instructional method and teach skills within supervision. A small number do not. Examples from the experience of the supervisor are sometimes shared as ways of helping supervisees learn, though one supervisor warned about the focus shifting from the client work of the supervisee to that of the supervisor.

A much-discussed area of learning in supervision is the use of tape-recorded sessions with the clients. Opinions did not always fall neatly into orientation lines: a strong psychodynamic counsellor said,

> *One of the ways to break the defensiveness is to hear a tape and pick up what's actually happening. If I think the counsellor is feeding me a line that they're doing all right but they're doing lots of questioning, I will sometimes ask for a tape and it usually reveals lots of questions, and we can work on technique as a learning thing.*

Interviewees tended to be either in favour of using taped sessions as a good learning methodology or against it as being either intrusive or time-consuming.

Other teaching/learning formats were introduced. Mention was made of a session 'devoid of supervision and then either they or I or together will produce papers and discuss particular areas', a 'psychodrama', ' . . . and if there was something like a visualization I would say "This is what I found useful . . . have you thought about that?" ' Some think that theory should follow practice. Others see instruction as helpful to practice.

Within the teaching task it is important to be seen to be genuine: 'What I don't do is I don't pretend I know everything.'

The need to teach supervisees how best to use supervision was voiced, 'People are not taught how to use supervision . . . this reflection and selection on what you bring to supervision . . . what do you want from supervision and how do you use it?'

Summary

Supervision is viewed by supervisors as akin to other teaching modalities. Individual supervisors have their own concepts of what makes good teaching, what teaching strategies they use and with which methods they feel comfortable and uncomfortable. Supervisors never doubt that teaching is a formal task of supervision, that it changes as the relationship changes. How teaching is operationalized and the methodologies adopted are more personal. It would be interesting to know if individual supervisors teach as they themselves have been taught, and supervise as they have been supervised (there are some hints of being victims of one's prior learning and previous experience of being supervised). It would also make interesting research to know how adaptable supervisors are to the learning styles of their supervisees and/or how much supervisees have to fit the teaching methods of their supervisors. There is a strong sense from these interviews that the teaching methodologies adopted by supervisors stem more from their own background, their beliefs and their counselling orientation than from the developmental learning needs of the supervisee.

The methods used by supervisors are many, and besides being methods they themselves seem to have inherited, there are strong connections between these methods and the counselling orientation from which the supervisor emerged. The data here would indicate the need for further training in teaching methods relevant to learning needs within a supervisory arrangement, to help the supervisor move from being primarily a therapist to also being a teacher of therapists.

TASK 3: THE COUNSELLING TASK OF SUPERVISION

The counselling task of supervision encourages supervisees to reflect on their personal reactions arising in working with clients or indeed supervisors. Even though this is called the 'counselling' role in supervision it is not therapy or personal counselling. In fact the most objectionable stance taken by supervisors (as reported by supervisees) is when the supervisor becomes or tries to become their therapist (Frankham, 1987; Rosenblatt and Mayer, 1975).

There is some agreement that the personal reactions of supervisees to clients, to themselves, to supervisors, to agencies in which they see clients, are valuable and positive aids for the therapeutic situation (Doehrman, 1976; Lesser, 1984; Searles, 1955). That they have a place in supervision is generally accepted, certainly within the psychodynamic and humanistic fields. Within behaviourial and cognitive-behaviourial orientations there is a place for its inclusion, even if on a limited basis (Wessler and Ellis, 1980).

The aim of supervision is to help supervisees become better therapeutic workers, whereas the aim in counselling stresses becoming a better person. The difference is not always so simple. Schlessinger (1966, p. 130) called this the 'most perplexing question in the supervision of psychotherapy – is it teaching or therapy?' But opinions vary on what it means. Some argue that there is no place for counselling in supervision (Altucher, 1967; Banikiotes, 1975; Blocher, 1983). Alongside that there is a strong body of opinion that sees supervision more akin to counselling and psychotherapy

(Arbuckle, 1963; Carkhuff, Kratochvil and Friel, 1968; Wessler and Ellis, 1980). Others point out that counselling is one amongst other tasks involved in supervision and has a definite place, though by no means a monopoly (Bernard, 1979; Hess, 1980).

Recent writings see this issue as unresolved. For example, Burns and Holloway argue that supervisors 'ethically cannot undertaking counselling relationships with their trainees' (1990, p. 48), basing their argument on the 'dual relationship' principle outlined in some ethical codes. The British Association for Counselling *Code of Ethics and Practice for Supervisors*, however, adopts a more flexible position, whereby:

> Supervisors and counsellors must distinguish between supervising and counselling the counsellor. They would not normally expect to mix the two. On the rare occasions when the supervisor might engage in counselling with the counsellor, a clear contract must be negotiated, and any counselling done must not be at the expense of supervision time. (1988, Section 2.4)

From the literature I have isolated four stances on how supervisors work with the personal reactions and feelings of supervisees emerging from their work with clients:

1. Working on an ad hoc basis and focusing on supervisee reactions when they interfere with client work. This view considers a counselling role within supervision but insists that it is a part of supervision and not the only focus. Searles (1962, p. 602) talked about this being done 'sparingly, if at all'.
2. Giving more time and emphasis to personal issues, leaving aside definite sessions in which to work with these. Lesser (1984) talks of a 'collaborative analysis' and Arbuckle (1963, 1965) was adamant that the counsellor–educator must be involved with students in a counselling role.
3. Issues of a personal nature arising in supervision should be taken to personal therapy (Lesser, 1984).
4. Supervisees should be trusted to deal with these issues in their own way and choose for themselves how and where they were considered (Crowley, 1984). Crowley (1984) contends that issues of a personal nature need not be dealt with necessarily in a counselling way but 'by educational methods'.

My interviews with BAC-recognized supervisors identified eleven themes on the counselling task:

1. Supervisors expect personal issues to emerge for their supervisees in their work with clients. This is part and parcel of the work itself and supervisors are very keen to monitor the extent and the consequences of those personal

issues. In general, when it is seen as a small matter it will be dealt with in supervision. A minimalist position is the most common:

> ... *as little work as possible, do the least possible. What is the minimum I need to do with this supervisee to help her deal with her personal problems?*

At other times supervisors differ in the amount of time they allocate to supervisees to work with personal issues. All have time limits and will begin to get anxious if these time boundaries are crossed. Some refer on for personal therapy, others suggest setting up personal therapy, some recommend it, some demand it. The counselling role of the supervisor is placed firmly within the professional, and not the private, development of the supervisee, even though these will have some overlap.

2. Supervisors are concerned with personal issues insofar as these issues affect the work with clients. Sometimes the client is at risk, in which case supervisors take decisive action:

> *I have stopped counsellors counselling because they themselves were in such a state of personal crisis that I felt it interfered with their work.*

At other times the work is affected and it is that impact that is the concern of the supervisor:

> *I would deal with whatever emerged from them (supervisees) wherever it came from, far enough to decide where it belongs ... I'll be concerned to know what the impact is on their work and where they can take it to deal with it better.*

3. Supervisors are clear as a body that they work only with personal issues emerging from client work:

> *You only become more involved with more personal stuff of the counsellor if you feel it's interfering with the work.*

The question for supervisors is how far and to what depth to deal with these personal issues as a task of supervision.

4. Personal issues emerge from work with clients and not all of them need be brought to personal therapy:

> *I don't think that everything that gets thrown up needs therapy, but some things get thrown up which indicate the counsellor's reached a point of development or a block that we can't possibly undo in the supervision, but we may be able to work with enough to at least help or prevent unhelpful things happening in the relationship.*

5. Some supervisors see their primary task as helping the supervisee monitor and learn from his or her own personal reactions or counter-transference:

If you are not really focusing on what is happening to you all that the client gets is the unfiltered stuff of his counsellor ... I think the second thing is the quality of the contact between my supervisee and their client.

6. Some supervisors are adamant that supervision concerns itself with client work and the personal issues of the supervisee are only considered insofar as they may throw light on what is happening to the client or may affect the client:

When I get it [a personal issue of the supervisee], I try to surface it as a personal issue. Then I'm only concerned in deciding with them where they take it, not in dealing with it ... I wouldn't accept supervision sessions being taken over, being hijacked into their personal work. I'm prepared to suspend that for five minutes or ten if they're very upset, but I wouldn't want to spend more than that really ... if they start going into their own stuff, I'd say, 'Well, hang on'. If I was the client I'd say, 'Bloody hell, you know, what about me?'

7. A second stance articulates and names the personal issue of the supervisee and then arranges for that to be dealt with somewhere else:

The task in supervision is to identify personal issues where they interfere with psychotherapy, explore them a bit and work at the consequences in terms of the relationship.

I distinguish between private personal development which in my book does not belong in supervision ... and professional counsellor development.

8. Another stance makes limited room for dealing with the personal issues:

Because if they don't have a place to take that [personal issues] to and it does happen too often I want to say to them, 'I think you need a place to take that to'. I think my boundaries are fairly flexible and I am prepared to give quite a lot of time to them working on an issue.

9. Supervisors differ too on the issue of personal counselling or psychotherapy as an essential ingredient of training:

I would only consult in supervision with those who were in personal therapy, or had access to it.

Others take a pragmatic view and, if supervisees are not in personal counselling or cannot afford to be, they will use some of the supervision time to deal with personal issues emerging from the work with clients.

10. Views on personal counselling as a requirement for training do not divide along orientation lines. Two psychodynamic supervisors responded:

> *I am not a believer myself personally that everybody who is a counsellor should have personal therapy. I've supervised a number of people who've done excellent work who've not actually had therapy.*

> *I feel very strongly on this one that people should only go into therapy because they are drawn to it by their own personal needs ... I like people to discover that they want therapy. If I really felt that this person just couldn't do without it [personal therapy] I would say it and be quite firm about it.*

The developmental stage of the supervisee was also seen as relevant:

> *It depends at what stage they are; in the early stages it would be desirable. On the other hand I've worked with voluntary counsellors who either don't have the time, or the money or the inclination or don't feel the need, and then one has to work without it. That would limit their counselling work.*

Equally passionate views are held from a humanistic supervisor:

> *I've got a very strong stand about that because all our trainees are in personal psychotherapy ... Otherwise I think what often happens is that supervision turns into psychotherapy and people don't actually get supervision and I think the clients suffer.*

11. Some supervisors feel very strongly about demanding action if they were worried about the work:

> *If I thought they were bad enough I would say, 'Go and get some therapy or you'll have to stop'*

Summary

The main conclusions drawn from reflections on the counselling task of supervision are:

- supervisors will only deal with the personal issues (counselling issues) of supervisees that arise from their work with clients;
- they will deal with them only insofar as necessary to help the supervisee become more effective as a counsellor, and not for issues of personal growth;
- they differ in how much time they will allow supervisees to work on his/her personal issues in counselling;

- they differ in how far they will demand personal therapy for those in supervision.

There are some hints that this divides along orientation lines, with the more psychodynamic supervisors prepared to do less 'counselling' work in supervision and those at the more humanistic end prepared to contract for personal time, sometimes quite substantial amounts of personal time.

My conclusions from the array of opinions and stances in the literature and from interviews with supervisors is that it is essential to have a counselling task as part of supervision, but that the emphasis for that task should be on what emerges from work with clients. This may seem more of a notional than a real distinction between counselling as personal therapy and counselling as a role within supervision. And yet it is a necessary distinction to make. Otherwise supervision can become either personal therapy or, at the other extreme, never deals with the personal reactions of supervisees.

TASK 4: MONITORING PROFESSIONAL/ETHICAL ISSUES AS A SUPERVISION TASK

The professional/ethical task of supervision ensures that clear boundaries are maintained within both counselling and supervision, that both client and supervisee are safe, that accountability is assured and that personal and organizational contexts are given reflective time. This normative function of supervision places supervisors in the role of monitors: supervisees become boundary and professional learners. It involves the 'quality control' function in working with people.

A further element is the issue of legal responsibility for clients of supervisees. This issue has not been addressed in Britain to date, but presumably it is only a matter of time until it needs clarification. Slovenko (1980) cited three cases in the USA where the supervisor was successfully sued for malpractice because of the actions of their supervisees. All three instances were in agency settings where managerial supervision was involved. He outlined the situation of 'vicarious liability' which means that 'one may be held legally responsible not only for one's own faulty conduct but also for that of others. By reason of certain relationships that may exist between parties, the negligence of one may be charged against the other, though the latter has played no part in it, has done nothing whatsoever to aid or encourage it, and in fact has done all that he possibly can to prevent it' (p. 453). The situation in Britain appears to be somewhat different. McCartney and O'Mahoney (1977) suggested that under the British Test of Negligence all actors are responsible for their own actions, a view confirmed in mental hospital practices (Nooder, 1978) and behaviour modification (Zangwill, 1980).

Nine themes emerged from my interviews with BAC-recognized supervisors.

1. Monitoring the ethical/professional aspects of supervisees' work is an essential ingredient of supervisors' work:

> *I feel very strongly about the professional part and the ethics. I'm always on the lookout for anything that is not at all professional.*

Besides the ethical codes, professional practice is seen as important here:

> *things like the number of hours of work being done and is somebody actually available given the kind of emotional availability and so on, suitability of their premises, kind of facilities being offered . . . fee levels . . .*

> *I mean if I felt that people were not keeping time properly, or boundaries, I can be very firm. I'm quite clear that the counselling profession depends to a large extent on boundaries.*

2. How that monitoring takes place differs quite a bit:

> *. . . to alert the counsellor to those (professional and ethical issues) and make sure the counsellor is taking responsibility for those.*

> *I challenge bad, I mean I challenge practice I'm not comfortable with.*

> *It's at the sexual level that the ethical thing will come up and then it's very important to encourage the counsellor to really talk about, you know, how they are actually feeling about their client and how they feel about their affection for the client, sexual desire for the client and how they are handling the client who wants to be sexual with them, loving with them . . . you know it's amazing when a supervisee is actually given permission to own their feelings as honourable, you know, even that they may be legitimately expressed.*

3. Many supervisors wait until professional and ethical issues arise from within the client work of the supervisee.

The rationale for this is that supervisors expect the training courses to teach ethical and professional standards and to acquaint supervisees with the various ethical codes. However, there are some exceptions, i.e. the beginning trainee and the trainee about whom the supervisor is worried:

> *. . . in supervising the person when they really should not be counselling, but you know they are going to, so you might as well try and help them make a not-bad job of it. In that case you probably are watching for those professional and ethical issues.*

I would see it as part of the contract that counsellors are working to British Association for Counselling ethics. That is something I would always ask and say that I would work with them on that condition.

4. Supervisors do not view their task as 'teaching' ethical codes and standards but rather to review their implementation:

... actually to make sure they have a professional body that they belong to and that they actually adhere to that particular code of practice.

I would do things like say, 'In your situation hadn't you better get some insurance?' and tell them about this cheap scheme.

I always ask them which code of ethics they work to ... I take a copy of the British Association for Counselling Code of Ethics and I give that to all the students.

5. Initially supervisors want to know that supervisees know, understand to some degree, and adhere to professional codes of practice. The developmental stage of the supervisee is seen as important here:

I mean for someone coming for consultative supervision after qualification or experienced then you might assume it until proved otherwise.

Supervisors monitor the work with antennae out for professional/ethical issues that could be potentially or actually harmful to clients,

With trainees I do spend time just helping them look at what their standards are, and how they know what's good enough practice for them ... and what are your values?

6. Several issues arise for the supervisor. First, what should I do when someone is not behaving ethically within a counselling relationship? Second, how can supervisee and supervisor work with values that differ across counselling orientations when they are from different counselling traditions? Third, how can a supervisor respond when his/her professional judgement is that the supervisee should not be seeing clients?

The first question is seen by supervisors in developmental terms. Supervisees are expected to make mistakes and the norm is to talk over the issue with the supervisee and help them reframe the issues and the dilemmas, to look at why they did what they did, and to help them learn other frameworks.

a. Supervisors with anxieties about a supervisee's professional conduct seem to have well-thought-out strategies for dealing with them. 'I would consult with my colleagues' is often given as a first step. A second step, or indeed a first step if the misconduct is not too serious, is to bring up the issue in supervision. One of the most difficult tasks for all supervisors is to share with a supervisee a decision that he/she (the trainee) is not perhaps suited for this role.

I really dread it. I'm very bad at it . . . it's the remaining part of my practice I feel least comfortable about and am most ambivalent about. I have done it.

Certainly in individual supervision I have stopped counsellors counselling because they themselves were in such a state of personal crisis that I felt it interfered with their work.

I'm saying to this supervisee, I don't feel I would want her to any long-term counselling at the moment.

If the worst came to the worst I think you would have to say I can't supervise you.

b. The second question of working across counselling orientations and the various value-conflicts that might emerge is generally not a major issue. Most supervisors feel they could supervise across orientations especially using the broad bands of psychodynamic, humanistic and behavioural counselling. Psychodynamic and humanistic supervisors seem to have little difficulty in supervising one another. Both feel hesitant to supervise from a purely cognitive–behavioural standpoint, though one talked about doing it. The latter articulated a broad principle that would well be subscribed to by most supervisors:

I don't see a difficulty. What you are doing is working for the client and it could be very limited if your supervision could only go to people who have been through the same process as yourself . . . I don't think there is only one way of working with clients. What is most important is that the counsellor is effective, whatever way they are using. Someone might be a wonderful behaviourist and very effective with clients and somebody may work psychodynamically and very effectively and somebody may be Gestalt and work very effectively and my job as supervisor is to enable them to do that to the best of their ability.

In some instances supervisors will be directive and tell the supervisee what to do if there is a possibility of harm to the client or harm to another person in the client's life, e.g. getting help for a suicidal client, whether or not physical contact with a client is therapeutic.

I would try to elicit that 'don't' or 'I shouldn't, should I' from the supervisee but in the end I would certainly say, 'Don't'.

The *modus agendi* for supervisors when faced with cross-orientation difference of values is to look at the motives of the supervisee:

Let's run through what is happening there to see what is happening in this situation. What's happening for you? What were you doing this for? What were your motives? What were you hoping for? ... what do you think the client would be thinking and feeling about that?

My supervisees are pretty good at touching and hugging and cuddling. The important thing that I would want to always ask is, for whose benefit are you doing this?

c. When there are serious doubts in the supervisor's mind about a supervisee's ability to work in counselling there are several viewpoints. One stance is somewhat fatalistic and works with what is there:

... I am never too happy with the response that says 'I would say I just couldn't supervise them' because then I ask what is going to happen to them ... I think it wouldn't be my first line of resort to stop supervision; it might be my last, or near the middle, or near the last.

Some supervisors demand that their supervisees either be within, or have access to, personal counselling as a way of dealing with the issues that could infringe on professional or ethical topics:

I would hesitate to take on somebody who wasn't ready or prepared to be in personal psychotherapy ... I wouldn't actually supervise someone who wasn't prepared to subscribe to a code of ethics.

My recommendation would be that at the moment, because his judgement is out of sync with what it should be, that he doesn't counsel at least for the time being. It wasn't a case of 'You're sacked forever' but that he's got needs that are not being met personally, that are now intruding into the work and he needs to sort that out if he is to make sounder judgements with clients.

Summary

Supervisors generally do not teach ethical/professional issues but monitor them for the welfare of the client and the development of the supervisee. They will confront bad practice, take steps when they have worries about the professional conduct or abilities of their supervisees, and in extreme cases, suggest someone give up counselling, at least for some time.

There was an element of anxiety expressed throughout the interviews about negative evaluation of ethical issues.

TASK 5: THE EVALUATION TASK OF SUPERVISION

There is some controversy around the task of evaluation within supervision. Some authors are in no doubt about its importance and centrality. Edelstein and Brasted (1983, p. 50) called clinical evaluation 'perhaps the most important and the most overlooked issue in clinical training'. Other supervisors have viewed formal evaluation as interfering with their teaching, counselling or consulting roles (Cohen, 1987; Wolberg, 1967) and have expressed anxiety lest they develop what Beardsley, Riggar and Hafer (1984) call 'the casework cop syndrome' (p. 59). How can supervisees trust their work, failures included, to supervisors who will have at least some influence on their overall assessment? Arbuckle (1965) has taken Patterson to task for trying to combine 'the two impossibilities' of providing a non-threatening atmosphere on one hand and evaluating the supervisee on the other. However, he too sees the evaluation role as an inevitable part of supervision.

Evaluation of supervisee's competency is still at an early stage of development. As yet there is no research to connect training with competence. The most alarming finding of the APA (American Psychological Association) Task Force on the Evaluation of Education, Training, and Service in Psychology (1982) was that 'there is no evidence that any specific educational or training programme or experience is related to professional competence' (Edelstein and Berler, 1987, p. xi). This is a rather frightening comment for supervisors who see themselves as helping supervisees connect theory and practice.

A distinction has been made between formative and summative evaluation. The former consists of ongoing feedback for and evaluation of the supervisee, taking into consideration his/her level of experience. Formative evaluation is informal and ongoing. Summative tends to end up as supervisory reports and contains the more formal assessment moments when an overall evaluation takes place.

The task of evaluation within supervision comprises:

a) Setting up the procedures by which the performance of the supervisee is described or judged to be competent or effective – professional or counsellor competence is not always a readily agreed procedure. A number of issues intrude to make evaluation a difficult process: e.g. what core competencies are considered essential for different counselling schools, what skills are seen to be necessary/essential for the different developmental stages through which supervisees travel, and what contexts and client groups demand further specific abilities?

b) Agreeing to the criteria on which judgements will be made.

c) Monitoring and evaluating the work of the supervisee with a view to final decision in respect of the student's future. Ekstein and Wallerstein (1972, p. 285) put it starkly: 'The supervisor is responsible, not only to the student, but to the training centre, as well. Has the supervisor successfully taught the student? Was the student able to make adequate use of the supervisor or did he fail at this task? . . . If

he [the student] has succeeded, what is the next step in his training?
... Has he failed and should he be discontinued from the program?'

d) Implementing evaluation procedures through ongoing feedback and
formal evaluation sessions and where applicable, written reports.

Evaluation procedures are usually one-way (i.e. directed towards the
supervisee). The 'You are up; I am down,' situation outlined by Rioch
(1980, p. 70) pertains in supervision and, in particular, with the tasks and
roles of supervision. However, evaluation does not have to be unidirectional
and effective supervisors create space for evaluation of themselves by
supervisees.

By its very nature evaluation creates power issues. Even when the
procedures are more desirable (i.e. a continuous process, discussed beforehand with the supervisee, where there is a positive relationship, where
evaluation is shared, and where the focus is the work and not the person of
the trainee there is still the inequality that one person is being judged and
the other judging. The issues become the more pertinent when the criteria
on which these judgements are made remain hazy or subjective.

Seven themes emerged from my interviews with BAC-recognized
supervisors:

1. There is general agreement amongst supervisors interviewed that evaluation is a task of supervision:

> *Under no circumstances do I want to be in a position where I feel inhibited
> from addressing or challenging or whatever, practice that isn't good enough
> to deliver a good enough service to the client.*

> *I actually think it's part of the supervisor's task [evaluation] and what
> they owe the supervisee quite apart from training ... I really expect my
> supervisor to be willing to tell me how they thought I was doing ... Indeed
> if they didn't I would ask.*

Others see informal evaluation (giving ongoing feedback) as part of supervision but formal evaluation (reports, written assessments, etc.) as not
necessary. One supervisor had never written formal evaluations and saw it
as changing the relationship:

> *That would put me in the same sort of thing as the managerial role ...
> which would change relationships, and I'd be there in a judgemental role as
> well.*

2. Feedback on all aspects of supervision is built into the contract with
supervisees:

> *I'd say it's an ongoing evaluation process.*

I think what it needs to be is constant specific feedback, right the way through, not an evaluation at the end of the course, but giving them constant feedback so that the student knows all the time.

I suggest to the supervisee, let's reflect back on what we've done and what the learning is that's taken place.

3. Evaluation is seen as the responsibility of the supervisor and undoubtedly creates a certain kind of relationship:

There is in all supervisory relationships some element of hierarchy or authority.

I think the supervisor's assessment is one of the most crucial because it is the supervisor actually who is aware of what is going on in the counsellor and I think that is really essential.

4. In all the tasks of supervision this is the one where the power element is most clear:

Evaluation does involve a power element. We cannot ignore that.

However, supervisors see the relationship between supervisor and supervisee as making all the difference in how evaluation takes place and how it is accepted:

I see myself as creating an atmosphere in which the supervisee is free to bring their full work; successes and failures. ... I am aware that supervisors can be punitive and if that happens it creates mistrust and the supervisee is anxious about sharing areas of weakness. A supervisor must not be naive about the power counsellors perceive them to have.

Making supervision a safe place for supervisees is high on the priority list for supervisors. Most would agree with the comment:

I actually see one of my fundamental tasks to make somebody feel safe enough to reveal themselves and their work ... I'm not too worried about it making a supervisee a bit anxious ... if you can't tolerate anxiety I don't know what you are going to do in your work with a client.

I create a climate where it is actually possible to look at positives and negatives in a way that is enabling, not threatening.

One supervisor talks about paranoia:

... the paranoia that surrounds having a supervisor maybe in a judgemental position. One of the difficult tasks is to balance one's critical role with one's encouraging role.

Another goes on to relate what could be a theoretical difference in supervision.

> *I'm a fairly analytic person and analytic responses can feel very persecutory so I have found that unless I watch that, counsellors get threatened.*

A further supervisor puts the welfare of the client as the chief aim of supervision.

> *When I take on a supervisee I tell them 'I do have to know how you practise because I feel I have a responsibility to your clients ... and I want to know what it is I'm endorsing, because if I am your supervisor I endorse you in something.'*

For all supervisors this is a serious obligation of their role and often placed within the realm of ethical responsibility.

> *I would say that that was part of my ethical responsibility ... I mean, your clinical responsibility is to evaluate the counsellor's work and I don't think that that has to be so destructive.*

It is hoped that supervision will be viewed within a 'learning/growing situation' and not 'seen like a school report', that it will be 'friendly information'. Interviewees were adamant that evaluation should not be a one-off assessment of the supervisee, but should be ongoing feedback which will be formalized, if needed, in a written document.

5. A well-trodden method of evaluation within supervision is common. Supervisors ask supervisees to evaluate themselves first of all. If supervision takes place within a small group then supervisees may evaluate each other. The supervisor then gives the formal evaluation which is often written. Interviewees specified their own way of working:

> *I get them to evaluate themselves. Sometimes I add some and sometimes I subtract some so that it is a joint evaluation.*

> *I either do it one of two ways. I'll either get them initially to write a report themselves and I will share it with them and amend it with them or I will write a report and share it with them.*

Some supervisors have clear criteria for evaluation:

> *I get to what I call the five-finger exercise: I want a diagnosis, I want strategy, I want their understanding the transference, the countertransference, and lastly the process ... at the end of it that is how we grade.*

Others keep it very open:

> *I don't have a checklist in my head or on a sheet of paper that I use afterwards . . . I think it is more intuitive . . . Is it feeling right?*

Some supervisors ask for evaluation on their role as supervisor:

> *I want feedback because I also need to know where I am.*

> *But the evaluation I see as also being from them to me . . . how has this been for you? How do you feel I have worked with you?*

> *. . . lastly they give a grade on how I've functioned.*

6. There is a marked difference in reaction to the use of taped material as a way of assessing how the supervisee is working with clients. Some see it as an essential way into the work:

> *That's why I think tapes help so much . . . sometimes people report something and it sounds dreadful and they play the tape and it's really good therapy . . . I want the tapes because I do not always trust their own judgement, one way or the other, of the way they work.*

Others see it as interfering with the process:

> *I'm a bit worried about how good it is for the client.*

> *I think I would prefer not [to use tapes], given my orientation and the emphasis and place here on the relationship and the transference and the countertransference. I think perhaps it could very well be an intrusion.*

It would be unwise to make a sweeping statement that psychodynamic approaches never use tapes. However, by and large that does seem to be the stance of the psychodynamic supervisors interviewed. Humanistic approaches often use taped material and in some instances supervisors require that supervisees tape sessions for supervision. In one instance the supervisory sessions were taped and the supervisee used the tape for their own learning. Stances on taping as a method of evaluating tended to be somewhat rigid on a continuum of always asking for tapes, to not condoning the use of taped material in either counselling or supervision. One supervisor who doesn't use tapes outlined the difficulty of assessment in this area and shared personal experience:

> *I did it when I was training [hid what I was doing from the supervisor] . . . I think most people do . . . I think perhaps we all do as I did.*

Those who do not use taped material claim that the client is represented in the supervisory session by the supervisee:

I see the client through the supervisee. It's an edited edition. You know the supervisee may try very hard not to reveal themselves, but it's difficult not to really.

7. Evaluation is a method by which supervisors let supervisees know they (supervisors) are unhappy about aspects of their (supervisees) work or, more finally they consider the supervisee should leave the profession or give up counselling for some time.

Yes, I would be quite straight with them ... once or twice I've said to people, 'Look, I don't think you are in the right business.'

There have been times when I have actually stopped counsellors from working because I have not felt that their standards were high enough.

Summary

From these interviews, evaluation can be viewed as either formal or informal. The latter, in which feedback on how the supervisee is working as a counsellor, and by which their learning takes place, takes place regularly in supervision (Chapter 5). Some supervisors build in review sessions as a regular feature of supervision. All attest to the anxiety raised by formal evaluation, i.e. where some report is given to the training organization.

There is a marked difference between those who have clear criteria by which they evaluate, and those who go more for the 'feel' of the work being done by the supervisee. This, again, seems to be an area where further training for supervisors in methods of evaluating trainees would be helpful, especially giving access to some of the supervisory rating forms available.

Formal evaluations should always be shared with the supervisee and something has gone wrong if the contents come as a surprise. Informal evaluation should be constantly feeding back what the formal reports summarize.

The quality of the supervisory relationship is seen as the context in which evaluation is itself evaluated. Where the relationship is safe, where the supervisee is expected to learn in a gradual way sometimes making mistakes, then the supervisee feels free to share these mistakes and learn from them.

Whilst evaluation is seen as an essential feature of effective supervision, there is still a lack of clarity about how it is carried out, and what criteria should characterize it formally. It is very easy for supervisors and supervisees to form a collusive relationship where evaluations are seen as positive, and negatives are not considered, especially any hint that supervisees may not be suitable for counselling.

TASK 6: THE CONSULTATION TASK OF SUPERVISION

Consultancy best describes the whole area of process in supervision. Besides considering client dynamics it includes the various relationships in the system (i.e. the relationship between the client and the supervisee and the relationship between supervisor and supervisee). Consultancy uses 'parallel process' as an information–gathering mechanism. Hawkins and Shohet deliberately named their model a 'process model of supervision' (1989) involving 'two interlocking systems or matrices; the therapy system . . . and the supervision system' (p. 56). From these two foci they outline six modes of supervision. Each is described according to the focus of the supervision:

When the focus is on the *counselling/therapy session*:

1. Reflection on the client and their dynamics. This is an effort to understand the client, make assessment/diagnosis, reflect on what was said, connect this to previous sessions, etc.
2. Reflection on the strategies/interventions of the supervisee (e.g. reviewing what the supervisee did, what they intended to do, looking at other possible interventions, designating a treatment plan).
3. Reflection on the relationship between client and counsellor/ therapist. This focus will dwell on transference/counter-transference, conscious and unconscious relationship issues, what kind of relationship is involved: working alliance, real relationship, transference relationship.

When the focus is on the *supervisory relationship*:

4. Reflection on the therapist's countertransference. The supervisee looks at issues carried from the counselling sessions, feelings for and towards the client, unresolved personal issues and feelings.
5. Reflection on the 'parallel process' (i.e. where the supervisee plays out the therapy relationship in the supervisory relationship).
6. Focus on the supervisor's countertransference. The supervisor dwells on his/her reactions, attitudes, feelings towards the client, the supervisee, their relationship, etc. as a means to understanding what is happening.

Five of these modes make up the 'consultancy' role of supervision, aimed at understanding all the processes of the system, examining them and looking at ways of influencing them, i.e. uncovering what is happening, understanding it and looking at other ways of intervening. Item 5 represents the 'counselling' role.

The consultative task of supervision is widely respected throughout the supervisory literature, ranging from those who see it as the underlying task to those who see it as one amongst other tasks. My own research (Carroll, 1995a) saw the consultative task as easily the most frequently used task in supervision. A mammoth 47.5 per cent of supervision time was spent in this task. The next most frequently used task was counselling, using up 17.9 per cent of supervisory time. Supervisees used the consultative aspects of supervision 54.3 per cent of the time, with counselling a distant second with 18.6 per cent of the time. Supervisors, on the other hand, used consultative interventions 27.25 per cent of the time with teaching a very close second with 26.9 per cent of time.

The consultation task comes to the fore with more experienced supervisees and begins to become the predominant focus of supervision when supervisees move from their training into full-time practice. In fact consultative supervision then becomes the professional activity rather than training supervision.

In interviews with BAC-recognized supervisors (Carroll, 1994c), the consulting task of supervision was presented in terms of systems involved: understanding the client as a system in his/her own right, the relationship between supervisee and client as another system, the supervisee as system, the relationship between the supervisor and the supervisee as a further system, and the supervisor as a system. The process of individual supervision involves three intermingling systems (supervisor, supervisee, client), a 'triadic' relationship. One supervisor suggested that a fourth very important system, easily overlooked, is the 'agency involved, like the college'. Eight themes emerged.

1. The consulting task is described by supervisors in various ways:

Freud talked about hovering . . . when I supervise I try to stay with what is actually happening, sort of reacting with the bit that seems appropriate at the time.

Having trained at the sociological end of the spectrum rather than the psychological end, I'm very systems aware . . . I think we tend to look too narrowly.

Supervision is almost . . . three- or four-dimensional . . .

I think one must be so very aware of the social system . . . in lots of psychotherapy or analysis the whole focus is on just those two, on what's going on between the client and the counsellor. I mean, that's drastic really . . .

2. There is a different emphasis on the various systems. All supervisors make it clear that they want to keep an eye on all aspects of what is happening, Psychodynamic counsellors stress two systems, the relationship between supervisees and clients and the relationship between supervisor and supervisee:

I have one predominant thing I do more than anything else which is to work with countertransference ... what the counsellor's feelings are in response to what is happening in the current counselling relationship.

However, supervisors who see themselves from orientations other than psychodynamic will often concentrate on similar systems:

I think I probably emphasize the counsellor/client one the most. I'm looking at that the most, at what's going on there.

3. Supervisors want to know what is happening with the client:

I need to know enough about the client ... there is the art of helping the supervisee to learn how to present in such a way that you get enough of the client.

Some see the relationship between supervisee and client as the key system in the chain, and concentrate on understanding and making it effective. Others view the diagnosis or the assessment of the clients as fundamental to the total process.

I want to know what the diagnosis is ... as long as it [what the supervisee is doing with the client] is based on a diagnosis, I am happy about that.

Others use their own feelings and reactions (their countertransference) as a crucial method of keeping in touch with the systems involved:

I am trying to work at what is happening to me ... be alertable to how my understanding of countertransference will alert me the whole process of what has been mirrored, reflected.

Are there any countertransference problems? Are they being reproduced here in the supervision process with me?

I can only discover the process in as far as I am in touch with myself.

For most supervisors the focus is not on the content of the counselling, though that is where it starts:

Yes, I would focus with what is going on with the client, but it's more. What I find a lot of supervisees are very keen on the content of the client and the client's life and everything, whereas I'm much more interested, not so much in the content, but very much more in the process.

4. How supervisees present their clients is agreed between supervisor and supervisee, and is important. There are supervisors who ask for audiotapes of sessions between clients and counsellors:

I find tapes very useful. Some people can describe what they are doing very well, but there's quite often a fair discrepancy between what they're describing and what's happening.

Other supervisors do not work with tapes:

I've never done that primarily because I had to supply tapes when I was training and I found the whole process terrifying, actually persecutory.

Others ask for notes kept by supervisees and sometimes require process notes of sessions, others again work solely with what the supervisee verbally presents within the supervision session. The latter is put well by one supervisor:

I certainly don't do anything that could remotely be called an assessment or a scientific measurement or anything alike that. I'm relying entirely on my sense which I guess could be very inaccurate and dangerous ... I'm really relying almost entirely on my countertransference and obviously that is linked to the parallel process which I really think is going on in a very powerful way.

Even though supervisors have clearly worked out ways of working with supervisees most are open to negotiating other formats with supervisees.

5. The parallel process, or reflection process, is seen by all supervisors as a real and workable phenomenon within supervision. It is described as:

monitoring the relationship between myself and the supervisee as a way of understanding what was happening between the supervisee and the client.

Its importance is described by supervisors:

The parallel process, the reflection process, that's there. I haven't spoken about it up to now, but that's of primary importance.

The countertransference is very key to me though I am not formally analytically trained. I'm a humanist therapist though I do see it as quite crucial.

What is going on with the client and what is going on with the supervisee is then going to be reflected in what is going on between me and the supervisee, so I can then be aware of what's going on for me to be able to feed that back.

Supervisors see the parallel process and the countertransference issues arising in them as supervisors as a main focus for monitoring what is happening with the clients:

My sense of what actually goes on in the session is very mediated through the supervisee's presentation and what they're saying and what they're not saying, so although I can say, yes, I'm an advocate of the client and monitoring the quality of the service I think it's very hard for me to do that, except indirectly by monitoring what I believe is the quality of how the process is being reflected in the session with me.

6. Some supervisors have reservations about how the parallel process is used in supervision:

I don't think the student has a clue what's being talked about. They just think they are being judged in some way.

Just recently in a group I had three new trainees joining and I could see that they were just so taken aback by it and I said at the end of the session, don't be too disconcerted, it will become clear to you eventually.

7. The developmental stage of the supervisee is seen as important in engaging in the consultative task:

... the idea for a brand-new trainee counsellor to say that I was bored by my client, they'd feel so guilty that they're failing, that they won't tell you. It's both in their development and in the development of the relationship between you and them or within the group.

8. The consultation task in supervision is seen by many as the key underlying task that determines other tasks. It is the task that involves the process and understanding what is needed to help the total system move. One supervisor put it well:

You see, I have that checklist: I'm constantly saying, What is the priority in this particular case? Is it a question of countertransference? Is that your main presenting problem or is it a question of treatment planning or is it a question of technique? Is it an ethics problem? ... Is it a theoretical problem? Is it a thinking problem?

Summary

There is general agreement amongst supervisors about the various systems involved in counselling and supervision and they wish and need to pay attention to all of them. Within that, supervisors have their preferred stances where they concentrate on what they consider to be the key systems. The relationship systems generally tend to be the one on which they mostly concentrate, certainly as supervision progresses, with psychodynamic supervisors paying particular attention to the transference/countertransference issues within these relationships.

All supervisors pay attention to the client and what is happening within their lives. After that, counselling orientation plays a part in the focus, with psychodynamic supervisors concentrating on the relationships involved (between the counsellor and client and between the counsellor and the supervisor) while humanistic supervisors are inclined towards what is happening to the counsellor. This is a matter of emphasis rather than a strict division.

TASK 7: THE ADMINISTRATIVE TASK OF SUPERVISION

As early as 1926, Dawson saw the administrative element in supervision as essential: 'the promotion and maintenance of good standards of work, coordination of practice with policies of administration, the assurance of an efficient and smooth-working office' (p. 14). However, Dawson was viewing supervision in the context of social work.

Administrative elements enter counselling supervision

a)   via the training course, which usually has the final say in whether or not a trainee is allowed to practise. Sometimes staff members supervise the client work of trainees and have to fulfil a number of roles vis-à-vis the students: teacher, tutor, administrator, supervisor.

b)   via the administration of the centre or agency in which the trainee sees clients. Often such placements are separate from the training centre; sometimes they are negotiated by the student alone, or by the training centre. In some instances the administration of the placement has little contact with the administrative personnel from the training course, and leaves all decisions and supervision to one of the staff members who has been appointed to have both clinical and administrative responsibility. This latter could be one of the administration staff. In other circumstances a trainee sees clients in settings that are not mainly counselling or therapeutic (e.g. doctors' surgeries, social work settings). There are further areas where a trainee sees clients where there is no administrative side (e.g. a trainee working in private practice).

For the above reasons, the organizational side of supervision is often vague or non-existent. And yet the institutional variables are critical points in the professional development of the trainee and in the service rendered to the clients who use the service. Trainee supervision always contains an organizational component.

Context gives meaning to and influences the process of counselling (Johnson and Gysbers, 1967). Supervisees work in agencies, relate to other staff members and with the management within the agency. Ekstein and Wallerstein (1972) talked about each clinical setting having its 'customs, rules, physical arrangements, and spirit that together constitute what we call its structure' (p. 36). Not only is there the structure but there exists 'the psychological meanings' that structure has for each individual involved. Even when supervisees work privately there is a management/ administrative side to their work: taking referrals from other professionals, making referrals, dealing with medical practitioners, psychiatrists, social workers, etc., who also work with their clients. Issues emerge from these areas that are not strictly work with clients, but have a vast influence on that work and on the context in which that work takes place. Several potential problem areas can be designated:

> issues of power and the style of leadership involved;
> the political climate of the agency;
> constraints on the agency, e.g. finance;
> the counselling orientation of the agency;
> who employs the supervisor for the agency client work.

The administrative task of supervision is about monitoring the various contexts in which the supervisee works. For some supervisors it may mean intervening in those situations, for others the task is about helping supervisees deal with whatever issues intrude on the work with clients.

Ekstein and Wallerstein (1972) pinpointed some of the problem areas that can arise and affect client work and trainee development:

> where the ideology of the administration in an agency differs from the ideology of the supervisor (and/or the supervisee);
> where the administrator undertakes administration for negative rather than positive reasons;
> where the administrator understands administration, but not counselling or psychotherapy;
> where the administrator cannot delegate but needs to do everything himself/herself.

A further area that influences the clinical work is the training course of which the supervisee is a member. The training course also has an administrative side. Carr (1989, pp. 2–3) summarizes some of the issues that can arise here:

> The training organization is a powerful, ever present force influencing the relationship between supervisor and supervisee. Both can feel judged in different ways, with their work in supervision, not only the work of the supervisee under examination. The supervisee can feel there is a strong bond between his supervisor and the training body, and he is excluded from this like a child is excluded from relationships between the adults. Difficulties can sometimes arise between supervisee and the training body, in which the supervisee can seek to

involve the supervisor in a collusive relationship against the training body. Supervisors can over-identify with their students and perhaps we are familiar with the supervisor, all of whose geese are swans.

Four themes arose in interviews with BAC-recognized supervisors (Carroll, 1994c):

1. Supervisors are very aware of the contextual issues in and around counselling. Contextual issues in supervision include the agency in which the supervisee works and sees clients, the educational training establishment in which the supervisee is a student, and the future training needs of the supervisee. Supervisors are aware of the many contexts that influence work with clients and see them as relevant material for supervision:

> *I don't see supervision as just talking about clients . . . sometimes it's talking about the way I manage my counselling work, or agency issues.*

> *. . . the agency issue, if that's interfering in some way with their work, then that's valuable work for supervision . . .*

> *I find an awful lot of time in supervision is taken up with actual stuff to do with relationships with colleagues and the institution and I'm very keen on systems work.*

In many instances clients are seen in agencies, mental health centres, as part of GP surgeries, community health centres, within the National Health Service, in employee counselling services and in various other institutional settings. Supervisors are clear that such settings affect the work with clients:

> *If you go to an organization for counselling . . . the organization affects what's going on.*

> *We have a misnomer that the client is coming just to the individual. I actually think clients come to agencies and the agency has a responsibility, and therefore the actual ethos of the agency and how that actually is carried through in very ordinary things like the policies of letter writing to clients . . . I can't divorce the client from those processes.*

Part of the supervisory task is to

> *alert the supervisee to the wider context, and to challenge them as to what they are going to do . . . so what does that mean in terms of you developing the most effective service you can for this client or these clients in this context.*

A cautionary note was mooted by one supervisor about the amount of time spent on administrative issues within supervision:

> *Yes, as long as it doesn't take up too much time.*

Another was more accepting:

Sometimes in supervision I find it's very hard to make a space for actual work with clients because they're so dominated with all the institutional, organizational systems dynamics that are going on ... I don't think it's a diversion from work with clients.

Another wanted to probe the reasons behind organizational issues emerging in supervision:

... but I would ask myself why they would want to talk to me about it, whether there is some splitting going on, whether they want me on their side against the institution.

2. Supervisors realize that the agency in which clients are seen affects the therapeutic relationship. Supervisees are contact points between the clients and the agency. They are conduits who carry the client into the agency and communicate the agency to the client. For this reason supervisors see supervision as a forum in which management issues are raised and dealt with, where agency relationships are considered and where policies and administration within the agency are important elements in how the client emerges from this experience:

I have process and management as two aspects of the supervisor's task and yes, I think the supervisor always is responsible for looking at management issues.

The general principle for supervisors is indicated in the following quotes.

To help the supervisee deal with whatever is part of their professional life as counsellors, and if agency or administrative matters are intruding on their learning or counselling then we deal with that.

I wouldn't start trying to change the organization, but I think it is important to find out what context they work in.

3. Some supervisors are paid by the agency to supervise counsellors within it. When their contract is with the agency supervisors have no problems in feeding back information affecting clients, and intervene with management to create more effective therapeutic conditions. They stress the importance of clarity within contracts:

If I was employed by an agency ... I would clarify the sort of contract of what the role was, to be very clear what the role was and what were the boundaries of confidentiality.

There are a variety of stances on what to do when the supervisory contract is with the supervisee who is working within an agency and problems and issues affecting client work emerge in supervision. The general approach seems to be something like:

> *The first thing was, I encouraged the person [the supervisee] to take responsibility for it and then when I saw that something really quite destructive was going on in that agency, I actually took it up. Because it seemed to me that the very nature of that particular agency was toxic and that they were not an enabling agency ... they were destructive.*

Some supervisors try to maintain contact with the agency in which the supervisee works:

> *I am in touch with him [the head of the agency in which the supervisee works]; I would get reports from that person, and I would liaise with that person.*

Others see their task to work with the supervisee, to deal with administrative and agency matters as they arise, but not to intervene as supervisor in the agency:

> *I never have [intervened in the context personally as supervisor]. I can't immediately see a place that I would do. I would hope we can talk it through and help them work into being assertive ... and perhaps take it on for themselves really.*
>
> *No, I would always get the supervisee to sort it out. I wouldn't go and do it over their heads or anything.*

Dealing directly with the agency as a counsellor is sometimes viewed as treating the supervisee as a child and not an adult, or analogous to interfering in the life of a client or a patient outside the counselling hour. All supervisors were prepared to view 'extreme situations' as possible moments in which they might intervene in an agency, though many could not conceptualize particular instances of this.

4. Tripartite meetings are a way of resolving problematic areas affecting the work with the clients. A number of supervisors felt that the clarity in contracts facilitates agreements and gives a basis for renegotiation, if needed.

> *I think they have to make an agreement or a contract with their agency and if that agreement isn't working out because they are having problems with the manager, that has to be sorted out.*

Some would wait for the counsellor to ask them to intervene with the agency. Tripartite meetings (supervisee, supervisor, members of the training team and/or the placement agency) were suggested as a way of working out difficult situations.

Summary

Whilst supervisors agree that the administrative task of supervision is crucial, they differ on how much time they allow it and how much they are prepared to intervene within the system affecting clients and supervisees. Again, it seems that counselling orientations may direct the approach to this, with psychodynamic supervisors less prepared to intervene directly outside the supervisory relationship whilst humanistic supervisors are more prepared to do so.

There is a sense, from the supervisory literature, that the importance of administrative and organizational aspects of supervision is still underrated. Systems approaches are continuing to educate supervisors to the role and effect that institutional structure, roles, responsibilities, and climate have on actual client work. Supervisors are becoming more aware of 'the helicopter ability', i.e. the ability to see problems and people in ever widening contexts, as a valuable resource for supervisors.

This chapter has presented each of the seven generic tasks, looking at what each involves, and at relevant definitions, discussions and controversies, and giving a review of related research. Below, in summary list form, are the seven tasks and the key themes within each, as generated from interview data with supervisors.

1. RELATIONSHIP TASK OF SUPERVISION

1.1. Little agreement on the 'kind' of relationship involved
1.2. A number of metaphors are used to describe the relationship
1.3. The relationship changes as supervision progresses
1.4. Supervisors feel able to combine other roles with supervisees
1.5. There is an element of power within supervision
1.6. The supervision relationship is characterized by choice, self-disclosure, transference/countertransference and contracts

2. THE TEACHING TASK OF SUPERVISION

2.1. Teaching is an essential task of supervision
2.2. Teaching is individualized within supervision
2.3. Teaching within supervision is more informal than formal
2.4. Modelling is seen as an important teaching method
2.5. Teaching recedes as the supervisee becomes more experienced
2.6. A number of teaching methods are used within supervision mostly determined by the supervisor
2.7. Some supervisors react negatively to formal teaching in supervision
2.8. Some teaching methods used, e.g. role-play, taping, psychodrama

3. THE COUNSELLING TASK OF SUPERVISION

3.1. Supervisors expect personal issues to arise from client work
3.2. Supervisors are concerned that supervisee personal issues might interfere with client work
3.3. Supervision deals with personal issues as they emerge from work with clients but not personal issues *per se*
3.4. Not all personal issues arising from client work require counselling
3.5. There is learning for supervisees from their own personal reactions
3.6. Some supervisors only work with personal issues when they throw light on work with the client
3.7. Other supervisors articulate personal issues but do not see supervision as the place to deal with them
3.8. Some supervisors give limited space to deal with personal issues
3.9. There are different stances on whether or not supervisors require supervisees to be in personal therapy alongside their supervision
3.10. Views on required personal counselling do not divide on orientation lines
3.11. Some supervisors demand action if they are worried about client work

4. MONITORING THE PROFESSIONAL/ETHICAL ASPECTS OF SUPERVISION

4.1. Monitoring the professional/ethical is seen as an essential task of supervision
4.2. There are different opinions on how to monitor this
4.3. Some supervisors wait till it emerges from client work
4.4. Supervisors do not see themselves as teaching the ethical dimension of client work
4.5. Supervisors need to assure themselves that their supervisees are working ethically
4.6. Some issues emerge around this for supervisors
4.6. Supervisors have worked-out strategies for dealing with supervisees when they are anxious about the ethical/professional side of their work
4.7. Supervisors move easily across counselling orientations when working with professional issues
4.8. Supervisors have several options when there is serious doubt about a supervisee

5. THE EVALUATION TASK OF SUPERVISION

5.1. Evaluation is seen as a key task within supervision

5.2. Ongoing feedback (evaluation) ought to be built into the supervisory contract

5.3. Evaluation is the responsibility of the supervisor and inevitably affects the supervisory relationship

5.4. In evaluation the power issues are very clear

5.5. Supervisors tend to have methods of formal evaluation

5.6. There are different stances on the use of taped material for evaluation purposes

5.7. Evaluation is used where supervisors are unhappy with the client work of supervisees or where they consider a supervisee may not be be suited to the role of counsellor

6. THE CONSULTATION TASKS OF SUPERVISION

6.1. The consultation task is described in various ways by supervisors

6.2. There is different emphasis on different systems

6.3. Supervisors want to know what is happening to clients

6.4. How supervisees present their clients is agreed between supervisor and supervisee and is important

6.5. Parallel process is a major part of supervision

6.6. Parallel process must be used with caution

6.7. Developmental stages are connected to the consultation task

6.8. The consultation task is seen by quite a number as the key underlying task of supervision

7. THE ADMINISTRATIVE TASK OF SUPERVISION

7.1. Supervisors are aware of the contextual issues in and around both counselling and supervision

7.2. The agency in which supervisees see clients affects the work with clients

7.3. Special considerations come into play when supervisors are part of the agency in which supervisees see clients

7.4. Tripartite meetings to discuss issues are sometimes used to facilitate working together

FIVE

Managing the supervisory process

If supervision is to become and remain a cooperative experience which allows for real, rather than token accountability, a clear – even tough – working agreement needs to be negotiated. (Proctor, 1986, p. 27)

Supervisors are responsible with counsellors for ensuring that they make best use of the supervision time. *Code of Ethics and Practice for the Supervision of Counsellors.* (BAC, 1988)

The supervisory process includes all aspects of setting up, maintaining and terminating a supervisory arrangement. Supervision does not 'just happen'; if left with unclear boundaries and unspoken agreements then it tends to disintegrate into a hurried chat over a cup of coffee, or will not happen at all. Supervision is a negotiated relationship which clarifies the roles and responsibilities of the participants and states its aims and objectives clearly.

In this chapter the supervisory process will be divided into five stages, (see below) with the one-to-one supervisory format as the underlying model, though the five stages can be adapted to other supervisory forms, such as group, peer or team supervision. It is presumed that both parties in the supervisory relationship are free to choose each other. This does not always happen, however. On some counselling training courses supervisees are allocated to supervisors in individual and group supervision. When this happens it is important that monitoring the relationship is continuous, and that some format be utilized to ascertain that supervision is working for both supervisor and supervisee. This arrangement can be particularly difficult for supervisees who are allocated to a supervisor with whom they find it difficult to work but cannot articulate their anxiety for fear of being seen as a 'difficult student', or fear that their 'resistance' might be held against them in their progress throughout the training course. Where possible, choice should be implemented.

The five stages of the supervisory process are:

Stage 1: Assessing
Stage 2: Contracting for supervision
Stage 3: Engaging in supervision
Stage 4: Evaluating supervisee, supervisor, and supervisor
Stage 5: Terminating the supervisory relationship

These are shown in Table 5.1. There is also a pre-assessment, or pre-supervision, stage in which supervisees and supervisors prepare for supervision.

These stages are not immutable. They are meant to be flexible and simply act as a guide. It is essential to get a balance between overmanaged supervision on one hand and understructured supervision on the other. The former removes all spontaneity while the latter can result in chaos, especially for beginning supervisees. Checklists, frameworks and methodologies are at our service and useful when they guide us, not when they imprison us.

At times supervision will take place on a short-term basis before formal contracting takes place: this enables both supervisor and supervisee to have experience of what supervision means before committing to it long term.

Table 5.1 *Five-stage model of the supervisory process*

Stage 1: Assessing	Stage 2: Contracting	Stage 3: Engaging	Stage 4: Evaluating	Stage 5: Terminating
Supervisee	Practicalities	Use of time	Supervisee	Review of work
Supervisor	Management of supervision	Presentation	Supervisor	Review of learning needs/objectives
Supervision context	Roles	Learning needs of supervisee	Supervision	Looking ahead
Roles/ responsibilities	Evaluation	Developmental stage of supervisee	Training course	References
Methods of evaluating	Appeals		Placement agency context	
	Emergencies	Parallel process		
Practicalities, e.g. availability, locality	Learning objectives	External influences		
		Focus of supervision		

PRE-ASSESSMENT

The pre-assessment stage involves different areas for supervisees and supervisors.

For supervisees

Several times throughout this book mention has been made of the need for supervisees to build up the skills necessary for the effective use of supervision. A number of authors have pointed out the dangers of presuming supervisees know what to expect from supervision (Carroll, 1994c; Feltham and Dryden, 1994; Inskipp and Proctor, 1993). Suggestions have been made that training courses ought to include a section on supervision for beginners. Certainly supervisors need to deal with how supervisees understand supervision, what has been, if any, their previous experience of it, and need to help supervisees prepare for their forthcoming experience of supervision. Whether provided by the training course or by supervisors, the following areas seem crucial for supervisees:

1. *Knowledge*
    a) about supervision (What is supervision? What are the roles/responsibilities of supervisees/supervisors? The various forms of supervision and the advantages and disadvantages of each form)
    b) about self (as a learner; as a counselling trainee)
2. *Skills*
    a) of assessing a supervisor
    b) of finding a suitable supervisor and an appropriate form of supervision
    c) of negotiating the setting up of supervision
    d) of writing learning objectives
    e) of preparing for supervision
    f) of presenting in supervision
    g) of transferring from supervision to counselling
    h) of receiving feedback
    i) of evaluating self and supervisor
    j) of terminating supervision

Feltham and Dryden (1994) give supervisors a number of useful ways of introducing supervisees to either their first or to a new supervision:

Finding out what supervisees understand by the term 'supervision'.
Creating room for explanation, discussion, and negotiation, even when the participants may not have choice.

Helping supervisees question on various aspects of supervision (they may not feel they have the right to, or may be anxious about asking question).

Describing your understanding of supervision, theoretical orientation, etc.

Clarifying assessment.

Discussing and exploring the issues involved in the BAC *Code of Ethics and Practice for the Supervision of Counsellors*.

Discussing and clarifying the boundaries between supervision, personal therapy and training.

Time spent helping supervisees understand supervision, helping them build up the skills they need to use supervision time effectively and supporting them as they find their roles and responsibilities within a supervisory relationship, is time well spent, and in the long term will reap rich rewards.

Supervisees can prepare themselves for supervision by finding out about supervision before it begins, by thinking through what they want from supervision, and from a supervisor, by reviewing varieties of supervisory contexts. Inskipp and Proctor (1993) have perhaps the most comprehensive and clear outline of this pre-supervision stage for supervisees. The first two and a half units of their work pertains to supervisees. The areas they cover are the following:

Unit 1: Supervision – for what purpose, in what way
Purposes of supervision
The working alliance
Tasks and roles of supervision
Responsibilities of supervisor and supervisee
Supervision in training and organizational contexts
Arrangements and structure

Unit 2: You as developing counsellor
Stage of development
Your theory and philosophy of counselling
You as an adult learner
Your interactive style
Staying sane and competent

Unit 3: Setting up the working alliance
Choosing your supervision arrangements and/or supervisor

In my research into counselling supervision amongst counselling trainees in Britain (Carroll, 1994c), I found that supervisees have very little understanding of what supervision means. This longitudinal research, which involved trainees filling in the 'Expectations of Supervision' questionnaire at the beginning of their course, after Year 1, and finally after Year 2, showed that trainees' expectations change very little over the course of their counselling training. It would seem that supervisees are very passive *vis-à-vis* supervision, have few expectations from which to negotiate with supervisors, and are prepared to 'fall in' with supervisor ways of setting up and engaging in supervision.

If supervision is of its very nature supervisee-centred, i.e. for the learning of supervisees, then it is essential that supervisees have some training in being supervisees. This training gives them power to negotiate to obtain what they want. It provides knowledge of a number of ways in which supervision takes place (individual, group, etc.) with an opportunity to find out which suits them best. With insight into their own way of learning, of their stage of development, they are in a better position to come to supervision with clearly outlined goals and learning objectives. They can be pro-active in negotiating their learning needs. And finally, knowing something about supervision makes supervisees stronger in assessing whether or not supervision is meeting their needs.

Before approaching a supervisor, supervisees may want to give some thought to practical considerations, such as travel, fees, how often they want to meet with a supervisor, whether individual or group supervision is best for them just now, what is required from the supervision by their training course.

For supervisors

The pre-assessment stage can be equally important for supervisors. With more training for supervisors now available, there is increased opportunity for them to articulate their philosophy and understanding of supervision, how they set up and maintain a supervisory relationship, their criteria for evaluation, and how they understand and implement their roles and responsibilities with supervisees. This can be either written out and made available for supervisees, should they desire prior knowledge of particular supervisors, or at least be clear to the supervisor so that it can be shared with supervisees when required. In particular, supervisors need to have worked out in advance their responsibilities vis-à-vis training courses and counselling agencies. I know of several supervisory arrangements that were up and running before such issues were even discussed and, when they were, the supervisor had a view that, had the supervisee known it in advance, would have influenced the supervisory contract. It is unfair for supervisees to gain such information after supervision has started, seeing that it could have affected their choice of supervisor if known earlier.

Although little research has been conducted on the stages supervisors go through as they move from beginners to experienced workers, there are two models that can help them anticipate the stages that lie ahead. Alonso (1983) depicts the life-chart of supervisors in a matrix relating supervisor issues (self and identity, interpersonal, and socio-political) to three developmental stages (novice, mid-career, and late-career supervisors). Hess (1986) has a simpler format which reviews three stages of supervisor development:

a) Stage 1 features the beginning supervisor, who is working through issues such as role, structuring and implementing supervision, how to work with supervisee resistance, anxiety about appropriate interventions, and stress around knowledge of models and research.

b) Stage 2 sees supervisors move beyond the novice stage to that of exploration. Here supervisors concentrate on working with their impact on supervisees, and build up their knowledge of supervision models and interventions. Pitfalls and weaknesses at this stage include restricting supervision to the use of one role rather than the ability to utilize a number of different roles, and being too intrusive.

c) Stage 3 confirms supervisors in their identity as competent supervisors. Supervision is exciting and interesting, there is less worry about relationships, supervisors share more on all fronts, and the key focus is on supervisees' agendas.

Knowledge of such stages can help supervisors monitor their own work. It can also help them anticipate the future and be somewhat prepared for what is to come.

STAGE 1: ASSESSMENT FOR SUPERVISION

Stage 1 allows supervisor and supervisee to generate information to help both make decisions to move to a contract phase. The assessment phase should end in a decision for supervisor and supervisee: to contract for supervision work or to decide that they will not/cannot work together. The decision not to work together should not be seen as a failure but viewed as a valuable outcome for both. The assessment time might convince a supervisee that he/she feels more comfortable working with a supervisor of the other sex at this stage, or that a group supervision experience will be more beneficial, or that a supervisor from within a particular counselling orientation might best serve his/her learning. Similar conclusions may be drawn by a supervisor in relation to a particular counsellor. A supervisor may decide that this counsellor is not yet ready to begin seeing clients, or is more in need of personal therapy than beginning client work.

Besides allowing for the gathering of information, the assessment time will allow both supervisor and supervisee to experience being together: already they are beginning to have a 'sense' of the other person, their personality, their interpersonal style and their way of engaging in supervision. This will play a large part, perhaps even the largest part, in the final decision on whether or not to work together.

Assessment takes place in three areas:

Assessing supervisees
Assessing supervisors
Assessing contexts

Assessing supervisees

Supervisors need information about supervisees in order to judge whether or not they can work with them, and to decide at what level they can 'pitch' supervision. Answers to the following questions will help:

- At what level of counsellor development is the supervisee (level of knowledge, skills, abilities)? What experiences as a counsellor do they have?
- What professional organizations does the supervisee belong to? What code of ethics does the supervisee subscribe to?
- What teaching/learning methods are best suited to this supervisee?
- What are the learning objectives of the supervisee at this stage of development?
- What has been their experience of supervision to date?
- Why are they coming for supervision to me?
- Is the counselling orientation of the supervisee similar to that of the supervisor or different? If different, what needs to be negotiated?
- When would I conclude that it would not be advisable to supervise this particular supervisee?
- What professional demands will there be on me from the counselling agency/the training course? For reports? For meetings?

Supervisors have different ways of generating the information they need. I know of one who asks supervisees for a tape of a recent counselling session. In this way she is able to ascertain the developmental level of the counsellor and how congruent that level is with how the counsellor has described their own work. Others ask for supervisor reports from previous supervision, or ask supervisees to fill in questionnaires on their work. In one instance a supervisor role-plays a client with a supervisee as a way of determining how the trainee works with clients.

There are a number of published formats available for assessing supervisees:

1. Stoltenberg and Delworth (1987, p. 36)
2. Counsellor competency (Couch, 1992)
3. Counselor competency scale for the analysis and assessment of counselor competencies (Bradley, 1989, p. 138)
4. Stages of psychological/professional development and matching supervisory techniques (Bradley, 1989, p. 264)

5. Assessment of supervisee development level (Borders and Leddick, 1987, p. 22)
6. Borders and Leddick (1987, Chapter 2) provide an overview of formal assessment tools for counselling skills and for what they call cognitive counselling skills (i.e. how supervisees think about clients)
7. Formats for determining learning styles: Kolb's (1984) experiential learning cycle
8. Inskipp and Proctor (1993)
9. Evaluation of counselor behaviours (Bernard and Goodyear, 1992, p. 283)

Whether they use formal assessment (questionnaires) or informal assessment (interview, tapes, role-play), supervisors want an overview of what experiences in supervision and counselling supervisees have had, what they have learnt from that, where they are in their training at this time and what they want from their present supervision.

Assessing supervisors

How can the supervisee assess whether or not this individual is the best supervisor for them? Some questions the supervisee might wants answers to are the following:

What qualities/skills/knowledge am I looking for in a supervisor?

What kind/sort of person would best meet my learning needs at the moment?

How does this supervisor work as a supervisor? What is his/her underlying philosophy of counselling and supervision?

What is the counselling background, theoretical orientation, and supervision training of this supervisor?

What experience does this supervisor have of supervising?

Is the supervisor supported in his/her role as supervisor?

What professional organizations does the supervisor belong to?

How does the supervisor handle such areas as:

evaluation within supervision?

contact with training institute and counselling agency in which the counsellor sees clients?

supervisee presentations?

Does the supervisor have any requirements from the supervisee (e.g. particular forms of client-presentation, length of supervision session, whether individually or in groups, etc.)?

What about practicalities, such as fees, location of supervision, times when the supervisor is free?

There are a number of published formats available for assessing supervisors:

1. Self-assessment of supervision-related knowledge and skills (Borders and Leddick, 1987, p. 8)
2. Competencies of supervisors (published in Borders and Leddick, 1987, p. 65)
3. Self-assessment questionnaire for supervisors (Hawkins and Shohet, 1989, p. 77)
4. Supervisory Styles Inventory (Friedlander and Ward, 1984): published in Bernard and Goodyear (1992, p. 288)
5. Supervisor Perception Form (Heppner and Roehlke, 1984)
6. Supervision Emphasis Scale (Lanning, 1986): published in Bernard and Goodyear (1992, p. 293)
7. Counselor Evaluation of Supervisors (Bernard and Goodyear, 1992, p. 289)

Supervisees will want to know what experience supervisors have had of supervising and especially if they are interested in individual and/or group supervision, in particular client groups or particular counselling contexts.

Besides the formal methods of assessing supervisors outlined above, there are a number of informal ways in which supervisees can ascertain whether or not this supervisor is suited to them. An exploratory interview is suggested by Inskipp and Proctor (1993). Here, not only is information traded, but both get a sense of the other person and their ability to work together. Recommendations from other supervisees is often a good way to begin the process of finding and assessing supervisors.

Assessing context

Context includes the place in which counselling takes place and the responsibilities of supervisor and supervisee.

Counsellors see clients in a number of contexts: privately, in mental health establishments, in GP's surgeries, in hospital settings and in organizations, both public and private. Clients can be restricted to age group (as in youth counselling services) or to particular problem areas (as in eating disorders clinics and cancer wards). Supervisor and supervisee will want to look in some detail at contextual factors so that they both agree that the supervision will address the needs of the client group and the needs of the counsellor. The following invite consideration:

1. What factors in the context will influence the counselling?
   client groups
   age groups
   special areas

2. What contextual issues will influence the counselling and the supervision?
   the counsellor having other roles with clients
   loyalties within the counselling provision (e.g. where a counsellor is employed by an organization to see members of the staff)
   ethical concerns
3. What organizational accountability is required from supervisors?

Stage 1 in the supervisory process is a way of generating sufficient information to help both participants in the supervisory relationship make decisions about whether or not to move to the contractual stage. If either decide to withdraw there should be some discussion of reasons. If the assessment process is seen as a way of finding the best supervision for a particular supervisee, then it can be experienced as a constructive dialogue even if it does not end in a contract.

STAGE 2: CONTRACTING FOR SUPERVISION

The aim of Stage 2 is to end with an agreed and negotiated contract that meets the needs of both supervisor and supervisee. At the end of Stage 1 the decision to set up a supervisory relationship has been made. In Stage 2 the focus is on capturing that decision in a working agreement which designates the roles and responsibilities of each participant. During the contracting phase similar areas to those covered in Stage 1 may re-emerge but this time with a view to negotiated decision about how they may be implemented to the satisfaction of both. As to the process of setting up a contract, a number of formats have been suggested:

1. Inskipp and Proctor (1993, p. 49) have suggested an exploratory contracting interview as a helpful way of contracting.
2. Borders and Leddick (1987) include a list of practicalities to be negotiated.
3. Page and Wosket (1994) call the first stage of their model contract and divide it into five subsections:
   Ground-rules: establishing principles to guide supervision.
   Boundaries: agreeing the rules and guidelines to structure the supervision.
   Accountability: how accountability will be managed.
   Expectations: clarifying and agreeing expectations from all parties involved in supervision (supervisee, supervisor, organizations).
   Relationship: establishing a supervisory relationship and what it means.
4. A checklist for the initial supervision session (Bradley, 1989, p. 331).

5. A checklist of fundamental tasks involved in the formation of a supervisory relationship (Bradley, 1989, p. 462).

Whichever the format/s followed, the contract can be divided into four areas: practicalities, working alliance, presenting in supervision, evaluation. Below is a list of some of the issues in these four areas:

1. Practicalities
   How frequently will meetings take place and where?
   What length of time will each supervision session take?
   If we meet in a group, how will time be allocated? Who will be responsible for time-keeping?
   What will supervision cost? How will payment be made? Will missed sessions need to be paid for?
   What will our holiday arrangements be?
   What arrangements do we need to implement in case of emergencies? If the supervisor is unavailable?
   Will we have an agreed termination date for supervision?

2. Working alliance
   What will be the roles and responsibilities of each person?
   How will feedback be given?
   How and when will we review our working alliance?
   What will we do if either party is dissatisfied with supervision?
   Can we negotiate and agree boundaries, and have an agreed code of ethics?
   What are the responsibilities of supervisors vis-à-vis the counselling course/the training agency?

3. Presenting in supervision
   How will supervision time be used?
   How will clients be presented?
   What is our agreement on taping counselling sessions?
   Will notes from supervision sessions be kept?

4. Evaluation in supervision
   When will formal evaluation take place?
   How will it take place?
   What will happen if there is disagreement over evaluation?
   What are the criteria to be used for evaluation?

At the end of this stage supervisor and supervisee should have a clear and negotiated contract that clarifies roles, responsibilities, boundaries, practicalities. Long-term and short-term goals in supervision will also be considered.

At the end of Stage 2 an agreed format for working together will be formulated. This may be flexible and open to ongoing negotiation, and is usually made for a certain amount of time (one year). It may be written or verbally agreed.

An example of a supervisory contract is given by Compton (1987), whose SLC (Supervisor Learning Contract) covers the following areas:

1. Purpose of the supervision
2. Expectations regarding clients
3. Expectations regarding agency
4. Format for presentations
5. Supervision schedule
6. Time frame
7. Location and setting
8. Taping expectations
9. Evaluation process
10. Fees and payment

Missing from this contract is any agreement on learning needs, goals and objectives for supervisees. Negotiating and contracting on these gives criteria against which evaluation can be measured.

In Stage 2 the contract between supervisor and supervisee is negotiated and agreed. This does not mean that changes cannot be made: it is always helpful to review the contract periodically to ensure that participants are still happy with its contents. Sometimes implementing contracts is the best way of realizing the weaknesses within them.

STAGE 3: ENGAGING IN SUPERVISION

Stage 3 implements the contract as agreed in Stage 2. Implementation may raise questions not considered in the first two stages and time will be set aside to negotiate these.

Supervision will take place in the context of:

- The learning goals of the supervisee: how will these be set up and monitored by both supervisor and supervisee?
- The learning experience of the supervisee: how will suitable methods be chosen and applied?
- The developmental stage of the supervisee: how will this influence the strategies of the supervisor? The supervisor will be eager to match supervision according to the level of the supervisee.
- The teaching/instructing mode of the supervisor: how will the supervisor's skills be used with the supervisee?
- The administrative influences on both: how will they affect supervision?

A number of formats for helping engaging in supervision are available:

1. Page and Wosket (1994) designate three stages of their model within the engagement section of supervision: what they call focus, space, and bridge. Focus is the subject or material under review, space is the environment provided where reflection takes place and bridge is the transfer back into client work.
2. Hawkins and Shohet (1989) provide six possible foci for supervision.
3. What intervention will the supervisor use? A number of authors have provided methods for thinking about supervisory interventions. These can be used by supervisors to review their own interventions. Heron (1977) has offered 'methods of facilitation' in his Six-Category Intervention Strategy. Holloway (1995) has a very useful matrix for naming supervisory interventions, and Carroll has outlined seven generic tasks (Chapter 4).
4. Bradley (1989, p. 467) has devised a short questionnaire entitled 'An evaluation of the dynamics of a supervisory learning environment' as a help to assessing the learning situation within supervision.
5. Supervision note-taking formats can help monitor engagement in supervision.

There are ways in which supervisors can monitor their supervision sessions to learn from their work:

a) tape a supervisory session and listen to it;
b) have a consultant occasionally listen to a taped supervisory session;
c) seek feedback from supervisees;
d) negotiate with supervisees what areas to work on: assessment methodologies, relationship, transference, countertransference, theoretical orientation, etc.;
e) build in feedback sessions when reviews take place;
f) look at the supervision format to see what areas are not being considered, and/or what tasks are not being used.

Engaging in the supervisory process contains different responsibilities for supervisors and supervisees. Supervisors are alert to the learning needs of supervisees, focusing on different aspects of work with clients, intervening to help supervisees reflect on their work, facilitating learning and monitoring the counselling work in respect of the welfare of both clients and supervisees. Supervisees on the other hand are choosing how and what to present in supervision, receiving feedback both informally and formally, processing their learning, and transferring that learning back to their client work.

Particular areas in engagement in supervision

Three areas in particular emerge in the engagement phase of supervision: supervisee reporting and presentation of issues (which will be dealt with in more detail in Chapter 7), meeting the developmental needs of supervisees (which includes linking developmental models with supervisor interventions), and working with parallel process. The latter two will be considered in more detail here.

The developmental needs of supervisees

A number of authors have attempted to trace the various stages that counselling trainees move through in their journey towards becoming professional counsellors. Borders (1989) counted twenty-five developmental models of supervision and asked for a 'moratorium' on further additions until the present ones have had some opportunity of being researched. To some degree her recommendation has been heeded and the only recent significant contribution to new developmental models has been that of Skovholt and Ronnestad (1992). While there is no space here to critique the various models, several themes will be offered as ways of understanding issues within developmental models and particularly ways of linking various supervisory interventions with relevant supervisee developmental stages:

1. There is no connection between stage of training and the developmental stage of supervisees. Length of time in training does not equate with movement through developmental stages. It would be wrong to think that after five years counselling training a supervisee should be at a particular level.
2. Developmental stages are very individual. Within the same supervision group, or a group of trainees belong to the one training group, there can be various developmental stages. Development through stages does not take place at the same rate for all individuals and seems connected to various factors: for example, age, ability to reflect on personal experience, gender, race, cognitive style, theoretical background, the training course and previous learning (Shovholt and Ronnestad, 1992).
3. Developmental models tend to be highly complex and often err on the side of being too dogmatic about stages and interventions related to stages. While knowledge about such models is helpful, it is the task of supervisees to monitor closely the learning needs of supervisees and to trust their own reactions to developmental tasks. What supervisors often lack are interventions geared to meeting the changing educational needs that come with different levels of training and expertise. There is some evidence that supervisors stagnate in ways of working and apply these irrespective of developmental needs in

supervisees (Carroll, 1994c). Without becoming obsessed with finding the perfect supervisory intervention to match the exact developmental stage of supervisees, it is worthwhile for supervisors to review their supervisory strategies with a view to increasing them.

Linking developmental models with supervisor interventions

There are various ways of understanding developmental models depending on emphasis: three in particular will be used here as examples. By far the simplest and the one most easily used is that of Hawkins and Shohet (1989), who, after describing the more complicated four-level stages of Stoltenberg and Delworth (1987), summarize them as:

Level 1: self-centred ('Can I make it in this work?')
Level 2: client-centred ('Can I help this client make it?')
Level 3: process-centred ('How are we relating together?')
Level 4: process-in-context-centred ('How do processes interpenetrate?')

This can be used as an easy way of monitoring where trainees are in their work with clients. Supervisees at level 1 often concentrate on the 'right way' of working with clients. As a result they watch themselves work. As one trainee said, 'I was watching myself listening so hard that I could not hear the client.' The focus is on the supervisee learning and doing. In level 2 emphasis shifts to the client, and supervisees can easily connect or identify too closely with clients. There is still the search for the correct way of counselling and supervisees struggle hard to find it. At level 3 supervisees become aware of the alliance with clients as a key fact in counselling and move away from simply working with problems. And finally at level 4 there is a growing awareness of how contexts and individual differences influence counselling work.

The second model is that of Stoltenberg and Delworth (1987), which presents under three areas, eight domains and four levels. This results in quite a complicated matrix where each level is connected to each domain and each area. Table 5.2 summarizes their work: Stoltenberg and Delworth match each domain with each area and suggest supervisor interventions to help supervisee learning at each stage of development.

And the third and most recent model is that of Skovholt and Ronnestad (1992). Based on their own research they outline eight stages with the various characteristics of each stage. Table 5.3 summarizes these under two headings: the stage with some key characteristics, and possible supervisor interventions (these latter are comments from Skovholt and Ronnestad (1992) plus my suggestions).

It must be stressed that the connects made in this table are general guidelines (in much the same way as general guidelines can be given to

Table 5.2

Areas	Domains	Levels
Autonomy	Intervention skills	Level 1 (Trainee)
Motivation	Assessment techniques	Level 2 (Trainee)
Self- and other-awareness	Interpersonal assessment	Level 3 (Trainee)
	Client conceptualization	Level 4 (Integrated counsellor)
	Individual differences	
	Theoretical orientation	
	Treatment goals and plans	
	Professional ethics	

anxious parents about how to work with a teenage son or daughter) and need to be adapted to individual circumstances.

In conclusion, effective supervision of developing supervisees requires a working knowledge of developmental models, an ability to monitor the supervisory relationship and the learning needs of supervisees, and a preparedness to continue widening supervisory interventions.

Parallel process in supervision

'Parallel process' is a fascinating yet little understood phenomenon of counselling supervision. It is somewhat like the 'Law of the Hammer': when first discovered the hammer solves all problems. It can too easily become a magical formula for clever interpretation and woolly connections. It can be utterly incomprehensible and threatening to supervisees, especially beginners. Some supervisors totally reject it as a viable factor in supervision, either because of its psychoanalytic overtones or because of its lack of value in learning about counselling.

Originating within psychoanalytic literature (Searles, 1955), parallel process (other terms used are 'reflective or reflection process', 'mirroring', 'parallel re-enactment') refers to the process whereby aspects of the counselling relationship are expressed in the supervisory relationship. Because supervision is a complex, triadic, multidirectional network or system (Gediman and Wokenfeld, 1980), elements of the counselling experience are transferred into the supervision relationship in ways that are not quite understood. In the early literature parallel process was seen as a form of transference with the features of transference: an unconscious process, unidirectional, and usually not beneficial to the relationship.

Table 5.3

Stage	Supervisor interventions
1. Conventional (no training): an individual helps from their own experience of life and their natural abilities	Offering support and encouragement Opportunity to reflect on the work done Create awareness of when to refer
2. Transition to training: formal training begins with enthusiasm and insecurity	What motivates the person to enter formal training? What information is needed? Reducing anxiety in seeing clients Structuring supervision clearly Helping supervisees use supervision Supporting the dream while testing reality
3. Imitation of experts: uncertain while developing mastery but dependent on the experts and how they do it	Facilitating supervisees' use of experts to find their personal way of working Helping supervisees discover the theoretical base to their work Understanding self becomes important
4. Conditional autonomy: a certain amount of independence while still relying on experts	Helping the supervisee function as an independent counsellor Strong feedback from supervisor needed Opportunity to dwell on the personal reaction side of counselling work Specific interventions are of high interest
5. Exploration: beginning to explore a personal way of working and reflection on other ways	Opportunity to explore more fully one's own way of working Confirmation and disillusionment enters at this stage: support needed from supervisor Some experimentation is supported: new experiences, client groups, etc. Group and peer supervision can be particularly helpful here Supervision encourages reflection

6. Integration: using personally chosen methods that are internalized: open to other approaches	Enables supervisees to develop professional authenticity Facilitating a conceptual system underlying client work Helping supervisees be aware and accept their limitations Use of different supervisors helps
7. Individual: individualized and person-alized way of working	Encourage highly individualized working Facilitating ongoing intellectual growth Monitoring personal growth and support (watch burn-out)
8. Integrity: congruence within oneself in working in a highly personalized, chosen and integrated manner	To help supervisees maintain the fulness of integrity To build a colleague/colleague supervisory relationship Facilitating the use of intuition and personal reaction

Source: Development model of supervision, Skovholt and Ronnestad (1992)

Even though it has now become a widely recognized phenomenon, not just by psychodynamic supervision, there is still no agreement, even within psychodynamic supervision, over why it happens. There is very little research on the process. Two empirical studies were found by McNeil and Worthen (1989): the seminal study by Doehrman (1976) and the 1989 study by Friedlander, Siegal and Brenock. Both were definite about the reality of parallel process, but not quite as conclusive about its causes.

Several explanations of parallel process have been offered, the majority of which are psychodynamic. Gray and Fiscalini (1987) summarize these explanations under the overall heading of identification but with several different emphases. Firstly, it is possible that supervisees identify with the defensive behaviour of clients and then represent that defensiveness in supervision. This is a form of communication with the supervisor. Not being able to verbalize unconscious issues, supervisees act them out, in much the same way as repressed memories are subject to repetition, according to Freud. So supervisors get a real live drama of what is happening in the counselling relationship. In a second explanation, projective identification is offered as a way of understanding what happens. The client projects feelings into the supervisee who in turn projects them into the supervisor, a sort of handing the problem down the line. What cannot be dealt with in counselling is passed on, acted out, in supervision.

Other explanations present parallel process as reflecting the impasse between counsellor and client (Mueller and Kell, 1972), or as representing that part of the supervisee's learning that is similar to the client's problem (Ekstein and Wallerstein, 1972).

So why does parallel process take place? Again, several reasons are offered. Some view it as a process of communication when words cannot be used: supervisees are telling supervisors what actually happened in their relationship with clients in action rather than words. It could also be a way of learning: if the supervisee does to the superior what has been done to them, then they can learn, hopefully, how to deal with the situation. A third explanation is that it is about concealing rather than communication (Bromberg, 1982): supervisees get anxious about working with certain clients and try to hide this anxiety, which then is revealed by acting out the whole process. A fourth explanation sees personality similarities as a basis for parallel process. Gray and Fiscalini (1987) offer their own reason (this may well be itself a form of parallel process) showing why investigating parallel process in counselling supervision is so difficult: 'We propose that parallel process integrations are brought about by interlocking security operations of neurotically similar individuals' (p. 135). Try unravelling that for supervisees! Doehrman (1976) has reviewed the unequal relationship between the two sets of participants, client/counsellor and counsellor/supervisor, as a possible reason for mirroring, especially when issues of authority and power emerge.

However it happens, and whatever explanations are offered for its occurrence, it does appear that paralleling in supervision takes place. Furthermore, there seems to be some benefit in looking at various explanations of why it happens. So far, these have been from a psychodynamic orientation but it seems likely (Gray and Fiscalini, 1987) that TA could offer an explanation in terms of transactions and games. Bernard and Goodyear (1992) introduce the term 'isomorphism' to help move away from understanding parallel process solely in intrapsychic terms. Isomorphism (which comes from mathematics) stresses the interrelationship side of parallel process. Systems theory and systemic approaches to counselling could well contribute to our understanding of parallel process, as could other counselling orientations: it would be interesting to investigate explanations from a cognitive–behavioural or humanistic background.

The best use of parallel process is to help supervisees understand what is happening within their counselling relationships. Supervisors can monitor their own relationships with supervisees and use that information to help supervisees be aware of the dynamics within counselling. There seem to be several factors worth remembering in using parallel process in supervision:

1. Parallel process is most effective, educationally, with more advanced supervisees: for beginning counsellors it can be either confusing or

meaningless, and sometimes interpreted as punitive. In Doerhman's (1976) research the least experienced supervisee was the only one who did not appreciate parallel process.

2. Parallel process is not just unidirectional: it works back through the system to the client. What happens in supervision will also be represented in the counselling relationship. In a rather dramatic example Doehrman (1976) points out that a cancelled session by the supervisor resulted in a cancelled session by the counsellor. Supervisees constantly remark that when they have dealt with something in supervision it seems to loosen up the counselling relationship. This, of course, is a good transfer of learning, and does not always require unconscious reference as a way of understanding what is happening.

3. There is a danger in ignoring parallel process in supervision just as there is a danger in seeing everything that happens in supervision as parallel process. Neither is very helpful. An awareness of its possibility, and a clear way of explaining it to supervisees to help their awareness and learning, is more useful. It is also helpful to alert supervisees to parallel process and ask them to monitor how they may be presenting their clients in supervision through this process. After an initial obsession with the concept they usually settle down to being excellent observers of their own processes.

4. The conduits for parallel process are supervisees: they are members of both systems (though with different roles) and carry one system into the other. They stand at the interface between counselling and supervision. Because of their centrality in both systems, there is a great deal of potential learning for them. It is possible to use the parallel process to understand the dynamics of what is happening to the client, or the relationship between client and counsellor. Both these are represented by the supervisee within supervision. However, potential learning can extend to supervisees' understanding of their own dynamics; how they work and how they identify with clients. Parallel process can be a source of help for supervisors as they monitor what is happening to them in their relationship with supervisees, noticing when they act unusually or when they get drawn into the dynamics of the client/counsellor relationship.

5. There are examples of parallel process in both individual and group supervision. Williams (1987) has given examples of parallel process in teaching a class about supervision. However, we know little about which settings trigger off parallel process, and whether or not it is more likely to occur within supervision where particular orientations are used.

There is a tendency to believe that parallel process disappears as soon as it reaches awareness. This would be a dangerous conclusion to draw.

Individuals seem to be stuck within parallel process even when they are alerted to it. Awareness and acknowledgement are not sufficient alone to break parallel process. Working effectively with parallel process entails being able to explain it clearly and tentatively. Timing is obviously important. To attempt an interpretation of parallel process while supervisees are still struggling with strong emotions connected to the experience may simply increase resistance and/or denial. In such instances trainees may feel they are being misunderstood or judged (Williams, 1987). Checking continually with supervisees is important if they are to learn effectively from the experience of parallel process.

One way of effectively working with parallel process is role-play. Role-playing clients by supervisees can be an effective method of accessing and learning from parallel process and takes the emphasis away from explanations by supervisors.

In conclusion, though there are several explanations, mostly psychodynamic, of parallel process, we still know little about it other than that it occurs. Caution must be advised in working with it so that it enhances rather than hinders learning for supervisees. And of course, the motivation of supervisors in dealing with it is important. Interpreting parallel process could too easily contribute to the megalomania of supervisors, giving them a role as all-important interpreters of the unconscious rather than as a means to the further training of supervisees and the increased welfare of clients.

STAGE 4: EVALUATING THE SUPERVISORY PROCESS

While the majority of supervisors and supervisees accept that evaluation and assessment is part of supervision, many agree that it is probably the most difficult aspect of it. Evaluation, especially formal evaluation, introduces the judgement (good/bad, examination, assessment) element into the supervisory relationship. Evaluation is particularly difficult where one or other of the participants is seen as lacking.

Evaluating is part of all stages of supervision and should be an ongoing process that characterizes the work together. It is both formal and informal, the latter characterizing the ongoing feedback that is part and parcel of each session. With trainee counsellors there is usually a report written for the training course which requires a formal evaluation.

Evaluation in supervision takes place in two ways: informal feedback (formative evaluation) and formal evaluation (summative evaluation). It is first of all part of every session. Supervisors are evaluating the work with clients constantly to make sure that clients and supervisees are safe, and also to see if other interventions might be more helpful to clients.

There is feedback from both participants on their work, their view of each other's work, and on their relationship. Obviously this feedback, and how it is delivered, is a key factor in learning. Supervisees learn by doing, by reflecting on that doing and by listening to others comment on their work. It is important not just to give feedback but to set up the environment in which feedback can be best used. A number of authors have commented on the skills and qualities involved in giving and receiving feedback (Borders and Leddick, 1987; Freeman, 1985; Hawkins and Shohet, 1989; Inskipp and Proctor, 1993; Page and Wosket, 1994). Below is a summary of the steps through which a feedback system can be set up, delivered and evaluated by supervisors:

1. Monitor the supervisory relationship to ensure that it can sustain feedback and to judge what feedback is suitable for this stage of the relationship. If the relationship is not sound and secure then positive feedback may be interpreted as 'being nice' and negative feedback seen as punitive.

2. Connect feedback to agreed learning needs and objectives. In this way it can be seen as more objective, rather than as representing the prejudices or bias of the supervisor.

3. Review your own motivation in giving this feedback at this stage to this supervisee. If you were totally free what would you like to say?

4. Deliver feedback in a way that is constructive and characterized by being:
   - clear
   - specific (and behavioural)
   - objective
   - owned by supervisor (take responsibility for the feedback)
   - balanced between positive and negative
   - focused on inconsistencies and incongruities
   - regular (not just a once-off)

5. Allow discussion of feedback. It is helpful to encourage supervisees to restate the feedback and share their reactions and feelings to it. This clarifies that it is understood. It also allows both parties to look at any blocks to feedback, e.g. counselling orientation, cultural issues, overloading by the amount of feedback.

6. Discuss how the feedback can be used to create more effective work. Does the supervisee need to work on some issues, e.g. skills, theoretical base, particular arrangements with clients? How can these be implemented with clients?

7. Look at ways in which feedback can be reciprocal between supervisors and supervisees. Supervisees may wish to give feedback on how feedback is delivered by supervisors or on the supervisory relationship or other aspects of the supervisory arrangements.

And the second way in which evaluation takes place in supervision is formal, when time is set aside explicitly to assess supervision, the supervisee, the supervisor. This evaluation may be needed for the training course on which the supervisee is a participant, for membership of certain organizations (e.g. BAC accreditation, BPS equivalency statements), or for an agency in which supervisees see clients. Whatever its purpose, it must be recognized that formal evaluation raises many issues for supervisors and supervisees. Supervisees are anxious that they will not live up to the standards required and often think they are not good enough. Even more seriously, they fantasize that evaluation will be used to interrupt their training or advise them to leave the counselling profession. Often supervisees hear the negatives and forget the positives. A supervisee put it well when he said, 'One negative evaluation equals 20 positives in supervision.'

Supervisors too are anxious about formal evaluation. They may be found wanting in meeting the needs of the supervisee, they may be very unsure of the criteria by which they are evaluating, and they may not want to disturb the positive quality of the relationship they have with their supervisees.

Page and Wosket (1994) outline a process for evaluation within supervision that can be used for all aspects of assessment:

1. Talk together about the areas of evaluation.
2. Write separately about what should be included.
3. Read and discuss the written material. Amend if needed.
4. Agree a statement, which is signed by both and outlines any areas of disagreement.

They offer a nine-point agenda (pp. 142–3) for this report:

- Range and approximate number of clients seen
- Variety of client issues and problems dealt with, together with an indication of any special areas of interest
- Main themes and issues dealt with in the supervision
- Developments made in terms of growing awareness, skills and competencies
- Particular strengths and areas of expertise shown
- Limitations, weaknesses and areas for further development
- Evaluation of the supervision experience from both the supervisor's and the supervisee's perspectives
- The counsellor's short- and long-term objectives for future development, consolidation of learning and further training
- A statement by the supervisor indicating his or her opinion of the counsellor's fitness to practise, outlining any reservations

An important issue in formal evaluation is that of 'due process'. Bernard and Goodyear (1992, p. 34) explain it well: 'The most blatant violation of a trainee's due process rights occurs when the trainee is given a negative final evaluation or dismissed from a training program or job without having had prior warning that performance was inadequate and without a reasonable amount of time to improve.' It is essential that formal evaluation is ongoing, is clear and gives focused feedback, outling clearly any areas which could affect the training or future career of the supervisee.

Setting up formal evaluation

Bernard and Goodyear (1992) draw on their experience as well as on the supervisory literature to summarize a number of factors that create favourable conditions for formal evaluation:

1. Supervisors must remember that supervision is an unequal relationship.
2. Who will see and use the written evaluation.
3. Defensiveness should be addressed openly.
4. Evaluation procedures should be spelled out in advance.
5. Evaluation should be a mutual and a continuous process.
6. There should be enough flexibility so that supervisees going through a difficult time will not be unjustly affected by evaluation.
7. The background to an evaluation must be a strong administrative structure, i.e. those receiving the report will treat it seriously.
8. Making stars of trainees should be avoided.
9. Supervisees need to witness the professional development of their supervisors.
10. Supervisors must always keep an eye to the relationship.
11. No one who does not enjoy supervising should supervise.

They suggest that criteria for evaluation should be no less than two and no more than ten, not so global as to be useless, and communicated clearly to supervisees. The formal evaluation experience needs to have a clear format. The following is one example of the steps involved:

1. Have agreed *criteria* for evaluation of supervisee, supervisor, supervision.
2. Have an agreed *method* for evaluation, e.g. self-evaluation by supervisee, peer evaluation if appropriate, supervisor evaluation.
3. Monitor the process and content of the evaluation.
4. Agree a written evaluation report.
5. Discuss and deal with any issues/reactions/feelings emerging from the evaluation process (particularly if there is a negative report or disagreements within the report).

Evaluation criteria

A number of methodologies have been forwarded to help evaluate supervisees, supervisors and supervision:

Evaluation of counsellors
Counseling Practicum Interview Rating Form (published in Borders and Leddick, 1987, pp. 20–1)
Practicum Student Counselor Form (Bradley, 1989, p. 148)
Evaluation of Counselor Behaviors (Bernard and Goodyear, 1992, p. 283)
Grann, Hendricks, Hoop, Jackson and Traunstein (1986)
Stoltenberg and Delworth (1989)
Practicum Student Counselor Form (Bradley, 1989, pp. 149ff)

Evaluation of supervisors
Bernard and Goodyear (1989, pp. 289ff)
Borders and Leddick (1989)
Hart (1982)
Page and Wosket (1994, p. 131)

Evaluation of supervision
Counselor evaluation of supervision (Borders and Leddick, 1987, p. 62)
An Evaluation of the Dynamics of a Supervisory Learning Environment (Bradley, 1989, p. 467)
Supervisory Working Alliance Inventory (Efstation *et al.*, 1990)

Supervisors need to have criteria for evaluation before supervision begins. These criteria can utilize already existing formats, or supervisors may create their own criteria in keeping with particular training course or counselling orientations.

STAGE 5: TERMINATING SUPERVISION

Given the importance of terminations/endings in counselling (Ward, 1989), it is surprising that there is so little written on termination in supervision. There is advice on how long a supervisory relationship should last, on recontracting in supervision and on changing supervisors (Inskipp and Proctor, 1993; Page and Wosket, 1994), but nothing to indicate how termination in supervision should be viewed or operationalized. We know from the literature that termination in human relationships needs to be handled carefully and termination in professional relationships needs to be considered systematically (Kell and Mueller, 1966). Endings in human relationships activate different issues for different people, growing up, separation, abandonment, loneliness, dependency, self-worth, choice, and most of them raise issues of loss. Perhaps this is one of the reasons why we are reluctant to address termination in too much detail. Ward (1989) points out some of the issues: 'One contributing factor (in the termination of counselling) is the strong human tendency to try to avoid issues of loss by not acknowledging or dealing with them.' Ending a supervisory relationship (one-to-one or group), brings with it a number of losses, especially if the supervisory experience has been a facilitative one. A trusted mentor is no longer there, the members of the group have disbanded.

Yalom (1975) has pointed out, in the counselling context, that termination is not only an integral part of therapy, but if managed well, is an important factor in the change process itself. The same is applicable to supervision. One of the main learning foci for supervisees is modelling by supervisors (Holloway, 1995). Supervisors model how to terminate relationships in the way they manage termination with their supervisees. They deal with their own feelings and reactions and enable supervisees to do the same.

But more. Trainees will have had to deal with client endings. And presumably they will have talked about these experiences in supervision. They will know already how both they and their clients imbue relationships with meaning, and they will have some insights (hopefully) into their own way of dealing effectively, or not dealing, with termination in counselling. By the time they come to end in supervision supervisees should be aware of their coping strategies and their characteristic ways of dealing with endings. From these experiences, and with the use of supervision, and even their own personal counselling, they will have learnt how to manage termination in counselling, and know something of their strengths and weaknesses in doing so.

Wall (1994) has given a fascinating twist to the issue of termination in supervision by connecting it to parallel process. Parallel process in supervision in respect of termination means that supervisees will reflect their problems with client termination in the supervisory relationship. Supervisors will already have an indication, through monitoring parallel process, of how supervisees are managing issues and conflicts with client termination. Wall (1994) has offered some hints on what to watch out for when parallel process is at work around termination: how are termination issues introduced into supervision and reported by supervisees, are there any inconsistencies or unusual behaviour by supervisees when working with termination, what timing is used to talk about termination (e.g. the end of the supervisory session when it cannot be worked with sufficiently)? Monitoring parallel process, and using it creatively with supervisees, will enable supervisees to have insight into themselves and their work with clients at the ending phase of counselling. Wall (1994, p. 32) puts it succinctly:

> If supervisors refrain from participating in the same dynamics as trainees and clients, but instead assist interns in recognizing the parallel process occurring in supervision, students can explore their

own feelings and conflicts about terminating with clients as well as ending the field placements and supervisory relationship.

And, of course, the parallel process will work both ways. When supervisor and supervisee do not deal effectively with termination in supervision then it is highly possible that ending will clients will be affected. Since a number of endings often coincide at this stage of development, training course, placement agency, members of the supervision group, clients, all these relationship may be affected adversely.

Practicalities often determine termination in supervision: the training course is coming to an end, a placement in a counselling agency is finishing, a supervision group is breaking up. Or termination can be a result of the time-limited contract between supervisor and supervisee. Unlike counselling, which speaks about assessing clients' readiness for termination (Mearns, 1993b), ending in supervision is generally more pre-arranged. Usually, a termination time is built into the supervisory contract and most supervisees are aware that the supervisory relationship will end at a specified time.

Process of termination

The process suggested below borrows the three 'areas' outlined by Borders and Leddick (1987).

Summarizing progress towards goals. It makes sense to build some form of evaluation of supervisees into the termination stage of supervision. This provides an opportunity to review what has happened, what learning has taken place and whether or not learning aims and objectives have been met. It also gives the chance to acknowledge the strengths and weaknesses of the supervision arrangement: what seems to have worked, what could have been handled differently/better. Termination time can be a valuable time for evaluations by supervisors as well as supervisees: coming to the end of the relationship is always a good time to take stock.

Discussing how changes will be maintained and identifying the next stage for growth. Part of the evaluation process is looking ahead for supervisees to their next stage of development. Termination in supervision is a golden chance to anticipate the future by considering the past. With the help of an effective supervisor, supervisees can summarize their learning and, using that as a springboard, anticipate their future learning, whether that is within a training ambience, or within supervision, or in a particular counselling agency.

Achieving a sense of closure. The final section is setting up an appropriate form of closure to end the relationship. This can be done in a number of ways:

a celebration of the time together;
an appreciation time, when individuals recount what they have appreciated about being together and each other;
a goodbye gesture, e.g. a handshake, a group hug.

Whatever method is used, it is important that the ending is clear and clean, and not avoided. It is certainly worthwhile to talk about the ending of the supervisory arrangement and what that ending means to all participants. McRoy, Freeman and Logan (1986) have pinpointed a number of strategies (below) for teaching students about termination within social work, which can easily be adapted to the supervisory relationship.

- Build termination into the contract: it should not be left unclarified.
- Use relevant theoretical material as a guide in planning the tasks of termination (such material can be found in the literature on attachment, separation-individuation, and loss and bereavement.
- Consider the influence of past experiences with separation/loss for self as well as for supervisee/s.
- Help supervisee/s be aware about predictable reactions to termination and aid them in identifying and normalizing such reactions when expressed.
- Review changes that have taken place throughout the supervisory experience.
- Acknowledge and work with those organizational factors which influence the content and process of the ending phase, e.g. ending of training, terminating a placement.
- Encourage supervisees to actively confront termination with clients.
- Help supervisees review both cognitive and emotional aspects of endings.
- Assist supervisees develop a written plan describing how they will deal with termination with one of their clients.
- Use the process in the group (when there is group supervision) to learn about issues of termination and its effects on individuals.

Stoltenberg and Delworth (1987) raise two issues regarding supervision termination. One concerns developmental stages of supervisees and termination. They suggest that different termination issues emerge for supervisees at various stages of their development: for the beginning supervisee there is often the loss of a trusted mentor, but generally a quick bonding with a new supervisee. Level 2 supervisees are more sceptical about new supervisors, and experienced supervisees (at what they call Level 3) experience termination in supervision as a parting of friends. The second issue they raise is that of gender and termination in supervision. Using the work of Gilligan (1982) and the emphasis she places on 'relationship' issues for women, Stoltenberg and Delworth suggest that women often experience problems 'saying goodbye' while men have more of a problem with 'saying hello'. Within supervision this could result in women being reluctant to terminate supervision (especially if there is a female supervisee and female supervisor), while male supervisees may take the 'goodbyes' too lightly, creating what they term a 'pseudotermination'.

Particular endings

Not all endings in supervision take place by mutual agreement, and not all endings are the result of positive feelings about supervision. There are times when the supervisory relationship breaks down. Sometimes it is a result of just being the wrong people at the wrong time. It may have something to do with chemistry, with the teaching style of the supervisor, with the learning needs of the supervisee. Training courses should not be hasty in blaming supervisees if their supervisory arrangements do not work out and they wish to change supervisors. Nor should they be naive in just accepting it as a *fait accompli*. Sometimes a three-way meeting between the training course, the supervisor and the supervisee can help resolve whatever issues are causing concern. Whatever the reason, if supervision is not working, then the participants need to talk about it, and honestly face why it is not working. Generally, it is the task of supervisors to provide this forum and initiate this conversation. It is a wasted opportunity for learning if both supervisor and supervisee deny what is happening: sometimes relationships that do not work teach us more about relationships than ones that work well. And unsatisfactory relationships, as much as satisfactory ones, need to end formally.

Another scenario arises when a supervisor decides that they no longer wish to engage in a particular supervisory relationship because they feel that the trainee in question should not be seeing clients, or should discontinue their counselling training. This is obviously a situation for concern, especially if there is disagreement between supervisor and supervisee. Supervisors need to be very clear about their reasons for discontinuing to supervise a particular supervisee, and should make those reasons known to supervisees. It is important that supervisees have a forum where the whole issues can be discussed.

Occasionally the unexpected/unanticipated ends the relationship, e.g. death of either participant, or one member moving away. Where death ends a supervisory relationship it is essential that the remaining member of the partnership should have the opportunity of dealing with this either within another supervisory relationship or within personal counselling. Within a group setting, the remaining group need to process their feelings and loss within the group. Where one party moves away, time must be set aside to deal with the reactions and issues emerging from this pre-mature ending.

After termination

After terminating the supervisory relationship it is possible that partici-pants in a supervisory arrangement create a new form of relationship. Estadt (1987, p. 36) has pointed out future possibilities: 'Shall the relationship continue in the future as supervisor-trainee? Will it move towards becom-ing professional colleagues? Is there a mutual desire to explore a relation-ship as friends?' If the relationship does continue, in whatever form other than the existing one, it needs to be talked through carefully so that it is not a way of avoiding ending the supervisory relationship. Sometimes a period of no contact, giving time for reflection, can be a helpful way of creating the necessary space to consider whether both parties wish to continue the relationship in another format.

Very often supervisees will require references, sometimes supervisory reports, for jobs or towards counselling accreditation. Supervisors are advised to keep notes and former reports so that they can have access easily to information for report-writing.

Stage 5 asks supervisors to organize termination in supervision so that it becomes systematic and not left to chance. Good supervisory endings are also about learning.

Like all professional relationships supervision has its beginning, middle and ending phases, each of which has its own characteristics. This model provides a systematic approach to the various stages and offers frameworks and checklists to guide supervisors as the plan reaches each stage.

SIX

Supervision in an organizational setting

It is our position that there is a strong and necessary component to
clinical supervision that is administrative or organizational in nature.
(Bernard and Goodyear, 1992, p. 151)

Where a counsellor works in an organization or agency, the lines of
accountability and responsibility need to be clearly defined, between:
counsellor/client; supervisor/counsellor; organization/client;
organization/supervisor; organization/counsellor; supervisor/client.
(BAC *Code of Ethics and Practice for Supervisors*, 1988, Section 2:11)

For some years now I have been supervising individuals and small groups
who work as counsellors in organizational settings. This group comprises
welfare officers/counsellors from within the Metropolitan Police, five
partners of an Outplacement Counselling Service, twelve outplacement
counsellors from an International Consultants Group, two counsellors from
a university counselling service and a number of individuals who work for
various employee assistance programmes (EAPs). I have been struck by the
'qualitative difference' of the counselling service offered by these
individuals compared to the counselling provided in other setting, e.g.
private practice. For most of them (the counsellors who work for EAP
providers are an exception), counselling is only one of many roles in which
they engage with clients. Furthermore, and this includes the group who
work within EAPs, there is an organizational aspect to their work often not
applicable in other settings. These two aspects of counselling work in
organizational settings (varying roles, and the influence of the organization)
are key to understanding what counselling means in these areas, and
fundamental backdrops against which counselling work must be evaluated.
It also affects the way supervisors work with counsellors from such
backgrounds and raises the question, What are the tasks of supervisors who
work with counsellors employed by organizations to see their employees?

Even though there has been an awareness of organizational influences on counselling work with clients, there is little research in this area. Holloway (1992) recently asserted that 'the influence of organization variables on supervision has rarely been studied'. Beginning the literature review of his recent dissertation, Waite confirms the situation: 'It is necessary to begin this literature review by acknowledging the paucity of material available on the topic of supervision of counselling at work. That this lack of material is real is supported by evidence from a number of sources, and is of interest in itself' (Waite, 1992, p. 10). A recent research dissertation, though not written specifically about supervision, provides some insight into how supervisors can work with counsellors in organizational settings. One of the few pieces of research done on counselling in organizations in Britain, it focused on workplace counselling (Carroll, 1994). Twelve in-house counsellors in private companies were interviewed to see how they understood their roles and responsibilities. Even though it was within a particular setting, the conclusions can be generalized to counselling in other organizational settings (the pilot interviews used counsellors from other contexts). Carroll (1994) concluded that counsellors in organizational settings had a number of characteristics different from counsellors who are self-employed. Under roles and responsibilities, all interviewees were clear that they had multiple roles within the organization and were unable simply to be counsellors. They were consultants, trainers, agents of change, welfare officers amongst other roles. What emerged very strongly was the role of the counsellor as a mediator between the organization and the individual client. It is impossible to work with individual clients as if the organization did not exist. Counsellors have responsibilities to organizations as well as to individual clients and problems can arise easily when there are clashes of values or loyalty between the organization and counsellors. Understanding the culture or ecology of an organization is essential if counsellors are to work with it effectively. Egan (1993) has drawn attention to what he calls the 'shadow-side' of organizational life, the underlying culture where the actual decisions are often made and where knowledge of the organization is circulated. The BAC *Code of Ethics and Practice for Supervisors* (1988) is explicit on the relationships involved, 'Supervisors who become aware of a conflict between their obligation to a counsellor and their obligation to an employing organization will make explicit to the counsellor the nature of the loyalties and responsibilities involved' (Section 2.12). This statement could go further and insist that such conflicts be made known to the organization also as a way of negotiating agreements.

Carroll's (1994) conclusions show that counsellors in organizational settings require more than one-to-one counselling training: they need to know how to work within an organization, how to control the flow of information, how to manage multiple roles, and how to combine loyalty to individuals with loyalty to the organization.

Crandall and Allen (1982) have used the concept of 'parallel process' to illuminate the relationship between organizational structures and client work, pointing out 'that in order to fully understand the development of a therapeutic relationship one much pay attention to the organizational context within which the helping occurs' (p. 431). Systems and systemic approaches are continuing to educate supervisors to the role and effect that institutional structures, roles, responsibilities and climate have on actual client work. Supervisors are becoming more aware of the 'most difficult new skill that supervision requires . . . the helicopter ability . . . the ability to see the client within their wider context and help the supervisees do likewise: and to see the work within the wider context of the organization and the inter-organizational issues' (Hawkins and Shohet, 1989, p. 37). Supervisors of the future will see the organizational side of supervision not as optional, but as an essential ingredient in all supervision, not just supervision of counsellors in organizational settings.

Inskipp and Proctor (1993, p. 13) outline the various relationships between counsellors in organizations and clients: counsellors who offer a service to organizational employees, or to consumers of the organization, or to the public, in general or specific groups. In reviewing the accountability the organization has to the counselling service they suggest that each organization should have a statement of ethics and practice which includes the following:

- a statement of its aims and its philosophy of counselling
- a description of administrative practice, e.g. record-keeping
- an account of the management arrangement for the delivery of work, day-to-day and overtime, e.g. case load, distribution of cases, boundaries of work
- an account of the arrangements for managerial and non-managerial supervision
- the relationship of those arrangements to appraisal

Such statements allow for negotiations and clarity over roles and responsibilities, a point argued by Feltham and Dryden (1994) in talking about supervision within the organization. They highlight a number of difficulties that can arise where organizational issues play a part in supervision: where managerial supervision is involved, where there are problems with managerial style, and when supervisory reports are required by the organization. They suggest that supervisors clarifying their roles with different individuals in the organization and 'do not underestimate the subtle areas in which boundaries may become dangerously blurred' (p. 24).

Supervision and organizations

The administrative or organizational side of supervision has been noted for some time. In 1964, Ekstein visualized the supervisor's tasks in terms of a

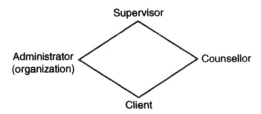

Figure 6.1 *The clinical rhombus (from Ekstein and Wallerstein, 1976)*

triangle with lines going to each of the three corners. In one corner was the client, in another the counsellor, and in the third the administrator. The third of these could quite easily be renamed the organization. Ekstein (1964) recognized that while there is a tendency to pull the supervisor in one or other of the corners, it is the supervisor's objective to remain 'equidistant' from all three. He viewed 'equidistancing' as a key supervisory function. Later Ekstein and Wallerstein (1976) outlined their clinical rhombus as a way of showing the various systems involved in the supervisory relationship (Figure 6.1).

Supervision is, of its very nature, a triadic relationship, with three systems involved: supervisors, supervisees and clients. When we widen these systems to look at contexts in which each is involved we become aware of the complexity of the supervisory system. Clients may live and work within an organization that pays for their counselling. That organization may be a work–company, an educational establishment, a GP surgery or a religious group. More and more organizations have set up counselling provision for the members of the organization (Reddy, 1993).

Figure 6.2 shows the relationship in a situation where both client and supervisee belong to the same organization. From this diagram it is clear that supervisors need to have a number of frameworks in mind when working with supervisees:

What client needs require consideration?
What counsellor needs must be attended to?
What is happening in the various systems that go to make up the counselling process: the relationship between the client and the counsellor, and the relationship between the counsellor and the supervisor?
What is the setting in which the counsellor/client relationship takes place and what influences does that setting have on the counselling work?

These four questions apply to supervisory work in whatever context counsellors work. However, the formulation of the answers will differ

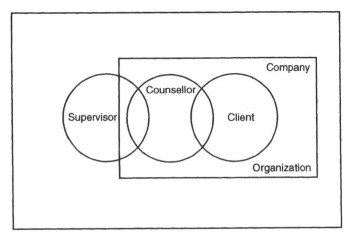

Figure 6.2 *Interrelationships between counsellors, clients and organizations*

depending on the setting. The organizational setting where counsellors work dramatically changes the counselling roles and tasks and require specific supervisory work.

Supervising counsellors in organizational settings

There are five areas of particular interest to the supervisor who is working with counsellors in organizational settings:

1. Enabling supervisees to live and work within organizations.
2. Helping supervisees control the flow of information within the organization.
3. Helping supervisees manage the delivery of counselling provision.
4. Working with supervisees at the interface between the individual and the organization.
5. Ensuring supervisees look after themselves while working within an organizational setting.

1. HELPING COUNSELLORS TO LIVE AND WORK WITHIN ORGANIZATIONS

Counsellors in organizations are employed by the organization, not by the client, and are both employees of the organization and counsellors to other employees within the company/institution. These roles demand clear thinking so that responsibilities to the organization are clear, as are the responsibilities to the individual clients. How these are viewed and decided by the counsellor may not be shared by the organization. There are many ethical dilemmas. Where does the counsellor's primary responsibility lie should there be situations where the good of the organization and the welfare of the client seem to be in conflict (i.e. where the counsellor is party to information shared by the client that is detrimental to the company)? What sort of independence does the counsellor have in making decision about referral without consent of the company? Although authors may sometimes claim that these are clear-cut, reality is often less simple. There is little agreement in the literature about where primary loyalties lie, with some writers being absolutely certain that the counsellors' major responsibility is to their clients, and others equally certain that the primary responsibility is to the organization (after all, it pays the salaries). Ethical codes do not give answers to many individual situations, and it is here that supervision can provide the forum that alerts to ethical sensitivity and allows for reflection preceding decisions. What is clear is that counsellors in organizational settings do more than engage in individual work with clients. They have a concern for the welfare of the organization, and in some sense 'counsel the organization' as well as the client. Otherwise they can get caught in the contradiction between helping to empower individuals to make decisions about their wellbeing and watching them adversely be influenced by a system that may be destructive of that wellbeing.

The supervisor is constantly monitoring the professional issue of relationships with the employee counsellor. A key question to the counsellor is: what relationship do you have with this person? Are you the trainer, the consultant, the advisor, the publicist, the counsellor, the advocate or the work colleague? Where relationships are not clear then all sorts of interpersonal games are played out. Especially difficult are areas where the relationship changes. A participant on a stress training course suggests coming for counselling, a counselling client wants an advocate in her forthcoming divorce court-case, a work-colleague hints that she wishes to talk about her personal problems, a client wants to form a closer interpersonal relationship, a manager who is being helped with personal problems asks for help with departmental relationships. Is it advisable to move from one set of relationship roles to another with this client? What are the implications? Would referral be better?

Since those who provide counselling from within organizational settings engage in a variety of roles and relationships, assessment of client needs becomes a key issue. Helping counsellors set up methods of initial and on-going assessment is crucial for clarifying intervention strategies and helping maintain the clarity of the helping relationship. Assessment can also be made from an organizational perspective. In other words is the client coming because of poor management within their division? Not all problems are intrapsychic: some are situational, some interpersonal, and not a few systemic.

2. HELPING SUPERVISEES CONTROL THE FLOW OF INFORMATION WITHIN THE ORGANIZATION

Supervision is the forum that helps the employee counsellor control the flow of information amongst the individuals in the organization. Redundancy counselling is an area particularly open to 'loose' information which creates double-binds for counsellors. The company-client often reveals information to the counsellor about the individual-client that the counsellor is unable to use. It may be about their personal life (e.g. he had a breakdown two years ago and saw a psychiatrist for six months; we have had a number of complaints about her way of dealing with subordinates) or about their professional life (e.g. she is a loner and unable to work within a team). What does the counsellor do with this information? In other circumstances the counsellor would feel free to share this with the client as a basis for their work together. From a company perspective it may not be possible to do so. The counsellor is caught with a 'secret': on one hand he/she has inside information about the client, on the other hand she/he cannot share it. And what happens when/if the client discovers that the counsellor knew and never disclosed that they knew?

Dealing with the flow of information, what information is required, what happens to information given from sources other than the individual client, becomes a key focus at times in supervision. Part of the supervision strategy is to help the counsellor control who knows what about whom, and direct how and what they want to know. Well-intentioned managers can burden counsellors with information they would be better not knowing. Part of the supervision is enabling the supervisee to educate the organization to information-flow.

On the other hand it is the task of the counsellor to feed back information into the organizational system. Of what use is a counselling provision if an organization cannot listen to the information from it and adapt its policies accordingly? Besides dealing with referring managers and work-supervisors, counsellors are in a prime position to make recommendations about life within the organization, about management styles, about team work and interpersonal relationships, and about the key problems faced by employees. This can be done in formal and informal ways: annual reports and statistics, training courses in counselling for managers. Supervision has a key role to play here and much valuable time can be spent on rehearsing methods of informing the company about issues that might help it change. Megranahan (1989) has quite rightly pointed out the key role that evaluation plays in counselling in the workplace. Supervision can help the employee counsellor review methods and research methodologies most suitable to realizing the kind of information needed by both counsellor and by the organization.

3. HELPING SUPERVISEES MANAGE THE DELIVERY OF COUNSELLING PROVISION

Supervising the counselling management function of the employee counsellor is a further element that becomes increasingly important in organizational settings. Counsellors not only see clients but manage the whole environment in which clients are seen. This involves simple practical arrangements (where will clients be seen, what furnishings are appropriate for this setting) to more complex issues, such as: who has access to counselling notes, will long-term counselling be offered to particular clients? The educational side of counselling provision is a major task in organizations that do not really understand counselling work. One counsellor who had just started as part of the Personnel Department (as the new counsellor) was amazed that her colleagues could not understand why she insisted on only five sessions with individual clients per day. They could not appreciate why she did not, like them, sift through 15 clients in a day. They began to interpret what she was doing as laziness and felt they were working hard while she was wasting much of her time with a few select individuals. This became a focal point in supervision.

Supervisors are unclear about whether or not it is part of their role to intervene in the work situation of their supervisees. Most prefer to work with counsellors to empower them to change the environment in which they work. However, I consider there are instances when counsellors need the support of their supervisor to intervene directly in a company in which unhelpful practices seem to be prevalent. In the instance given above I was invited to talk to the Personnel Department about counselling and supervision.

4. WORKING WITH SUPERVISEES AT THE INTERFACE BETWEEN THE INDIVIDUAL AND THE ORGANIZATION

Supervision is located at the interface between the counsellor and the organization. Organizations have their own cultures, some of which are supportive of counselling, some of which tolerate it, and some of which are embarrassed by it. Ekstein and Wallerstein (1972, p. 36) talked about each counselling setting having its 'customs, rules, physical arrangements, and spirit that together constitute what we call its structure'. Alongside that structure, and sometimes intertwined with it, are the 'psychological meanings' the structure has for each individual involved. These are connected to: issues of power and styles of leadership within the organization; the political climate of the company; constraints on the organization, e.g. finance, recession, etc.

A number of authors have addressed the organizational culture and its influence on counselling and/or supervision (Lane, 1990; Hawkins and Shohet, 1989; Randall, Southgate and Tomlinson, 1980). Hawkins and

Shohet (1989) talk of five organizational cultures: the personal pathology culture, which sees all problems as emanating from within the individual; the bureaucratic culture, which is high on task and low on personal relatedness; the watch-your-back culture, which is highly competitive or rife with internal politics and sacrifices individuals easily; reactive/crisis-driven culture, which lives and breathes by creating ongoing crisis situations; the learning/developmental culture, which creates the kind of environment suitable for learning and growing. They indicate how supervision can exist in these cultures. From a slightly different angle Lane (1990) outlines four organizational cultures and shows how counselling fares within each. The four he depicts are: power culture, role culture, achievement culture, support culture. Randall *et al.* (1980), while not applying counselling/supervisory elements to their work, document the types of culture that will have an impact on this: 'the founder's syndrome ... the charismatic leader ... the compulsive collective ... the bureaucrats and the bored ... the love is all ... and the nothing but the task' (quoted in Waite, 1992, p. 17).

Helping counsellors to understand the kind of organizational culture in which they are involved will enable them to be realistic about expectations. For a year I supervised a small team of counsellors who were constantly frustrated that management never listened to their suggestions. Management was not interested in the kinds of problem being brought to the counselling service. The counsellors felt they had some valuable feedback that could influence management decisions but could not, for the life of them, understand why no-one was willing to hear what they had to say. Understanding that the culture of this organization was based on power, and was bureaucratic and somewhat crisis-driven, was some help in explaining how management viewed counselling. Supervision sessions spent on ways of getting the information into the system other than through management were helpful. Waite (1992) concludes his research with a number of recommendations. One is very pertinent here: 'Supervision for those who counsel at work needs to embrace the specific demands, opportunities and ethical issues of the setting, and to be responsive to whatever acceptable arrangements it is possible to negotiate in different organizations' (p. 53).

Supervision keeps a focused eye on client work, but also on organizational structures and ecology, and furthermore on how the counselling provision can be of help to the organization as such, not just to the individuals within it. Supervision may well spend time on how this effect can be achieved and, at some stage, if the employee counsellor is not knowledgeable in management consultancy (e.g. diagnosing the organization to see what form of counselling may be best suited to it), then supervisory help in this area may be important. Supervisors who move from supervising within a purely clinical setting to one that involves organizational structures can be quite naive about the influence of the latter and concentrate solely on work with the client almost as if the organization did not exist. Supervision of employee counsellors and organizational workers is about reviewing their work with 'clients-in-this-organization'. The situational and contextual surrounds are not mere interest points but at the very heart of the counselling, and therefore the supervisory, work. Carroll and Carroll and Walton (both in preparation) are looking in more detail at the impact organizations have on counselling provision.

5. ENSURING SUPERVISEES LOOK AFTER THEMSELVES WHILE WORKING WITHIN AN ORGANIZATIONAL SETTING

Supervisors monitor what is happening to counsellors as a result of working within the organization. Counsellors in organizational settings may not have the support of other counsellors. Many work alone. They need a forum that allows them to express what is happening to them, to off-load issues that clients may leave with them. Hawkins and Shohet (1987, p. 121) use the term 'bucket theory' to illustrate how an individual (in this case the organizational counsellor) will carry the 'distress disturbance, fragmentation, and need' of the organization that comes to them through clients. Waite (1992) quotes the term 'institutional transference' from Gendel and Reiser (1981) to illustrate how clients sometimes transfer onto the counsellor their feelings towards the organization. Supervision allows the counsellor the 'space' needed to reflect on personal reactions and the areas of life from which they emerge, whether from the counsellor's own issues, resolved or unresolved, or from the client's ability to project onto and into the counsellor their feelings from the relationship between counsellor and client, and/or from the organization and organizational context of which both are a part. Supervision becomes a forum where personal reactions and feelings can be contained and dissolved before having deleterious effects on the worker. It is also the place where supervisors ensure that supervisees are not working beyond their limitations, or working beyond their limits. Burnout is all too common in industry and counsellors need to be aware of how it can infiltrate their own work.

Thus there are areas of particular importance for the supervisor who works with counsellors whose clients are 'organizational'. First of all it seems important that the supervisor should have some understanding and working knowledge of organizations – how they work, their varying cultures. Second, a good background in counselling management and how to set up counselling provision is especially helpful. So many supervisory issues emerging from this work relate to managing the counselling provision within the organization. And third, the supervisor needs a keen insight into how to maintain and support the counsellor as he/she works in an area between the organization and the employee, and how to separate and work within the differing roles and relationships that inevitably arise.

SEVEN

Forms of supervision and presentation in supervision

Each method of supervision has advantages and opportunities, disadvantages and obstacles. None of the suggested methods can meet all the needs of counsellors. (Cloud, 1986, p. 41)

Supervision takes place in a number of ways: self-supervision, one-to-one, co-supervision, small group, peer group, team/staff, organizational supervision. One or more supervisors may be involved, the supervision may be live, or deal with reported material. What is important is that different forms of supervision are not presented as if they were in competition, and one form was better than another. All have strengths and weaknesses and the skill needed is the ability to know which format is most suitable for this supervisee at this stage in their development. It is also important for supervisors to ask themselves which forms of supervision they feel comfortable with, and which they consider to be either beyond their competence, or outside their beliefs.

This chapter will describe a number of supervisory formats, reviewing the strengths and weaknesses of each, and look at issues emerging from that particular form of supervision. However, it must be remembered that strengths and weaknesses are often interchangeable concepts dependent on the context and what is stated here as a strength of a particular form of supervision may easily be a weakness in a different situation.

SELF-SUPERVISION

A number of authors have referred to the use of self-supervision (Bernstein *et al.*, 1986) or used the term 'internal supervisor' (Casement, 1985) to describe the ability to monitor one's own counselling work. One of the reasons for moving towards supervisees as their own supervisors has been a reaction to supervision as a life-long commitment. Getzel and Salmon (1985) articulate the adverse effects of counsellors *having* to be in supervision even after qualification. They suggest it creates dependency within counsellors, and never allows them to have the sense of their own abilities and powers. However, a more acceptable reason for self-supervision is the need to create a reflective forum where supervisees are able to examine their own work, evaluate it effectively, and move towards different interventions with clients. While most supervisors see this as admirable and very necessary, they consider self-supervision as a preparation for supervision, rather than a substitute for it.

Table 7.1 outlines the strengths and weaknesses of self-supervision when it is used as a form of supervision on its own, without reference to other supervisory arrangements.

Table 7.1 The strengths and weaknesses of self-supervision

Strengths	Weaknesses
Involves oneself alone	Counsellor may not be in touch with what is happening within themselves
No financial commitment	
Can utilize one's own time	Counsellor may miss significant factors in the relationship with clients
Builds up confidence in counsellor's own reflections	Counsellor may deny their own issues
Great independency	Counsellor may be impulsive in inter-ventions with clients during the sessions
Proactive rather than passive response to supervision	
Can be used as counselling is taking place	
It encourages reflexity	

Bernstein and Lecomte (1978) describe self-supervision as 'a set of procedures the counsellor uses to modify self-selected professional attitudes or behaviours', and Bernstein, Hofmann and Wade (1986) have outlined the steps through which it proceeds:

Self-observation: the counsellor observes self on video or audiotape in a session with the client
Self-assessment: the counsellor chooses criteria and assesses self against them
Selecting a goal: a behaviour is chosen as a goal to be changed (reflective listening)
Planning for change: the change is planned
Implementation: and implemented
Readjustment: and reformulated according to what happens with the client

As can be seen from the above, this set of steps is an invaluable tool for counsellors, and indeed for supervisors, with which to self-monitor the work they are doing in a systematic manner. The term counsellor could easily be changed to supervisor in the above outline and we have an excellent instrument for monitoring supervision sessions.

Interpersonal Process Recall (IPR) is a further method very helpful to students monitoring their work, and not unlike the method outlined above by Bernstein, Hofmann and Wade. A number of reviews of IPR have described it in detail (Bernard and Goodyear, 1992; Cashwell, 1994; Kagan, 1980), and it was always intended to be used in conjunction with an external supervisor. However, it can easily be adapted to supervisee work alone, and the questions asked by supervisors could be self-administered by supervisees. A tape of a counselling session is reviewed (the recall session), and segments chosen by the supervisee. The supervisor (or, as I am suggesting, the supervisee in some instances) then facilitates the reflection process with questions such as:

- What do you wish you had said to him/her?
- How do you think he/she would have reacted if you had said that?
- What would have been the risk in saying what you wanted to say?
- If you had the chance now, how might you tell him/her what you are thinking and feeling?
- Were there any other thoughts going through your mind?
- How did you want the other person to perceive you?
- Were those feelings located somewhere physically in your body?
- Were you aware of any feelings? Does that feeling have any special meaning for you?
- What did you want him/her to tell you?
- What do you think he/she wanted from you?
- Did he/she remind you of anyone in your life? (Cashwell, 1994)

Issues arising

Self-supervision seems to be a valuable tool for counsellors in general, and a goal that can be worked towards during counselling training. Since it is dependent on counsellors setting up and marshalling their own time, resources and motivation, and creating the structures in which their learning takes place, it is dependent on their resourcefulness. However, it is used most effectively when allied to other approaches, e.g. as a preparation for supervision in a one-to-one or, indeed, group setting. Its major weakness, where it is the only method of supervision used, is the possibility that, being blind to our own issues, we do not see areas for concern. Hawkins and Shohet (1987) have outlined some of the 'blocks' to arranging supervision that apply to self-supervision: previous experience, personal inhibition, the supervisory relationship, organizational issues, practical problems and cultural concerns and have indicated that the ability to recognize and manage these blocks is a way of caring for ourselves. It is possible that a counsellor would choose self-supervision as a way of denying possible problems and a way of avoiding having to face them if confronted by another. In brief, self-supervision is not advised for beginning counsellors, or indeed for counsellors in training, other than as a preparation for supervision with another/others. However, from the beginning of training, it is essential that supervisees be taught a method of monitoring their own work. They do not come with a handbook of how best to use supervision (Carroll, 1994c), and it falls to either the training course or the supervisor to help them devise strategies to monitor their counselling sessions.

ONE-TO-ONE SUPERVISION

As the words imply, one-to-one, or individual, supervision is a supervisory arrangement involving one supervisor and one supervisee. Probably, though there is little research to allow one to draw specific conclusions, one-to-one supervision is the most popular form. In some instances it is required by training, in others the choice is left to supervisees. Table 7.2 shows the strengths and weaknesses of one-to-one supervision.

Table 7.2 *The strengths and weaknesses of individual supervision*

Strengths	Weaknesses
More time for the supervisee	Full focus is on the individual supervisee
More opportunity for supervisees to hear about and experience a particular counselling approach	Isolated context
	Input from only one person (supervisor)
Gives the opportunity to create clearer and more focused learning objectives	Becomes difficult if the supervisory relationship breaks down
Highly personalized	Evaluation and feedback from one perspective
Can more easily parallel individual counselling	Can become collusive with very little challenge
Allows for strong mentoring	Can create dependency in supervisees
Allows supervisees to concentrate on a number of their clients	Can concentrate on one counselling approach
Supervisee can work at his/her own pace	No comparison for supervisees on other ways of working
A non-competitive environment (no sibling rivalry)	
Development of the supervisee can be monitored more easily	
Supervisor interventions can be geared more specifically towards the learning of this supervisee	

Individual supervision is expensive in terms of time and sometimes of economics. It is of particular benefit to those who are at the beginning of their client work and who are seeing several clients, and is also often the choice of full-time experienced counsellors who spend a lot of time in client work. In giving individual attention to the supervisee it provides a systematic and ongoing forum that is highly educational. Every counsellor should have the opportunity of experiencing individual supervision at some stage in their training.

ONE-TO-ONE CO-SUPERVISION

Individual co-supervision is an opportunity for two individuals to take turns in being supervisor and supervisee. In alternating the roles of supervisor and supervisee they share the time together within one session or take sessions in turn in being supervisor/supervisee. Table 7.3 outlines the strengths and weaknesses of this form of supervision.

Table 7.3 *The strengths and weaknesses of one-to-one peer supervision*

Strengths	Weaknesses
Can be easily set up	May be loose around boundaries, e.g. social roles involved
Works well where both participants are about equal levels of development	Can easily become collusive and lacks challenge
Experienced counsellors can find this empowering	Can become competitive
Eliminates the 'expert' side from supervision	Has to deal with the difficulty of changing roles within one relationship
Inexpensive	

Because of the need to change roles, and the need to trust one another, it is highly advisable that one-to-one co-supervision be not the only form of supervision open to supervisees. Certainly, at the beginning of counselling training supervisees need a stronger structure in which they can feel secure, and where they do not have to take on the quite difficult role of supervisor when they are still learning how to be supervisees.

These are some of the issues which need to be addressed when individual co-supervision is being set up:

a) Choosing the correct partner as supervisory partner. Remley *et al.* (1987) consider that different levels of training and experience may not be a disadvantage. Participants learn in different ways even when there are differences of experience. However, they stress that issues need to be negotiated, in particular where there is a difference in

theoretical orientation. They also review the advantages and disadvantages of having a peer co-supervisor from within one's work
setting or from outside it, and discuss the conflicting evidence on the
advisability of same-sex versus cross-sex of the peer-pair.
b) Ability of both to create a learning relationship.
c) Successfully negotiating roles and responsibilities.
d) Clarifying counselling orientations and how to work together if from
   different theoretical backgrounds.
e) Negotiating a supervisory contract that fits in with the abilities of
   both.
f) Dealing with possible difficult points, e.g. times, evaluation process,
   etc.

A model for this supervisory format is offered by Remley *et al.* (1987). They
propose a ten-session (one hour each) programme, with evaluation built in
so that modifications can be made to suit the needs of the participants.

Session 1: Background information and goal-setting
Session 2: Each presents a client case (orally) with an exchange of audio/
videotapes
Session 3: Tape review for counsellor 1
Session 4: Tape review for counsellor 2
Session 5: Discussion of readings
Session 6: Intermediate evaluation
Session 7 and 8: Second tape of each counsellor
Session 9: Case presentations and current issues
Session 10: Evaluation

The participants may decide to end the sessions at this stage or a new
agreement may be proposed and accepted.

GROUP SUPERVISION

Interestingly, the history of supervision within social work shows a move
from individual to group work supervision based on a fear of the supervisee
becoming dependent on the supervisor ('interminable supervision') and
never quite able to be an independent practitioner (Getzel and Salmon,
1985). Group supervision provided the supportive and administrative
domain with the realization that the supervisee was no longer in need of
formal education in the profession.
   Group supervision is perhaps the most widely practised form of supervision. Holloway and Johnson (1985) entitled their article 'Group supervision: widely practised but poorly understood' and have pointed out that
group supervision is still at a rudimentary stage of development. They
concluded with five questions that need to be asked from this form of
supervision:

1. What should be the goals of group supervision?
2. What roles should the group supervisor adopt to promote the realization of these goals?
3. What balance between didactic material, case conceptualization and interpersonal process is most productive for trainee learning?
4. What is the role of evaluation in group supervision?
5. What unique contribution does group supervision make to a training programme?

Holloway and Johnson also indicate that the term 'group supervision' covers a wide range of supervision practices. Early forms of group supervision combined case presentation, group dynamics within the supervision group and didactic material (Orton, 1965) while more up-to-date models use the therapeutic power of the group and stress the developmental stages of the supervisees (Patterson, 1982; Sansbury, 1982; Yogev, 1982).

Group supervision can be seen as a generic term that covers a number of supervision formats.

a) *A supervisor, designated as leader of the group, works with individuals within a group setting.* What characterizes this form of group supervision is its lack of use of group process within the learning alliance. Individuals are allocated time within the group and the supervisor works with the individual supervisee but within the group. Other members of the group may share their thoughts and reflections but group process is not the focus of learning within supervision. Most group supervisors will use group process when it is *interfering* with learning but not as itself a focus for learning.

b) *There is a designated leader* but *the group process within supervision is used as a learning focus.* Obviously, this can be a particularly powerful way of learning for supervisees involved in group counselling. Bernard and Goodyear (1992, p. 69) make this emphasis on group process a condition for group supervision: 'In order to qualify as group supervision, therefore, the procedure must depend on the interaction of group members and must have at its core the dynamics of group process, including the delicate balance between individual growth and development and group growth and development.'

Where supervisors use the group process as a learning focus in the supervisory group, it is essential that they have some understanding (and hopefully) training in working with groups, in understanding group dynamics and knowing when and how to intervene effectively. Just as individual supervisees move through developmental stages on their journey towards mastering their art, so groups have defined stages. There seems to be little research on the stages that supervisory groups go through, and conclusions are applied to them from the literature and research on therapy groups and groups in general. Table 7.4 present the strengths and weaknesses of group supervision.

Table 7.4 *The strengths and weaknesses of group supervision*

Strengths	Weaknesses
Input from a number of people (supervisor is not the only person with knowledge and experience)	Individuals can be sacrificed to the group
Opportunity to experience other counselling orientations	Individual can get lost (or hide) within the group
Supportive atmosphere from peers, especially for beginning counsellors	Scapegoating can take place (sibling rivalry)
The value of listening to others describe how they work and the problems they face	Supervisees who carry heavy case-loads may not have enough time
Cost-effective in terms of both time (supervisor) and economics (supervisees)	May be less time for experimenting with other supervisory interventions
Allows experimentation with other supervisory interventions, e.g. drama-therapy	Not all individuals are suited to group work
Can help supervisees deal with issues of dependency on supervisors	Personal growth takes over from client-work
Evaluation and feedback from a number of people	Some use the group as a dumping ground for feelings
Risk-taking can be higher in a group setting	Group dynamics can interfere with individual learning
Help from others as they share their failures	Pressure to conform to group norms
Emotional support from peers who are in similar learning situations	Difficulty of entering an already-established group by a newcomer
Can address issues arising from within the group that may affect work with clients, e.g. competitiveness, dealing with stress, self-disclosure, interpersonal style	Time spent on areas not of interest to other group members
Dilutes the power of supervisor	May be too much happening (overload) for individual to process
Someone of the same age, gender, race	Confidentiality is less secure
	More experienced supervisees tend to lose out in group supervision
	Less likely to mirror individual counselling session

We still await documentation on:

How do we select suitable participants for group supervision?
What is the most suitable size for a supervision group?
Should a supervision group be open, or closed?
What group norms need to be negotiated?

How do group stages affect supervisory interventions?
How long should a supervision group last?

Issues emerging from group supervision

The supervisor can either take responsibility for apportioning time amongst the supervisees, or allow them to negotiate time on their own behalf, or leave time open for those who wish to use it. Whatever process is decided or required by the supervisor the following needs to be agreed:

1. Will group process be used as part of supervision?
2. How will time be allocated?
3. What form of client-presentation will be used within group supervision?
4. How will evaluation/feedback take place?
5. How will selection of participants for group supervision take place? Will this be decided by counselling orientation, developmental level of trainee, type of clients seen, location?

Setting up group supervision

In setting up and maintaining a group supervision arrangement a number of factors need to be reviewed. A knowledge of group dynamics on the part of the supervisor is essential in order that the group work well, and in particular that the group process assists the learning of the supervisees and does not interfere with it. A clear and negotiated format of how time will be used (allocated by supervisor, negotiated at the beginning, left open for individuals to use at will) helps the flow of the group. Review times, where the group process is evaluated, where individuals needs are re-considered and where supervision is evaluated, allows for formal feedback and necessary changes.

Ellis and Douce (1991) have identified eight issues that tend to characterize group supervision. These need to be considered in the preparatory stage of setting up the group:

Supervisor issues: supervisor anxiety; choice of interventions
Group process issues: competition versus team support
Counsellor–supervisor process issues: balancing responsibility; parallel process; power struggles; individual differences; sexual attraction

These are not unlike issues that can arise in any form of group work.

PEER GROUP SUPERVISION

Like one-to-one peer supervision, a peer group supervision is an arrangement where 'three or more counsellors share the responsibility for providing each other's supervision within the group context. Normally they will consider themselves to be broadly of equal status, training, or experience' (*Information Sheet No. 8*: BAC, 1990). Peer group supervision usually involves experienced or qualified counsellors who want to share experiences and do not have the same need for the 'expert' guide as supervisor. Participants fulfil roles of supervisor and supervisee.

The aim of the peer supervision group is to create a forum where counsellors share their client work and problems with other experienced counsellors. Not only does it allow the group to deal with issues arising from client work but it can also be a forum for exchange of ideas, a referral network, sharing of news from within the counselling profession and a mutual support for the members. Table 7.5 shows the strengths and weaknesses of peer group supervision.

Table 7.5 *The strengths and weaknesses of peer group supervision*

Strengths	Weaknesses
Equal power sharing for experienced counsellors	No final responsibility for client welfare
More empowerment for participants and less dependency on a single leader	Individuals may not be equal in respect of training or experience
More in keeping with the principles of adult learning	Excessive competitiveness, criticalness and/or lack of concern for individuals
Non-hierarchical relationships within group	Group dynamics take over
Cost-effective in time and finance	No one to monitor the group process over and above the participants
Cohesiveness within group when members are chosen	Individual may join to get help with personal problems
Shared values	Becomes a friendship rather than a supervision group
Giving and receiving mutual support and encouragement	No confrontation or reluctant to challenge
Creating a referral network	No formal evaluation
Can create a place for friendship and exchange in what can be an isolated profession	Becomes too informal
Can use the group process to learn	Becomes a 'moan' group

Issues arising

Peer groups need to be carefully planned. Key questions to be decided are:

Will the group be an open or closed group?

If an open group, how will new members join?

How will members leave the peer group?

How will the group be organized and structured?

Will the group be leaderless or should there be a 'rotating' leader? If the latter, what are the responsibilities of the leader?

What ground rules will characterize the group, e.g. confidentiality, referral of clients within the group, use of the group to deal with personal issues, etc.?

Goldberg (1981) has pointed to the possibility of having 'difficult' group members who can be very demanding, either bringing their own issues and insisting the group deals with them, or in demanding an inordinate amount of time for themselves, and/or being very destructive in their relationship with other group members. Such people may represent the 'implicit conflicts experienced and denied by their colleagues' (p. 31) and their dropping out of the group does not solve the issues within the group. He has also considered the issue of group membership suggesting that peer group involvement demands a certain level of psychological maturity and group members may wish to decide whether or not participants have had personal therapy as a prerequisite to joining.

Hints for setting up peer-group supervision

Hawkins and Shohet (1989) summarize suggestions on forming a peer-supervision group:

- try to form a group that has shared values but a range of approaches;
- have no more than seven people in the group;
- be clear about commitment (it is a recipe for disaster to allow members to attend at their own convenience);
- make a clear contract (negotiations will include venue for meeting, how often the group meets, how long the supervision sessions last, how the time will be used, how individuals will contact group members if they will be absent, etc.);
- be clear about the different expectations (reasons for being part of a peer supervision group ought to be declared at the group's inception;
- be clear about role expectation;
- give time to the supervisory process within each session;
- have periodic review sessions.

These hints are translated into a model for organizing a peer supervision group:

set ground rules;

negotiate time according to set criteria;

encourage clarity around expectations and needs;
decide about informal time.

TEAM OR STAFF SUPERVISION

Team or staff supervision normally involves a group of individuals who work together and who employ an outside supervisor to help them with their client work. It is a particular kind of group supervision, where the group is the same staff team. The supervisor may also help them work through the inter-personal and group issues arising from their being a staff team.

Occasionally staff group meet on their own as a sort of peer supervision group but this is rare, and is vulnerable to adverse group dynamics taking over. The strengths and weaknesses of a staff/team group meeting with an outside supervisor are set out in Table 7.6.

Table 7.6 The strengths and weaknesses of team/staff supervision

Strengths	Weaknesses
Individuals know each other	Individuals are afraid to share weaknesses because of career implications
All are committed to the same organizational goals	Competition and politics within the team distract from learning
Can decide policy as well as look at clients	Management uses the supervision to monitor what is happening
Can create a sense of organizational responsibility for clients	Difficult to confront individuals in front of their peers
Can develop as a team	Acting-out takes place through absenteeism, etc.
Can deal with problems that move back into the system from clients	
Can check out perceptions, distortions, assumptions with other group members	

Shulman (1982) asks some questions that need to be clarified with team supervision:

1. Who should/will attend? Should management be there? Should clerical, administrative, support staff also attend?
2. To whom is the supervisor responsible (what reports will be written, what feedback given)?
3. How will reports be used?
4. What kind of meeting is this: is it a staff meeting, an in-service training, case-consultation of clients, or group supervision focused on supervisee growth?

Team/staff supervision requires clear boundaries and negotiated contracts, especially in teams where this is not the norm. Particular attention needs to be directed towards the dynamics and politics within the working group. Not to deal with these openly and directly is to allow them to influence, and sometimes take over and/or sabotage supervision.

OTHER FORMATS

While looking at a number of forms of supervision, it must be pointed out that there are variations, some quite creative, on how supervision formats are utilized. One group in the north of England had a peer group process whereby the full group of six people met for a full day every two months. In the intervening time, they met in pairs fortnightly for co-supervision, these pairs revolving every so often. Others have combined peer supervision with supervision from a designated supervisor. I know of one supervisee who spends two full days a year with her supervisor: she lives overseas and visits London once a year, during the summer. This is her only opportunity to meet with a supervisor she trusts.

Hawkins and Shohet (1989) have used the terms 'supervising networks' and 'supervising organizations' to show the supervision need not be confined to individuals and/or small groups, but can be applied to wider contexts. However, it is difficult to see this as actual organizational supervision rather than supervision of people who are creating change within organizations. It looks more like organizational consultancy and/or organizational development rather than supervision as understood here. Besides the skills of supervision it would appear that such work involved a strong knowledge of organizations, organizational culture and of facilitating change within organizations.

Which form of supervision is most suitable for this supervisee? – in this training? – at this developmental level? – working with these clients? – who learns this way? are the key questions when seeking supervision. Answers to these questions will go a long way in determining which form best suits whom. It is valuable to have such a rich choice at this stage in the development of supervision.

RECORDING AND PRESENTING CLIENTS IN SUPERVISION

There are a number of methods used by supervisees to record their client work and present clients in supervision. Methods adopted are sometimes related to counselling orientation (e.g. psychodynamic approaches tend to favour supervisee verbal reports and, by and large, dissuade the use of audio- or videotaping client sessions). Tradition can also be a factor in the choice of method (family and systemic approaches to counselling are strong adherents to 'live supervision' and have a well-established tradition of using one-way mirrors, bug-in-the-ear, etc.); and/or the use of particular methods may be related to supervisors' preferences (some supervisors demand tapes of client sessions) or indeed supervisees' preferences (e.g. some would prefer to avoid role-playing).

There are arguments for and against the various presentation methods. Goldberg (1985) has pointed out that it is easy to get into a 'which-is-the-best' mode of presentation with individuals taking strong and sometimes exclusive positions. He asks instead (p. 4):

> which mode is most useful given specific educational objectives? . . .
> process notes, audio, and video-tape can be utilized in a mutually
> enhancing way rather than being seen as competing choices which
> depend solely on the supervisor's style and his or her philosophical
> orientation towards teaching . . . at times one mode shows obvious
> advantage, in some instances a combination of modes is helpful, and
> there are also areas in which no specific mode appears to have a clear
> advantage . . . the underlying principle applied here is that specific
> educational objectives determine the most desirable mode of
> presentation to be used.

Goldberg has stressed the need to connect presentation method with educational needs. This may well be a far cry from how presentation methods are actually chosen in supervision. A sensible evaluation question for both supervisors and supervisees is: 'How have we come to choose these methods of client presentation in our supervision?' Inevitably, that will raise the question of what methods are not being used, and why not. Articulating how the methods have been chosen allows some insight into the amount of thought and time given to this area. Methods are often chosen by default, i.e. supervisors either dictate what will happen, or allow supervisees to present as they wish.

Goldberg (1985) has suggested a sensible three-step approach on how to connect method with educational aims:

1. Select and agree an area of learning for the supervisee.
2. Determine what data are needed from client-work to best meet the learning need.
3. Choose a method of recording and presentation that best presents these data.

The next section will review some of the advantages and disadvantages of different forms of presentation.

Verbal reports

Verbal reports present the client/clients orally, using the memory of the supervisee as the main source of information about clients, and about what happened between the client and the trainee. There is no doubt that this mode of presentation indicates 'how the client has entered into the intrapsychic life of the supervisee' (Hawkins and Shohet, 1989, p. 102). For this reason, a number of authors have questioned the reliability of such accounts, pointing out that what supervisors receive is the client as perceived by the supervisee. While this is a valuable source of information with which to work, what is often missing is what *actually happened* and what the client is *actually like*. We know that supervisees can deliberately misrepresent what happened with clients (Chrzanowski, 1984). But they can also, like witnesses, present what they interpret as happening. Verbal reports are interpretations and one question for supervisors must be: Is there a relationship between what actually happens and this supervisee's report on what happened? Several times I have listened to supervisees describe an event in counselling that I subsequently listened to on audiotape. I have been amazed at the differences between their interpretation and my interpretation of events. In one instance the end result of the intervention by the supervisee, reported by him as beneficial, seemed to me to be the direct opposite of what he intended.

Verbal reports emerge from supervisees' memories of the session/s with clients, from notes written after the session/s, and/or from notes written during the session/s. Supervisors may or may not ask to see notes of counselling sessions before the supervisory session. Others recommend that supervisees review their notes with a number of clients with a view to co-ordinating any counselling themes for presentation in supervision. Table 7.7 shows the strengths and weaknesses of verbal reports.

Table 7.7 *The strengths and weaknesses of verbal reports in supervision*

Strengths	Weaknesses
Forces the counsellor to remember actual details	The counsellor can miss the client in trying to remember the words
Demands that the counsellor pay strict attention to what is said	The report does not capture the non-verbals in the actual counselling encounter
Captures as much as possible of the counselling process	The supervisee records selectively
May help the supervisee review progress if the reports are in a written format that is similar after each session	The supervisor can never be sure from the report that the client is not being harmed
Can be a valuable way of helping supervisees know how they interpret what happens	Report can miss essential information

Verbal reports are probably the most frequently used method of client-presentation in supervision. With experienced supervisees they can be highly effective, especially if there is no formal evaluation as part of the supervisory contract. With trainees, however, it would seem more helpful to combine verbal reports with other forms of accessing clients. Not only does this help them widen their methods of learning, but it allows both supervisors and supervisees to concentrate on the development of supervisees. Role-playing a particular skill with an individual client in mind (e.g. challenging) can focus on skills learning while listening to audiotapes can allow supervisees to choose other ways of intervening.

Process notes

Verbal reports can provide details in a number of ways. They can offer information on the client's life, a short history, the presenting problem and interventions by the supervisee. They can offer reflections and opinions on what is happening. Or they can contain a moment-by-moment account of the counselling conversation. Process notes are a form of verbal reporting in which the supervisee writes out, word for word, what is remembered of the actual dialogue between supervisee and client. It is as full an account as possible of the conversation between the participants in the counselling relationship. This can be a very helpful exercise and has a number of advantages for supervisees. Table 7.8. presents some of these advantages as well as the disadvantages.

Table 7.8 *The strengths and weaknesses of process reports*

Strengths	Weaknesses
Gives a full overview of the remembered session	Very time-consuming
Documents the conversation as it is remembered	Depends on the ability to remember a full counselling session of conversation
Forces supervisees to build up their memory and observation skills	Can distort what actually happened
Can use the notes to look at other possible interventions	No way of verifying the supervisee's account
Can review patterns and themes over time	
Can review parallel process between the two relationships (counselling and supervision)	

Process notes tend to be used mostly, but not exclusively, within the psychodynamic tradition. Supervisors often see it as of occasional use rather than demand that supervisees produce such notes all the time. And that seems to be its main value, as an occasional way of reproducing the counselling dialogue in written form.

Audiotaping

Taping counselling sessions has been used in counselling training since 1950, when taping machines first became available. Viewed as a blessing by some (Rice, 1980) and a burden by others (Carroll, 1994c), discussion has continued on the value of taping counselling sessions and the use of such tapes in supervision. Table 7.9 shows the strengths and weaknesses of using audiotapes in supervision.

Table 7.9 The strengths and weaknesses of using audiotapes

Strengths	Weaknesses
Direct access to counselling session	Costly in time and sometimes involves financial costs
Supervisees don't have to worry about remembering details	How much does it intrude on the counselling content?
Can keep tapes and review the process over time	Can raise confidentiality issues (Is there a technician present? Who has access to the tape?)
Ensures more safety for clients	
Can compare what actually happens with what is reported by the supervisee	The wealth of material thrown up can overwhelm
Can use the tape to look at supervisee intentions	Can end up fragmenting the session (microdissection)
Can help the supervisee learn about their own interpersonal dynamics, e.g. mannerisms, ways of talking, their use of language	Can be uncomfortable for supervisees
	Can break down (mechanical failure)
Can move back and forth throughout the session for learning purposes	Can involve more time trying to get a good recording than concentrating on clients
Can monitor progress for both supervisee and client	Use of mechanics to record sessions can reduce the observational skills of supervisees
Can use in a variety of learning ways (e.g. IPR)	
Can facilitate self-supervision	
Can isolate latent messages within the relationship	
Can be used by clients	

There are a number of ways in which tapes, either video or audio, can be used in supervision. The first method is controlled by supervisees; they monitor the tape, choose what to play, and determine the length of time for which tapes will be used. The second is supervisor-controlled. Some supervisors will listen to a full taped session and give feedback to supervisees, others will listen to part of a tape, e.g. beginning or ending either within the supervision session, or outside of it. Either way, what is important is that supervisors and supervisees have negotiated and reached agreement on how tapes will be used in supervision.

To make the use of tapes effective in supervision, supervisees ought to know their machinery well. There are few more frustrating aspects of supervision than trying to listen to a badly recorded tape of a counselling session. The permission of clients to tape their counselling sessions, and use that tape for supervision purposes, needs to be explained and agreed with them. Some authors suggest a written agreement. It also needs to be agreed clearly with clients and supervisors what will happen to tapes when they are not being used any longer for supervision purposes.

Videotaping

This procedure shares many of the strengths and weaknesses of audio recording. There are some extra features that need consideration when video is used (see Table 7.10). There is no doubt that videotapes give the added dimension of visual representation. However, other than in training courses, many of which use video in their role-plays, the use of video in supervision is not widespread in Britain. This is because having video equipment on a private basis is expensive, and its effective use requires technical expertise.

Table 7.10 *Strengths and weaknesses of using videotapes in supervision*

Strengths	Weaknesses
Can see as well as hear what is happening	Can become artificial as participants play to camera
Have a visual recording of non-verbals, interventions, strategies, etc.	Can create anxiety for clients and/or supervisees
Can link language with actions	
Can reveal underlying dynamics not always accessible in the words	

Live supervision

Traditionally live supervision in Britain has been confined to a particular counselling tradition, that of family therapy. Few other trainings use it other than for skills training, either because of the expense of setting it up, or because of the difficulty of getting all parties together: clients, supervisees and supervisors.

A number of methods can be used in live supervision, such as:

one–way mirrors;
supervisor in room with the trainee;
bug–in–the–ear.

Live supervision often has more than one supervisor (a team), and often takes place watched by a group of trainees (see Table 7.11).

Table 7.11 *Strengths and weaknesses of live supervision*

Strengths	Weaknesses
Can intervene and change interventions as counselling takes place	Can be very costly to set up (one-way mirrors, bug-in-ear)
Immediate learning for supervisees	Can be very threatening for clients and/or supervisees
Benefit of a number of perspectives from supervisor/s	
Provides an objective view	Can be intrusive on the dynamics of counselling
Observers have time to formulate interventions	Possible breaches of confidentiality are substantially widened
Can use the supervision in a variety of creative ways	

Other methods of recording and presenting clients

The three methods of recording and presenting clients outlined above are not the only ones available. Supervisors and supervisees can be creative in finding their own ways that best suit the learning. Page and Wosket (1994) have talked of sculpting and drawing in supervision as a method of client presentation. Psychodrama and role-playing have also been made use of in supervision for some time. Hawkins and Shohet (1989) have used what they call the 'Brandenburg Concerto' as a method of client presentation in group supervision. Briefly, after a client is presented in supervision by one of the supervisees, the other members of the group take on roles/relationships within the life of the client. They then speak from within these roles. From this material the supervisee is able to get an overview of possible reactions from significant relationships in the client's life. The possibilities for presenting clients in supervision and learning from the method of presentation is endless, and supervisors and supervisees can spend valuable time reviewing the methods used and other possible ways of learning.

Casey, Bloom and Moan (1994) have introduced modern technology into supervision in ways which will affect the presentation of clients in the future (see Chapter 2 for a short summary of their work). While methods of presentation are linked strongly to how supervisees learn most effectively, they are also tied to how comfortable supervisors are with their use.

Many counselling orientations originated before direct access to counselling sessions was available. Knowing what happened in counselling was largely dependent on supervisees' accounts of that process. Unlike most other professions which observe their trainees in action, and indeed allow their trainees to watch the teachers at work, counselling has a tradition of keeping the therapeutic session private. Some counselling traditions are adamant that any intrusion into the counselling session is harmful to the therapeutic relationship. However, modern technology has confronted us with machinery for accessing counselling directly. How that is being used, and how it will be used in the future, is still being debated. Perhaps an emphasis on the education of the supervisee rather than on the origins of the counselling theory might help supervisors consider the learning possibilities available today.

EIGHT

Ethical dimensions of counselling supervision

> In summary, approximately 5 per cent of respondents indicated they had experienced sexual contact with their supervisors. (Bartell and Rubin, 1990, p. 444)

The above quotation is a rather pessimistic note on which to begin a chapter on the ethical aspects of supervision. We know, from recent literature on both counselling and counselling supervision, that unethical behaviour exists. Counsellors abuse clients, not just sexually, but in numerous other ways, and supervisors abuse supervisees (Feltham and Dryden, 1994; Kaberry, 1995). Why unethical behaviour takes place cannot be attributed to any one reason. It is too simple to claim that human nature is of itself inherently weak. Bernard and Goodyear (1992) make the point that much unethical behaviour is a result of omission, not so much what is done, as what is not done. Unethical behaviour could be the result of an inability to connect ethical principles with live situations, or because of the unmet needs of supervisors and/or supervisees, or because of lack of training or personal therapy. This chapter will look at the background to ethical decision-making within supervision. It will apply ethical principles to supervision and look in particular at five areas: supervisors' ethical responsibilities to clients, supervisees, the supervisory relationship, training/placement agencies, and to themselves.

TRAINING IN ETHICAL BEHAVIOUR AND ETHICAL DECISION-MAKING

Most professional training in counselling and counselling supervision requires trainees adhere to ethical codes and demand that ethical issues arising in supervision be addressed. However, few courses spend substantial time on training in the ethical/professional aspects of counselling and supervision, and fewer still on educating students in methods of ethical decision-making. The result is that students are left to discover ethical solutions by 'osmosis' (Handelsman, 1986). Gawthrop and Uhlemann (1992) discuss the drawbacks of this method of education by default: simply providing ethical information is not enough, students end up without sufficient skills to make ethical decisions. They suggest, quite rightly, that education in ethical decision-making should be a *formal* part of the counselling training curriculum, a section of the taught course in its own right and not contained within another course or left to supervision. They recommend, from their own study, the use of problem-solving approaches to teaching ethical decision-making. Their research is indicative of the value of training in ethical decision-making. One group of trainees were give a three-hour workshop on ethical decision-making, another group were given the workshop handouts but not the workshop, and the third group were given neither. All three groups were then given brief instructions and requested to respond to a case vignette containing ethical dilemmas. The treatment group scored significantly higher on decision-making quality than did either of the other groups. How can supervisors be helped to deal with ethical issues emerging from the client work of their supervisees, and furthermore how can they receive help in ethical decision-making for dealing with professional/ethical problems and dilemmas within the supervisory arrangement? How can they, in turn, work with supervisees to help them understand and make professional and ethical decisions regarding clients? Fine and Ulrich (1988) have used an integrated psychology and philosophy approach to decision-making within the ethical domain. Arguing that ethics historically belongs within the domain of philosophy, they outlined a four-stage model:

1. Ethical theories
2. Ethical principles
3. Ethical codes
4. Ethical decisions

1. Ethical theories. In Stage 1 Fine and Ulrich (1988) review ethical frameworks and theories (in particular utilitarianism and deontology). The existence of several ethical theories explains why such fierce debates often occur on the definition of 'ethical'. What ethical interpretation do we place upon an action? Do we evaluate it by its consequences, or by some inherent quality of right or wrong, or by its benefits to others? A knowledge of ethical theories, and particular the ethical theory underlying our own way of working, is helpful when it comes to making particular decisions. Sometimes when ethical dilemmas cannot be resolved it is necessary to return to ethical theories.

2. Ethical principles. In Stage 2 they review ethical principles that are derived from ethical frameworks and theories:

> beneficence (engaging in what is good for clients);
> non–malevolence (not doing harm to people);
> autonomy (the principle that people are free to act as they judge fit, provided this is not harmful to others);
> justice (being fair in the way I deal with people);
> fidelity (about keeping promises, being faithful, loyal).

Page and Wosket (1994) use these five principles as the basis for their chapter on ethical and professional issues. It must be remembered that they are 'principles' and as such open to interpretation. Two counsellors could well disagree about whether a certain action (e.g. sending a client for a psychiatric assessment) was for the good or could lead towards harm for this particular client. The principles are accepted as good, but defy clear and definitive application. A number of factors can influence an actual ethical decision, e.g. different counselling orientations can have radically opposing views of what is 'beneficient for clients'.

3. Ethical codes. Stage 3 consists of looking at ethical codes (i.e. rules to help the practitioner) and how they emerge from principles. While ethical codes involve translating ethical principles into rules, by and large these 'rules' are guidelines. A few are absolute and are intended to cover all instances, e.g. 'Supervisors should not participate in any form of sexual contact with supervisees' (ACES, *Ethical Guidelines for Counseling Supervisors*, Section 2.10). But these are unusual: most are relative, and guidelines rather than rules. When guidelines exist (BAC, *Code of Ethics and Practice for the Supervision of Counsellors*, 1988; ACES, *Ethical Guidelines for Counseling Supervisors*, 1993), rarely do they give answers to particular problem areas. This is no bad thing. Given the complexity of counselling situations, ethical guidelines need to be applied in each particular situation, with each particular client.

Few supervisors or counsellors would disagree with Section 2.1 (b) of the BAC *Code of Ethics and Practice for the Supervision of Counsellors* (1988) that, 'supervisors are responsible for helping counsellors reflect critically upon that work.' What does this mean in practice? Are supervisors obliged to set up training in 'critical reflection' for supervisees? Does it mean supervisors confront supervisees who never claim to make mistakes? Or does it mean that supervisors allow space for consideration and evaluation of supervisee client work? There is room here for stringent or lenient interpretation. Other sections of the *Code* require similar interpretations. Section 2.15 contains a statement that is very acceptable to most supervisors: 'Supervisors should, whenever possible, seek further training experience that is relevant to their supervision work.' Again, what does it mean in practice?

Should supervisors see this as a non-negotiable dictate and book in for ongoing training in supervision on a regular (a month, a year, every five years) basis? Is consultation with another supervisor sufficient to fulfil this? These are two examples (almost all the guidelines could be dealt with in the same way) indicating the relativity of ethical codes and how important it is to interpret them. Bishop and D'Rozario (1990) understand the need practitioners have for absolute standards but argue 'in most situations ethical decisions are relative . . . to operate as if there were absolutes is naive' (p. 215).

4. Ethical decision. Finally, Stage 4 involves looking at specific ethical decisions and using the knowledge of ethical theories, ethical principles, ethical codes and reflection on the issues to make decisions for action.

Keeping in mind these four stages of ethical decision-making, we can now look at the ethical responsibilities of supervisors in five areas.

SUPERVISORS' ETHICAL RESPONSIBILITIES TO AND FOR CLIENTS

There seems to be a difference between British and American views on what responsibilities supervisors need to shoulder in respect of clients seen by their supervisees. Several authors have reviewed the US situation comprehensively (Bernard, 1994a; Bernard and Goodyear, 1992; Disney and Stephens, 1994). The latters' monograph, entitled *Legal Issues in Clinical Supervision*, is an up-to-date review of both ethical and legal responsibilities of supervisors.

In the USA vicarious responsibility (*respondeat superior* is its legal terminology) maintains that one person who holds a position of authority over another can be held legally responsible for damage perpetrated by the latter. This damage could be negligence, malpractice or unprofessional behaviour. Obviously, a number of issues would need to be considered before supervisors would be held responsible (e.g. the motivation of the supervisee, the place and purpose of the behaviour, whether or not the supervisor could reasonably anticipate that a supervisee might engage in such an action). But, in principle, supervisors could be held responsible for actions of supervisees *vis-à-vis* clients.

In Britain, to date, unlike the USA, there has been no litigation in this area. At the moment supervisees are legally responsible for their own behaviour. However, supervisors have ethical responsibility for the clients of supervisees, especially where supervisees are in training. The BAC and ACES codes, as well as the AACD *Standards for Counseling Supervisors* (1989) stress that one of the main purposes of supervision is the welfare of clients. Section 1 of the ACES document is entirely devoted to 'Client Welfare and Rights'. What responsibilities do supervisors have towards the clients of their supervisees?

Managerial responsibility

In most instances supervision is non-managerial, i.e. the supervisor is not a staff member of the counselling agency in which supervisees see clients, and there are no line-management responsibilities. Where there are, then there may well be managerial responsibility. Managerial responsibility entails keeping an eye on the welfare of the agency, as well as the client, and on the career of the supervisee, as well as on the clinical work with clients. Where this pertains boundaries need to be clear. It has to be recognized that supervisees will monitor what they bring when their supervisor is in a position to affect their career, and/or their job: Chrzanowski (1984) records that some of his students confessed to falsifying what they brought to supervision because of their fear of negative appraisal.

Non-managerial responsibility

Where supervisors have no managerial responsibility, they are still ethically bound to ensure that clients are receiving a good service from supervisees. This will entail accountability in a number of domains.

a) How do supervisors monitor client work so that they are assured that clients are not being harmed? In most supervision, verbal reports from supervisees are the norm, and supervisors have to use these reports, and their relationship with their supervisees, as a way of monitoring what is happening within the counsellor/client relationship. There is still disagreement on the use of taping client sessions. Page and Wosket (1994) suggest that a good supervisory relationship will eliminate difficulties here. It is always valuable for supervisees to ask themselves how they would know if a client was being harmed in some way.

b) How can supervisors be assured that clients receive certain information?

c) How are clients and their problems evaluated, and what decisions are made in respect of counselling provision? Feltham and Dryden (1994) have complained about counsellors' temptation to put counselling theory ahead of client needs, ignoring informed consent and choice on the part of the clients. Supervisors are in good position to monitor that clients are not fitted to theory or problem, or indeed counselling approach, but that they get a suitable treatment for the issues they bring.

The theoretical orientation of supervisees and supervisors sometimes dictates ways of working with clients that make establishing common norms difficult, e.g. counsellors from some counselling orientations do not, as a matter of principle, let clients know they will be discussed within supervision, or how they work, or give certain personal information. At times this is very sensible and at other times is less than helpful. Practitioners from particular counselling orientations can get caught in a 'time-warp' and engage with clients as their predecessors did, say 50 years ago. Modern requirements, and indeed contemporary legal requirements (consumer rights, data protection, citizen charters) and the use of modern technology, have been slow to find their way into counselling work. Today they need to be considered.

In brief, supervisors are ethically responsible to the clients of their supervisees for the service received. It is their task to monitor that service, to know what it is, and to intervene when the welfare of clients is not being maintained.

SUPERVISORS' ETHICAL RESPONSIBILITIES TO AND FOR SUPERVISEES

What are the responsibilities of supervisors vis-à-vis the ethical and professional dimensions of supervisees' work with clients? There seems little doubt that there is a 'gatekeeping' function of supervisors ensuring that clients receive the most effective counselling provision, and that supervisees are working within guidelines and boundaries that create a safe therapeutic environment for clients. Within this role there is some debate (see Chapter 4) on whether or not supervisors ought to teach ethical principles or whether they simply ascertain that the supervisee is aware of ethical codes and is working within them.

Supervisors see their role as monitoring ethical/professional dimensions of counselling practice. However, they are adamant that they do not see their job as teaching ethics and ethical practice to supervisees (Carroll, 1994c). They deal with professional/ethical issues as they arise from client work rather than being proactive with such issues. Several areas of interest emerge from research into supervisors' perceptions of their own role as monitors of the ethical dimension of the work of their supervisees. Almost all supervisors surveyed (Carroll, 1994c) agree that their task is to monitor ethical/professional aspects of the supervisees' work. But how that takes place is debated. Some challenge when practice is seen as unethical, others alert the supervisee to ethical issues and help them take responsibility for them, others encourage the supervisee to talk about all aspects of their work with clients. The majority wait until such issues arise within supervision. They consider it the task of the training course to provide ethical education and acquaintance with ethical codes. Some insist on ensuring that trainees understand and work with a certain ethical framework, to the extent occasionally of providing them with counselling codes of ethics.

A further area of concern to professional practice is the ongoing need for training within the context of ethical issues. It is not enough to include training in ethical issues within counselling courses. There is a demand to keep up-to-date with what is happening. Changes within the profession and within society are asking new ethical questions from counsellors. The Data Protection Act is one such new dimension, involving new legislation and new ethical issues. New legislation makes further and novel ethical demands on counsellors. Jenkins (1992, p. 165) has looked at 'the apparent lack of interest in developing a knowledge base or practice competency in relating to legal matters affecting counselling' and made a strong and substantiated plea for the ability 'to deal competently with situations . . . which pose real ethical dilemmas with a legal dimension'. It is not sufficient to know the content of ethical codes. What is needed is a method of making ethical decisions in counselling contexts.

Supervisors need to be sure that supervisees:

a) Know ethical codes (Feltham and Dryden, 1994, recommend discussing the BAC code of ethics with supervisees).
b) Have a method of making ethical decisions.
c) Belong to relevant professional bodies, and subscribe to appropriate codes of ethics and practice for counsellors.
d) Are not overworking, have reasonable case-loads and are looking after themselves. Inskipp and Proctor (1993, p. 34) state this very well:

> It is your ethical responsibility to your clients, and your human right for yourself, to nurture and maintain your physical, emotional, intellectual and spiritual well-being.
> Counselling can be demanding and can be stressful in different ways at different stages of your development.
> Supervision is one major resource: it cannot fulfil all your needs for support and development.
> You may surprise yourself by realizing how many opportunities you already use for replenishment – and how many more there are to use.

e) Have adequate insurance (Mearns, 1993).
f) Are able to reflect critically on their interventions with clients.
g) Are free to bring their 'bad' work to supervision.
h) Are aware of ways in which they can abuse clients (Feltham and Dryden, 1994).
i) Are aware of the stresses of their life and work at different stages of their development as counsellors.

Even though supervisors have ethical responsibilities *for* supervisees they also have ethical responsibilities *to* them. The ethical principles mentioned on p. 150 apply here.

Beneficence. Supervisors do what is good (beneficial) for supervisees.

Non-malevolence. They do not do harm to supervisees.
Autonomy. They help supervisees move towards autonomy.
Justice. They are fair in how they work with supervisees.
Fidelity. They keep promises and are loyal to contracts.

These, of course, are open to some interpretation and what one supervisor might consider beneficial to supervisees could be considered by another as malevolent. However, keeping the principles at the forefront of their work enables supervisors to monitor their ethical responsibilities to supervisees.

It is worth mentioning, again, the issue of abuse in supervision. Awareness of abuse, how it occurs, its effects on supervisees, and why it occurs can be of help in avoiding it. Kaberry (1995) has completed one of the few research projects (and the only one I know of in Britain) specifically dealing with this theme. The conclusions of her work are very apt here. She interviewed fourteen individuals (thirteen women and one man) who felt they had had the experience of being abused by a supervisor (there were seven male and seven female supervisors). Two main areas of abuse emerged: the sexualization of the supervisory relationship or some form of persecution within supervision (derogation, intrusion, invasion, scapegoating). The following were among the features that emerged from the interviews:

- nine out of the fourteen supervisees were allocated supervisors;
- five experienced abuse within group supervision;
- breaching of boundaries between roles (counselling, supervising, socializing, teaching) was not uncommon;
- supervisors used supervisory material for their own gratification;
- rigid and authoritarian stances were taken by supervisors;
- there was a tendency to 'pathologize' the supervisee;
- feedback was always negative, never positive;
- the supervisory contract was unclear and never clarified.

Kaberry suggests that abuse can be avoided within supervision if:

- supervisors have the ability to deal with transference, countertransference and parallel process in supervision;
- supervisors know about and can deal with their own 'unresolved' issues;
- supervisors manage their own anxiety;
- supervisors know how to manage group process so that scapegoating does not take place;
- supervisors are trained;
- supervisees are allowed to choose their supervisor, or at least can trust them when the supervisory relationship is not working out or is conflictual;

- supervisees are prepared so that they know what to expect from supervision and can be assertive about poor supervision;
- it is accepted that abuse does occur, the forms of abuse are known and their effects on supervisees recognized.

In brief, supervisors today need to be aware of their ethical responsibilities for supervisees and also their responsibilities to them. As counsellors are accountable for their work with clients so supervisors are accountable for their work with supervisees.

SUPERVISORS' ETHICAL RESPONSIBILITIES FOR THE SUPERVISORY RELATIONSHIP

The relationship between supervisors and supervisees as a professional and ethically sound relationship also raises issues. A number of ethical codes have formally addressed these areas (BAC, 1988; ACES, 1993) and several key articles dwell on specific ethical areas within this domain (Bernard, 1994b; Bernard and Goodyear, 1992).

Supervisors are responsible for:

a) Contracting for a supervisory relationship where roles/responsibilities are clear.
b) Dealing with difficulties in the supervisory relationship.
c) Evaluating supervisees, supervision and self. Issues of 'due process' may enter the field here. Bernard and Goodyear (1992, p. 134) describe 'due process' by showing how it can be violated:

> The most blatant violation of a trainee's due process rights occurs when the trainee is given a negative final evaluation or dismissed from a training program or job without having had prior warning that performance was inadequate and without a reasonable amount of time to improve.

d) Not engaging in ongoing counselling with supervisees. The ACES ethical code sees this as 'dual relationships', and the BAC code suggests that if supervision and counselling are mixed then clear boundaries be defined and that counselling does not take place to the determinant of supervision.
e) Working in an 'equal opportunities' manner where the supervisory relationship does not suffer because of gender, race, disability, sexual orientation.
f) Clarifying the meaning of confidentiality with supervisees, and when it will be broken, with or without the consent of the supervisee.
g) Raising issues of informed consent. Informed consent is a procedure whereby patients have a right to know what is happening to them that could be potentially harmful. Disney and Stephens (1994) state four elements that are necessary for informed consent:

competency: that a person is able to make sensible and rational decisions about what affects them;
understanding: that a person understands what is being said;
disclosure of material information (there is no agreement on how much information should be given);
voluntary consent means that agreement was given freely and without coercion.

It makes eminent sense to apply informed consent to supervisees within the context of the supervisory relationship. It is too easily taken for granted that supervisees know what is involved in supervision, and that they agree to it. Many do not (Carroll, 1994c), and care needs to be taken that there is a basis of understanding. After a substantial time talking about supervision and about the need to 'bring clients to supervision', I was surprised when one new trainee, who kept shaking her head, eventually blurted out, 'I don't know how I can get all my clients together to bring across here from North London.' 'Bringing clients to supervision' can naturally be understood in different ways.

SUPERVISORS' ETHICAL RESPONSIBILITIES TOWARDS TRAINING COURSES/PLACEMENT AGENCIES

Many training courses in counselling are demanding that supervisors be part of the ongoing and sometimes final assessment of their trainees, and supervisor reports are taken seriously in that assessment. This brings an added dynamic into supervision with a further system that needs to be seen in relationship to the participants. A number of situations can further complicate the issues:

1. Where the supervisor is employed by the agency in which trainees see clients.
2. Where the supervisor is employed by the training course, and where the supervisee sees clients in an agency which has little formal contact with the training course.
3. Where the supervisor is employed by the supervisee alone on a one-to-one basis and where the supervisor has no formal connections with the training course or the placement agency.

What is vital in these circumstances is that contracts are clear and the parties – supervisor, supervisee, training course, placement agency – know their role/s and responsibilities. Before a supervisory contract is set up the supervisor ought to know what is required from the other three participants in this arrangement, and have agreed to it. I know of some instances in which supervisors billed training courses for time spent on supervisory report writing, while billing supervisees for their actual supervision. Such an arrangement had not been agreed in advance and gave rise to a lot of unnecessary resentment on all parts, with the unfortunate supervisee caught somewhere in the middle.

Page and Wosket (1994) make the point that training courses ought to monitor the choice of supervisors to ensure competency. This is certainly an ideal, and where possible ought to pertain. Often it is not possible because of the few requirements within this area for supervisors (the only forum which has any kind of supervisor accreditation is the BAC recognition scheme, which to date has something like forty-seven accredited supervisors). It is too easy to create collusive relationships where we think certain supervisors are 'good' without any criteria for suggesting they might or might not be.

What are the responsibilities of supervisors in respect of the training course and the placement agency? The following are a few:

a) *Honesty in reports.* It seems to me, and this is an impression rather than an evidenced fact, that supervisors are extremely reluctant to give reports on supervisees that indicate they have reservations about their work. It seems that supervisory reports have reached the status of references, which may require to be read between the lines. In any case, let the buyer beware. Supervisors have an ethical requirement to be honest in supervisory reports and to state clearly what they want to say.

b) *Clear relationships and boundaries with all four parties in the supervisory arrangement:* supervisor, supervisee, training course, placement agency. Clear procedures for reporting back, contacting the course where there are problems, what to do in emergencies, etc. need to be considered beforehand and clarified.

c) *Having supervision reports as part of the assessment procedure.* The role of supervisors in assessment, and in particular the role of reports, needs to be clarified. Also needing clarification is the response of the course managers should problems arise with the client work of the trainee. The course managers need to consult the supervisor if for any reason there are doubts about the trainee's progression.

SUPERVISORS' ETHICAL RESPONSIBILITIES FOR THEMSELVES

Supervisors need to be concerned about themselves, their own welfare, and development as supervisors. There is some evidence that 'modelling' plays a large part in supervision and that supervisors become models of good (or bad) practice for supervisees (Holloway, 1995). Modelling concern for one's own health and safety, and ongoing involvement in professional development, can be a stronger lesson to supervisees than many words.

Carroll (1995a) has outlined three areas of potential stress for supervisors: stresses within supervisors themselves, those that emerge from the supervisory relationship and those that are extraneous to the participants. Supervisors need to look after themselves and manage creatively the stresses that come as part of the job.

The various codes of ethics for supervisors emphasize the need for supervisors to be alert to their own competency and involved in their ongoing training. This training is fast becoming a requirement for supervisors, rather than an optional extra. The days of inheriting the supervisory mantle, and requiring no initial and ongoing training in supervision, are disappearing.

Isolation can become a danger area for supervisors and they need to protect themselves from becoming too alone in their work. Creating a forum for their own consultation is one way of dealing with isolation, as is ongoing training, peer group supervision, and going to conferences.

Standards for Counseling Supervisors (ACES, 1989) sees one of the personal traits and characteristics of a counselling supervisor as having a sense of humour (Section 2.5). And indeed this seems to be an essential ingredient not just for the sanity of the supervisor but also for the learning of supervisees. Not taking ourselves too seriously, realizing as humans we make mistakes, being able to accept our own limitations, can allow us to laugh more readily at the foibles of human nature that find their way into supervision. Humour is not about trivializing clients or their problems, nor about not taking them and supervisees seriously. Quite the reverse. It is the realization that as we struggle with the pain and anguish of life and life's problems we know there are moments for lightening the loads, for letting go and laughing.

Ethical decision-making for supervisors

How can supervisors make ethical decisions within their own areas of responsibilities, and help supervisees, not to depend on them for judgement, but to be able to make their own decisions in conjunction with the supervisor? Below is a four-stage model of ethical decision-making for supervisors.

A first step in the ethical decision process is a realization that there are no 'simple' interpersonal solutions to problems; there only appear to be. Agony aunts are notorious for offering simple solutions, the problem being taken out of their personal and situational contexts. What do you do if someone is depressed? Answer: Tell them to be happy. Problem: If they were happy they would not be depressed. Same question. Ethical dilemmas are highly complex situations that demand a lot of thought, a lot of feeling, and a lot of courage to make and stay with decisions (Dryden, 1986).

Facing ethical issues is a daily event for most supervisors and counsellors. Questions such as: Should I reach out and touch this client? Ought I to continue working with this supervisee when I do not think he/she ought to see clients just now? Am I competent to deal with this issue as a counsellor/ supervisor? Having to reach a decision is the key to moving forward ethically. How that decision is reached, within counselling, within supervision in respect of counselling work, or within supervision in respect of supervision itself, cannot be haphazard or simply intuitive, right though the final action may be. Providing frameworks to guide decision-making is fundamental for building confidence but most particularly for helping individual supervisors and supervisees live with the consequences of decisions that sometimes only time will see as the most helpful.

Using the work of Austin, Moline and Williams (1990), Beauchamp and Walters (1989), Corey, Corey and Callahan (1993), Eberlein (1987), and Kitchener (1984, 1986), Carroll (1994b) has outlined a four-stage model of ethical decision-making, which applies to supervision, as well as counselling:

1. Creating ethical sensitivity
2. Formulating a moral course of action
3. Implementing an ethical decision
4. Living with the ambiguities of an ethical decision

Stage 1: Creating ethical sensitivity

Ethical sensitivity involves becoming aware of the implications of behaviour for others and insight into the possibility of ethical demands within interpersonal situations. Very early in counselling development, trainees are often unaware of ethical implications. I remember one counsellor, when a client did not appear for a session, going to visit her in her home. Another counsellor was telephoned by a client's wife and listened to what she had to say about an affair her husband had had some time earlier; a third passed on information from a manager to the client. None of these three counsellors, who were at the start of their training, were aware of the ethical dilemmas involved. Developing as a counsellor involves become more acute to the complexity of interpersonal issues involved in counselling, and the above examples are not unusual as trainees struggle to learn about the boundary issues in counselling. As learning progresses, understanding when ethical issues/dilemmas are present becomes more focused. However, as Kitchener (1991, p. 237) points out, 'many counsellors do not have a mind-set when they leave graduate school that includes looking for ethical problems'. Pryor (1989, p. 303) uses the term 'ethical watchfulness' to portray the sensitivity needed by the counsellor. He sees this watchfulness based on five components:

a) Familiarity with ethical codes
b) Ability to anticipate and foresee possible ethical problem-areas
c) Ethical evaluation of new techniques before they are adopted

d) Outlining conflicting responsibilities
e) Creating thoughtful delays to consider all aspects when ethical issues emerge

How to create this mind-set, this 'ethical watchfulness'? How sensitize to underlying ethical issues? A number of suggestions have been made:

Legitimize ethical questions as a part of case reviews (Kitchener, 1991)
Ask students to identify ethical issues arising from their client work (Kitchener, 1991)
Use reading and discussion of ethical codes (Gawthrop and Uhlemann, 1992)
Case vignettes (Gawthrop and Uhlemann, 1992)
Self-generation of ethical dilemmas from experience (Gawthrop and Uhlemann, 1992)
Explore how values underlie ethical codes (Gawthrop and Uhlemann, 1992)
Offer training in values clarification and promote understanding of the counsellor's own value system and how it influences work with clients. Tennyson and Strom (1986, p. 300) put this well: 'The responsible counselor must engage in reflective activity. This is an individual matter involving self-confrontation. Self-confrontation entails systematic questioning to discover possible contradictions, distortions, discrepancies, and hidden meanings in beliefs and values underlying practice.'
Review issues of power within counselling and how the social influence involved works with clients (Karasu, 1981)

All of these areas can be part of supervision.

Stage 2: Formulating a moral course of action

Stage 2 involves making a decision on what is the moral course of action to take in this particular situation. Kitchener (1991, p. 240) considers this stage as an interplay between 'the facts of the situation, ethical rules that govern our professional behaviour, and ethical principles from which our professional codes are derived'.

In line with the ethical principles above (autonomy, beneficence, non-maleficence, justice and fidelity) a number of areas may be tapped to help decide what course of action is most appropriate. These include common-sense. (Hayman and Covert, 1986, p. 319) indicate that counsellors in their study of College Counselling Centres 'most often resolved ethical dilemmas by relying on common sense'. Other sources used in decision-making include clinical and administrative supervisors, peers, codes of ethics and practice, literature. Of considerable importance in this context is the self-awareness of the counsellor and an understanding of his/her motivation in intervening. Formulating a course of action will be somewhat dependent on the motivation of the counsellor. For example, there is some evidence that counsellors will not allow clients to deal with issues that they themselves (the counsellors) have dealt with.

Stage 3: Implementing an ethical decision

Even when counsellors are sensitive to the moral implications of the situation, and even when they make ethical decisions, they do not always follow them through with action. In an article entitled 'The failure of clinical psychology graduate students to apply understood ethical principles', Bernard and Jara (1986) point out that 'at least half the students stated that they would not live up to their own interpretation of what the ethical principles required of them as professionals. Most simply put, this amounts to saying, "I know what I should do as an ethical psychologist, but I wouldn't do it" ' (p. 315). The problem here, as pointed out by Bernard and Jara, is how to motivate counsellors to implement ethical principles they already understand.

There may be a number of reasons why ethical decisions are not implemented: the politics of the situation, the rationalizations of the counsellor, protection of a colleague, or self-interest on the part of the counsellor. Rest (1984) sees 'ego strength' as a necessary component to implement the decision made. This can be built up through supportive colleagues, supervision, peer group work and support outside the work situation.

Stage 4: Living with the ambiguities of an ethical decision

Even when decisions are made and implemented there is always the 'left-over ambiguity' of wondering if one has done the right thing. Having made a decision to implement the process of hospitalizing a suicidal client against her will, the supervisor and the counsellor will not rest easily at night. Did they act too impulsively? Would it have been better to wait and not risk endangering the working alliance? The opposite decision, not to hospitalize, results in a equally sleepless night: will the client be alive tomorrow? Have adequate precautions been taken to protect the client? Perhaps more time should be spent in supervision on this client? Ethical dilemmas do not result in decisions that sit easily within the counsellor's life. Karasu (1981) ends his chapter with a quotation from Bernal and Del Rio V (1967, p. 2546): 'By definition, ethical problems remain unresolved. By their unresolved quality, they provoke a continuous anxiety in the practising psychiatrist, and concomitantly a desire to search, to oppose, to think and to research.'

The chart belows gives a summarized model of ethical decision-making in supervision, with suggestions for methods within each section.

A four-stage model for ethical decision-making in supervision

STAGE 1: *CREATING ETHICAL SENSITIVITY (WATCHFULNESS)*

Case reviews
Identifying ethical issues arising from counselling work
Reading ethical codes and related literature
Case vignettes (what would you do?)
Exploring value-issues arising from counselling work
Clarifying and confronting one's own values
Creating awareness around the 'power' issues involved in counselling
Reviewing critical incidents within counselling
Evaluating ethical frameworks and theories
Ascertaining levels of moral development and how this affects ethical decision-making

STAGE 2: *FORMULATING A MORAL COURSE OF ACTION*

1. **Identify the ethical problem, or dilemma**

   What are the parameters of the situation?
   What is the source of conflict for the client, or for the counsellor?
   Is the conflict with another person, group of people, or family member, or with the organization?
   Is the conflict between the client and the counsellor?
   Does the conflict involve legal, moral, ethical, religious, cultural, gender or value issues?
   What are the counsellor's feelings about what is happening?
   How may the problem be clearly defined, especially where terms are emotionally charged?

2. **Identify the potential issues involved**

   What is the worst possible outcome?
   What could happen if nothing is done?
   What are the implications involved in this problem or dilemma?
   What are the rights, responsibilities and welfare of all affected parties?

3. **Review the relevant ethical guidelines**

   Do guidelines, principles, or laws exist that are relevant to the dilemmas and may provide a possible solution?

Are the counsellor's values, ethics, or morals in conflict with the relevant principles or guidelines?
Is the counsellor aware of the effect of values and does he or she have a rationale for the behaviour?
Are there relevant codes, sections, chapters of books, etc. pertinent to this issue?
What further information is needed to help resolve the issues?

4. **Obtain consultation**

Bring the situation to supervision
Talk with colleagues, where appropriate
Consult line-managers, if appropriate
Talk to a lawyer (or an expert from another profession), again if appropriate

5. **Consider possible and probable courses of action**

What are the alternatives? (Brainstorming without evaluating is helpful.)

6. **Enumerate the consequences of various decisions**

What are the implications for the client?
What are the implications for others?
What are the implications for the counsellor?

7. **Decide on what appears to be the best course of action**

Could I recommend this action to other counsellors in similar circumstances?
Would I condone this behaviour in another counsellor?
Can I defend this behaviour if it were made public?
Would I treat other clients in the same situation differently?

STAGE 3: *IMPLEMENTING AN ETHICAL DECISION*

What steps need to be taken to implement the decision?
What people are involved and who needs to be told what?
What restraints are there not to implement the ethical decision (e.g. politics of the situation, protection of a client, rationalization, etc.)?
What support is needed (by the counsellor, by the client, by others) to implement and to live with the results?

STAGE 4: *LIVING WITH THE AMBIGUITIES OF AN ETHICAL DECISION*

Dealing with anxiety attending the final decision
Letting go of the situation and the dilemma
Accepting the limitations involved
Formulating learnings from the experience
Using personal and professional support to live with the consequences of the decision

Conclusion

Every human encounter raises professional issues that require ethical decisions. It is not always possible to have the luxury of time, and consultation, and discussion as ways of helping make effective ethical decisions. Being prepared, and having worked through some of the principles underlying ethical issues, can be a headstart when decisions are imminent.

Epilogue

This book has taken a 'broad-brush' approach to counselling supervision, opting to cover many supervision areas within a short space. In being brief, injustice can be done too easily to supervision topics that deserve more elaborate consideration. Summarizing cross-cultural supervision, group supervision, engaging in the supervision process, to mention just a few, gives a taste of what they are about but inevitably misses out large essential areas. My hope is that this book, and these topics, may give rise to more detailed publications. We are ready in Britain for further work on group supervision, on multicultural supervision, on the various stages of supervision, as well as detailed understanding of peer supervision and work on both the ethical and the organizational dimensions of supervision work. We have just begun to apply supervision to different contexts, e.g. counselling in the workplace. With our rich tradition of practice, and theory emerging from practice, I consider British supervision to be poised for an increase in knowledge, and hopefully publications, on all these topics. If this book brings that future closer to realization then it will have met a need. My hope is that we can share ideas, be generous with practice and theories, forget some of our unhelpful differences and work together towards a technology of supervision that combines its artistry and its scientific base.

BAC Code of Ethics and Practice for Supervisors of Counsellors*

1. Status of the Code

1.1   In response to the experience of members of BAC, this Code is a revision of the 1988 Code of Ethics & Practice for the Supervision of Counsellors.

2. Introduction

2.1   The purpose of the Code is to establish and maintain standards for supervisors who are members of BAC and to inform and protect counsellors seeking supervision. Throughout this Code the terms Counsellor and Counselling are used in accordance with the definition of counselling in the Code of Ethics & Practice for Counsellors.

2.2   All members of this Association are required to abide by existing Codes appropriate to them. They thereby accept a common frame of reference within which to manage their responsibilities to supervisees and their clients, colleagues, members of the Association and the wider community. Whilst this Code cannot resolve all ethical and practice related issues, it aims to provide a framework for addressing ethical issues and to encourage optimum levels of practice. Supervisors and supervisees (counsellors) will need to judge which parts of this Code apply to particular situations. They may have to decide between conflicting responsibilities.

2.3   Counselling Supervision is a formal and mutually agreed arrangement for counsellors to discuss their work regularly with someone who is normally an experienced and competent counsellor and familiar with the process of counselling supervision. The task is to work together to ensure and develop the efficacy of the supervisee's counselling practice.

Counselling Supervision is the term that will be used throughout this Code. It is also known as supervision, consultative support, clinical supervision or non-managerial supervision. It is an essential part of good practice for counselling. It is different from training, personal development and line management accountability.

2.4 This Association has a Complaints Procedure which can lead to the expulsion of members for breaches of its Codes of Ethics & Practice.

3. Nature of Counselling Supervision

3.1 Counselling supervision provides supervisees with the opportunity on a regular basis to discuss and monitor their work with clients. It should take account of the setting in which supervisees practise. Counselling supervision is intended to ensure that the needs of the clients are being addressed and to monitor the effectiveness of the therapeutic interventions.

3.2 Counselling supervision may contain some elements of training, personal development or line-management, but counselling supervision is not primarily intended for these purposes and appropriate management of these issues should be observed.

3.3 Counselling supervision is a formal collaborative process intended to help supervisees maintain ethical and professional standards of practice and to enhance creativity.

3.4 It is essential that counsellor and supervisor are able to work together constructively as counselling supervision includes supportive and challenging elements.

3.5 There are several modes of counselling supervision (see 5), which vary in appropriateness according to the needs of supervisees. More than one mode of counselling supervision may be used concurrently. This Code applies to all counselling supervision arrangements.

3.6 The frequency of counselling supervision will vary according to the volume of counselling, the experience of supervisees and their work setting.

4. Anti-discriminatory Practice in Counselling Supervision

4.1 Anti-discriminatory practice underpins the basic values of counselling and counselling supervision as stated in this document and in the Code of Ethics & Practice for Counsellors. It also addresses the issue of the client's social context, B.2.7.3 of that Code (1993).

4.2 Supervisors have a responsibility to be aware of their own issues of prejudice and stereotyping, and particularly to consider ways in which this may be affecting the supervisory relationship. Discussion of this is part of the counselling supervision process.

4.3 Supervisors need to be alert to any prejudices and assumptions that counsellors reveal in their work with clients and to raise awareness of these so that the needs of clients may be met with more sensitivity. One purpose of counselling supervision is to enable supervisees to recognise and value difference. Supervisors have a responsibility to challenge the appropriateness of the work of a supervisee whose own belief system interferes with the acceptance of clients.

4.4 Attitudes, assumptions and prejudices can be identified by the language used, and by paying attention to the selectivity of material brought to counselling supervision.

5. Modes of Counselling Supervision

There are different modes of counselling supervision. The particular features of some of these modes are outlined below. Some counsellors use combinations of these for their counselling supervision.

5.1 **One to One, Supervisor-Supervisee**

This involves a supervisor providing counselling supervision on an individual basis for an individual counsellor who is usually less experienced than the supervisor. This is the most widely used mode of counselling supervision.

5.2 **Group Counselling Supervision with Identified Counselling Supervisor(s)**

There are several ways of providing this form of counselling supervision. In one approach the supervisor acts as the leader, takes responsibility for organising the time equally between the supervisees, and concentrates on the work of each individual in turn. Using another approach the supervisees allocate counselling supervision time between themselves with the supervisor as a technical resource.

5.3 **One to One Peer Counselling Supervision**

This involves two participants providing counselling supervision for each other by alternating the roles of supervisor and supervisee.

Typically, the time available for counselling supervision is divided equally between them. This mode on its own is not suitable for all practitioners.

5.4 **Peer Group Counselling Supervision**

This takes place when three or more counsellors share the responsibility for providing each other's counselling supervision within the group. Typically, they will consider themselves to be of broadly equal status, training and/or experience. This mode on its own is unsuitable for inexperienced practitioners.

5.5 Particular issues of competence for each mode are detailed in the Code of Practice B.2.6.

6. The Structure of this Code

6.1 This Code has two sections. Section A, the Code of Ethics, outlines the fundamental values of counselling supervision and a number of general principles arising from these. Section B, the Code of Practice, applies these principles to counselling supervision.

A   CODE OF ETHICS

A.1 Counselling supervision is a non-exploitative activity. Its basic values are integrity, responsibility, impartiality and respect. Supervisors must take the same degree of care to work ethically whether they are paid or work voluntarily and irrespective of the mode of counselling supervision used.

A.2 Confidentiality

The content of counselling supervision is highly confidential. Supervisors must clarify their limits of confidentiality.

A.3 Safety

All reasonable steps must be taken to ensure the safety of supervisees and their clients during their work together.

A.4 Effectiveness

All reasonable steps must be taken by supervisors to encourage optimum levels of practice by supervisees.

A.5 Contracts

The terms and conditions on which counselling supervision is offered must be made clear to supervisees at the outset. Subsequent revisions of these terms must be agreed in advance of any change.

A.6 Competence

Supervisors must take all reasonable steps to monitor and develop their own competence and to work within the limits of that competence. This includes having supervision of their supervision work.

B   CODE OF PRACTICE

B.1 Issues of Responsibility

B.1.1   Supervisors are responsible for ensuring that an individual contract is worked out with their supervisees which will allow them to present and explore their work as honestly as possible.

B.1.2   Within this contract supervisors are responsible for helping supervisees to reflect critically upon their work, while at the same time acknowledging that clinical responsibility remains with the counsellor.

B.1.3   Supervisors are responsible, together with their supervisees, for ensuring that the best use is made of counselling supervision time, in order to address the needs of clients.

B.1.4   Supervisors are responsible for setting and maintaining the boundaries between the counselling supervision relationship and other professional relationships, e.g. training and management.

B.1.5   Supervisors and supervisees should take all reasonable steps to ensure that any personal or social contact between them does not adversely influence the effectiveness of the counselling supervision.

B.1.6   A supervisor must not have a counselling supervision and a personal counselling contract with the same supervisee over the same period of time.

B.1.7   Supervisors must not exploit their supervisees financially, sexually, emotionally or in any other way. It is unethical for supervisors to engage in sexual activity with their supervisee.

B.1.8   Supervisors have a responsibility to enquire about any other relationships which may exist between supervisees and their clients as these may impair the objectivity and professional judgement of supervisees.

B.1.9   Supervisors must recognise, and work in ways that respect, the value and dignity of supervisees and their clients with due regard to issues such as origin, status, race, gender, age, beliefs, sexual orientation and disability. This must include raising awareness of any discriminatory practices that may exist between supervisees and their clients, or between supervisor and supervisee.

B.1.10 Supervisors must ensure that together with their supervisees they consider their respective legal liabilities to each other, to the employing or training organisation, if any, and to clients.

B.1.11 Supervisors are responsible for taking action if they are aware that their supervisees' practice is not in accordance with BAC's Codes of Ethics & Practice for Counsellors.

B.1.12 Supervisors are responsible for helping their supervisees recognise when their functioning as counsellors is impaired due to personal or emotional difficulties, any condition that affects judgement, illness, the influence of alcohol or drugs, or for any other reason, and for ensuring that appropriate action is taken.

B.1.13 Supervisors must conduct themselves in their supervision-related activities in ways which do not undermine public confidence in either their role as a supervisor or in the work of other supervisors.

B.1.14 If a supervisor is aware of possible misconduct by another supervisor which cannot be resolved or remedied after discussion with the supervisor concerned, they should implement the Complaints Procedure, doing so within the boundaries of confidentiality required by the Complaints Procedure.

B.1.15 Supervisors are responsible for ensuring that their emotional needs are met outside the counselling supervision work and are not solely dependent on their relationship with supervisees.

B.1.16 Supervisors are responsible for consulting with their own supervisor before former clients are taken on as supervisees or former supervisees are taken on as clients.

B.2 Issues of Competence

B.2.1 Under all of the modes of counselling supervision listed above, supervisors should normally be practising and experienced counsellors.

B.2.2 Supervisors are responsible for seeking ways to further their own professional development.

B.2.3 Supervisors are responsible for making arrangements for their own supervision in order to support their counselling supervision work and to help them to evaluate their competence.

B.2.4 Supervisors are responsible for monitoring and working within the limits of their competence.

B.2.5 Supervisors are responsible for withdrawing from counselling supervision work either temporarily or permanently when their functioning is impaired due to personal or emotional difficulties, illness, the influence of alcohol or drugs, or for any other reason.

B.2.6 Some modes require extra consideration and these are detailed in this section.

	A	B	C	D	E	F	G	H
One to one supervisor-supervisee	X							
Group counselling supervision with identified and more experienced supervisor	X	X		X	X			
One to one peer counselling supervision	X	X	X	X			X	X
Peer group counselling supervision	X	X	X	X		X	X	X

A. All points contained elsewhere within the Code of Practice should be considered.

B. Sufficient time must be allocated to each counsellor to ensure adequate supervision of their counselling work.

C. This method on its own is particularly unsuitable for trainees, recently trained or inexperienced counsellors.

D. Care needs to be taken to develop an atmosphere conducive to sharing, questioning and challenging each others' practice in a constructive and supportive way.

E. As well as having a background in counselling work, supervisors should have appropriate groupwork experience in order to facilitate this kind of group.

F. All participants should have sufficient groupwork experience to be able to engage the group process in ways which facilitate effective counselling supervision.

G. Explicit consideration should be given to deciding who is responsible for providing the counselling supervision, and how the task of counselling supervision will be carried out.

H. It is good practice to have an independent consultant to visit regularly to observe and monitor the process and quality of the counselling supervision.

B.3 Management of Work

B.3.1 THE COUNSELLING SUPERVISION CONTRACT

3.1.1 Where supervisors and supervisees work for the same agency or organisation the supervisor is responsible for clarifying all contractual obligations.

3.1.2   Supervisors must inform their supervisee, as appropriate, about their own training, philosophy and theoretical position, qualifications, approach to anti-discriminatory practice and the methods of counselling supervision they use.

3.1.3   Supervisors must be explicit regarding practical arrangements for counselling supervision, paying particular regard to the length of contact time, the frequency of contact, policy and practice regarding record keeping, and the privacy of the venue.

3.1.4   Fees and fee increases must be arranged and agreed in advance.

3.1.5   Supervisors and supervisees must make explicit the expectations and requirements they have of each other. This should include the manner in which any formal assessment of the supervisee's work will be conducted. Each party should assess the value of working with the other, and review this regularly.

3.1.6   Supervisors must discuss their policy regarding giving references and any fees that may be charged for this or for any other work done outside counselling supervision time.

3.1.7   Before formalising a counselling supervision contract supervisors must ascertain what personal counselling the supervisee has or has had. This is in order to take into account any effect this may have on the supervisee's counselling work.

3.1.8   Supervisors working with trainee counsellors must clarify the boundaries of their responsibility and their accountability to their supervisee and to the training course and any agency/placement involved. This should include any formal assessment required.

B.3.2 CONFIDENTIALITY

3.2.1   As a general principle, supervisors must not reveal confidential material concerning the supervisee or their clients to any other person without the express consent of all parties concerned. Exceptions to this general principle are contained within this Code.

3.2.2   When initial contracts are being made, agreements about the people to whom supervisors may speak about their supervisees' work must include those on whom the supervisors rely for support, supervision or consultancy. There must also be clarity at this stage about the boundaries of confidentiality having regard for the supervisor's own framework of accountability. This is particularly relevant when providing counselling supervision to a trainee counsellor.

3.2.3   Supervisors should take all reasonable steps to encourage supervisees to present their work in ways which protect the personal identity of clients, or to get their client's informed consent to present information which could lead to personal identification.

3.2.4 Supervisors must not reveal confidential information concerning supervisees or their clients to any person or through any public medium except:

a. When it is clearly stated in the counselling supervision contract and it is in accordance with all BAC Codes of Ethics & Practice.

b. When the supervisor considers it necessary to prevent serious emotional or physical damage to the client, the supervisee or a third party. In such circumstances the supervisee's consent to a change in the agreement about confidentiality should be sought, unless there are good grounds for believing that the supervisee is no longer able to take responsibility for his/her own actions. Whenever possible, the decision to break confidentiality in any circumstances should be made after consultation with another experienced supervisor.

3.2.5 The disclosure of confidential information relating to supervisees is permissible when relevant to the following situations:

a. Recommendations concerning supervisees for professional purposes, e.g. references and assessments.

b. Pursuit of disciplinary action involving supervisees in matters pertaining to standards of ethics and practice.

In the latter instance, any breaking of confidentiality should be minimised by conveying only information pertinent to the immediate situation on a need-to-know basis. The ethical considerations needing to be taken into account are:

i. Maintaining the best interests of the supervisee

ii. Enabling the supervisee to take responsibility for their actions

iii. Taking full account of the supervisor's responsibility to the client and to the wider community.

3.2.6 Information about work with a supervisee may be used for publication or in meetings only with the supervisee's permission and with anonymity preserved.

3.2.7 On occasions when it is necessary to consult with professional colleagues, supervisors ensure that their discussion is purposeful and not trivialising.

B.3.3 THE MANAGEMENT OF COUNSELLING SUPERVISION

3.3.1 Supervisors must encourage the supervisee to belong to an association or organisation with a Code of Ethics & Practice and a

Complaints Procedure. This provides additional safeguards for the supervisor, supervisee and client in the event of a complaint.

3.3.2　If, in the course of counselling supervision, it appears that personal counselling may be necessary for the supervisee to be able to continue working effectively, the supervisor should raise this issue with the supervisee.

3.3.3　Supervisors must monitor regularly how their supervisees engage in self-assessment and the self-evaluation of their work.

3.3.4　Supervisors must ensure that their supervisees acknowledge their individual responsibility for ongoing professional development and for participating in further training programmes.

3.3.5　Supervisors must ensure that their supervisees are aware of the distinction between counselling, accountability to management, counselling supervision and training.

3.3.6　Supervisors must ensure with a supervisee who works in an organisation or agency that the lines of accountability and responsibility are clearly defined: supervisee/client; supervisor/supervisee; supervisor/client; organisation/supervisor; organisation/supervisee; organisation/client. There is a distinction between line management supervision and counselling supervision.

3.3.7　Best practice is that the same person should not act as both line manager and counselling supervisor to the same supervisee. However, where the counselling supervisor is also the line manager, the supervisee should have access to independent counselling supervision.

3.3.8　Supervisors who become aware of a conflict between an obligation to a supervisee and an obligation to an employing agency must make explicit to the supervisee the nature of the loyalties and responsibilities involved.

3.3.9　Supervisors who have concerns about a supervisee's work with clients must be clear how they will pursue this if discussion in counselling supervision fails to resolve the situation.

3.3.10　Where disagreements cannot be resolved by discussions between supervisor and supervisee, the supervisor should consult with a fellow professional and, if appropriate, recommend that the supervisee be referred to another supervisor.

3.3.11　Supervisors must discuss with supervisees the need to have arrangements in place to take care of the immediate needs of clients in the event of a sudden and unplanned ending to the counselling relationship. It is good practice for the supervisor to be informed about these arrangements.

References

Alonso, A. (1983) A developmental theory of psychodynamic supervision. *Clinical Supervisor* 1 (3), 23–36.

Alonso, A. (1985) *The Quiet Profession*. New York: Macmillan.

Altucher, N. (1967) Constructive use of the supervisory relationship. *Journal of Counseling Psychology* 14, 165–70.

Arbuckle, D.S. (1963) The learning of counseling: process not product. *Journal of Counseling Psychology* 10, 163–8.

Arbuckle, D.S. (1965) Supervision: learning, not counseling. *Journal of Counseling Psychology* 12, 90–4.

Arundale, J. (1993) *Psychotherapy Supervision: Impact, Practice and Expectations*. Ph.D. thesis, University of London.

American Association for Counseling and Development (1989) *Standards for Counseling Supervisors*. AACD.

Association for Counselor Education and Supervision (1989) *Standards for Counseling Supervisors*. Alexandria, VA: ACES.

Association for Counselor Education and Supervision (1993) *Ethical Guidelines for Counseling Supervisors*. Alexandria, VA: ACES.

Austin, K.M., Moline, M.E. and Williams, G.T. (1990) *Confronting Malpractice: Legal and Ethical Dilemmas in Psychotherapy*. Thousand Oaks, CA: Sage.

Banikiotes, P. (1975) Personal growth and professional training. *Counselor Education and Supervision* 15, 149–51.

Bartell, P.A. and Rubin, L.J. (1990) Dangerous liaisons: sexual intimacies in supervision. *Professional Psychology: Research and Practice* 21(6), 442–50.

Beardsley, M., Riggar, T.F. and Hafer, M. (1984) Rehabilitation supervision: a case for counselor training. *Clinical Supervisor* 2(3), 55–63.

Beauchamp, T.L. and Walters, L. (eds) (1989) *Contemporary Issues in Bioethics* (3rd edn). Belmont, CA: Wadsworth.

Beier, E.B. and Young, D.M. (1980) Supervision in communications analytic therapy. In A.K. Hess (ed.), *Psychotherapy Supervision: Theory, Research and Practice.* New York: Wiley.

Bernal, Y. and Del Rio, V. (1967) Psychiatric ethics. In A.M. Freedman and H.I. Kaplan (eds), *Textbook of Psychiatry.* Baltimore, MA: Williams & Wilkins.

Bernard, J.M. (undated) Clinical supervision: impending issues. Unpublished paper.

Bernard, J.M. (1979) Supervisor training: a discrimination model. *Counselor Education and Supervision* 19, 60–8.

Bernard, J.M. (1981) Inservice training for clinical supervisors, *Professional Psychology* 12, 740–48.

Bernard, J.M. (1987) Ethical and legal considerations for supervisors. In L.D. Borders and G.R. Leddick, *Handbook of Counseling Supervision.* Alexandria, VA: ACES.

Bernard, J.M. (1994a) Ethical and legal dimensions of supervision. In L.D. Borders (ed.), *Supervision: Exploring the Effective Components.* ERIC/CASS Digest Series. University of North Carolina at Greensboro.

Bernard, J.M. (1994b) Multicultural supervision: a reaction to Leong and Wagner, Cook, Priest and Fukuyama. *Counselor Education and Supervision* 34, 159–71.

Bernard, J. and Jara, C.S. (1986) The failure of clinical psychology graduate students to apply understood ethical principles. *Professional Psychology, Research and Practice* 17(4), 313–15.

Bernard, J.M. and Goodyear, R. (1992) *Fundamentals of Clinical Supervision.* Boston: Allyn & Bacon.

Bernstein, B.L. and Lecomte, C. (1978) Counselor self-supervision as a strategy for self-renewal: a model for integrating self-development with accountability. Paper given at pre-convention workshop. Washington, DC: American Personnel and Guidance Association.

Bernstein, B.L., Hofmann, B. and Wade, P. (1986) Counselor self-supervision: beyond traditional approaches to practicum supervision. *Michigan Journal of Counseling and Development* 17(2), 13–17.

Bibring, E. (1937) Report of four centres' conferences: ITC, methods and techniques of control analysis. *International Journal of Psychoanalysis* 18, 369.

Bishop, B. and D'Rozario, P. (1990) A matter of ethics? A comment on Pryor (1989). *Australian Psychologist* 25(2), 215–19.

Blocher, D.H. (1983) Towards a cognitive developmental approach to counseling supervision. *Counseling Psychologist* 11, 27–34.

Borders, L.D. (undated) *Supervision Evaluation*. University of North Carolina at Greensboro (private publication).

Borders, L.D. (1989a) Structured peer group supervision. Paper presented at the annual meeting of the American Association for Counseling and Development, Boston (March, 1989).

Borders, L.D. (1989b) A pragmatic agenda for developmental supervision research. *Counselor Education and Supervision* 29, 16–24.

Borders, L.D. (1994) The good supervisor. In L.D. Borders (ed.), *Supervision: Exploring the Effective Components*. ERIC/CASS Digest Series. University of North Carolina at Greensboro.

Borders, L.D. (1994) (ed.), *Supervision: Exploring the Effective Components*. ERIC/CASS Digest Series. University of North Carolina at Greensboro.

Borders, L.D. and Leddick, G.R. (1987) *Handbook of Counseling Supervision*. Alexandria, VA: ACES.

Bordin, E.S. (1983) A working alliance-based model of supervision. *Counseling Psychologist* 11(1), 35–43.

Boyd J.D. (1978) *Counselor Supervision: Approaches, Preparation, Practices*. Muncie, IN: Accelerated Development Inc.

Bradley, L. (ed.) (1989) *Counselor Supervision: Principles, Process and Practice*. Muncie, IN: Accelerated Development Inc.

British Association for Counselling (1988, rev: 1990) *Code of Ethics and Practice for the Supervision of Counsellors*. Rugby: BAC.

British Association for Counselling (1995) *Code of Ethics and Practice for Supervisors of Counsellors*. Rugby: BAC.

British Association for Counselling (1990) *Information Sheet No. 8: Supervision*. Rugby: BAC.

British Psychological Society (1995) *Regulations and Syllabus for the Diploma in Counselling Psychology*. Leicester: British Psychological Society.

Bromberg, P.M. (1982) The supervisory process and parallel process in psychoanalysis. *Contemporary Psychoanalysis* 18, 92–111.

Brown, D. (1985) The preservice training of supervision of consultants. *Counseling Psychologist* 13(3), 410–25.

Burns, C.I. and Holloway, E.L. (1990) Therapy in supervision: an unresolved issue. *Clinical Supervisor* 7(4), 47–60.

Butterworth, C.A. and Faugier, J. (eds) (1992) *Clinical Supervision and Mentorship in Nursing*. London: Chapman & Hall.

Carifio, M. and Hess, A. (1987) Who is the ideal supervisor? *Professional Psychology* 18(3), 244–50.

Carkhuff, R.R., Kratochvil, D. and Friel, T. (1968) Effects of professional training: communication and discrimination of facilitative conditions. *Journal of Counseling Psychology* 15, 68–74.

Carney, C.G. and Kahn, K.B. (1984) Building competencies for effective cross-cultural counselling: a developmental view. *Counseling Psychologist*, 12(1), 111–19.

Carr, J. (1989) A model of clinical supervision. In *Clinical Supervision: Issues and Techniques* (papers from the public conference, April, 1988). London: Jungian Training Committee.

Carroll, C. (1994) *Building Bridges: A Study of Employee Counsellors in the Private Sector*. M.Sc. thesis, City University, London.

Carroll, M. (1988) Counselling supervision: the British context. *Counselling Psychology Quarterly* 1(4), 387–96.

Carroll, M. (1993) Trainee counsellors' clients. In W. Dryden (ed.), *Questions and Answers on Counselling in Action*. London: Sage.

Carroll, M. (1994a) Counselling supervision: international perspectives. In L.D. Borders (ed.), *Supervision: Exploring the Effective Components*. ERIC/CASS Digest Series. University of North Carolina at Greensboro.

Carroll, M. (1994b) Making ethical decision in organizational counselling. *EAP International*, 1(4), 26–30.

Carroll, M. (1994c) *The Generic Tasks of Supervision: An Analysis of Supervisee Expectations, Supervisor Interviews and Supervisory Audio-taped Sessions*. Ph.D. thesis, University of Surrey, Guildford.

Carroll, M. (1995a) The stresses of supervising counsellors. In W. Dryden (ed.), *The Stresses of Counselling in Action*. London: Sage.

Carroll, M. (1995b) The counsellor in organizations: some reflections. *Employee Counselling Today* 7(1), 23–9.

Carroll, M. (in preparation) *Workplace Counselling: A Systematic Approach to Employee Care*. London: Sage.

Carroll, M. and Walton, M. (eds) (in preparation) *The Handbook of Counselling in Organizations*. London: Sage.

Casement, P. (1985) *On Learning from the Patient*. London: Tavistock.

Casey, J.A., Bloom, J.W. and Moan, E.R. (1994) Use of technology in counselor supervision. In L.D. Borders (ed.), *Supervision: Exploring the Effective Components*. ERIC/CASS Digest Series. University of North Carolina at Greensboro.

Cashwell, C.S. (1994) Interpersonal process recall. In L.D. Borders (ed.), *Supervision: Exploring the Effective Components*. ERIC/CASS Digest Series. University of North Carolina at Greensboro.

Cherniss, C. and Egnatios, E. (1977) Styles of clinical supervision in community mental health programs. *Journal of Consulting and Clinical Psychology* 45, 1195–6.

Chrzanowski, G. (1984) Can psychoanalysis be taught? In L. Caligor, P.M. Bromberg and J.D. Meltzer (eds), *Clinical Perspectives on the Supervision of Psychoanalysis and Psychotherapy*. New York: Plenum Press.

Clarkson, P. and Gilbert, M. (1991) Training counsellor trainers and supervisors. In W. Dryden and B. Thorne (eds), *Training and Supervision for Counselling in Action*. London: Sage.

Cloud, J. (1986) Supervision for the counselor in private practice. *Michigan Journal of Counseling and Development* 17(2), 39–42.

Cohen, B.Z. (1987) The ethics of social work supervision revisited. *Social Work* 32, 194–6.

Cohen L. (1980) The new supervisee views supervision. In A. Hess (ed.), *Psychotherapy Supervision: Theory, Research and Practice*. New York: Wiley.

Compton, J.R. (1987) The supervisory learning contract. In B.K. Estadt, J.R. Compton and M.C. Blancette (eds), *The Art of Clinical Supervision*. New Jersey: Paulist Press.

Connor, M. (1994) *Training the Counsellor*. London: Routledge.

Cook, D.A. (1994) Racial identity in supervision. *Counselor Education and Supervision* **34**, 132–9.

Cook, D.A. and Helms, J.E. (1988) Visible racial/ethnic group supervisees' satisfaction with cross-cultural supervision as predicted by relationship characteristics. *Journal of Counseling Psychology* 35(3), 268–74.

Cooper, S.E. (1984) A spiral-ecological approach to supervision. *Clinical Supervisor* 2(3), 79–87.

Corey, G., Corey, M.S. and Callahan, P. (1993) *Issues and Ethics in the Helping Professions* (4th edn). Pacific Grove: Brooks/Cole.

Cormier, S. and Bernard, J. (1982) Ethical and legal responsibilities of clinical supervisors. *Personnel and Guidance Journal* **60**, 486–91.

Couch, A. (1992) The competent counsellor: An open-ended competency framework designed to enhance counsellor training. Paper delivered to the BPS Counselling Psychology Conference, Birmingham, May 1992.

Crandall, R. and Allen, R.D. (1982) The organizational context of helping relationships. In T.A. Wills, (ed.), *Basic Processes in Helping Relationships*. London: Academic Press.

Crowley, R.M. (1984) Being and doing in continuous consultation for psychoanalytic education. In L. Caligor, P.M. Bromberg and J.M. Meltzer (eds), *Clinical Perspectives on the Supervision of Psychoanalysis and Psychotherapy*. New York: Plenum Press.

Davis, K.I. and Arvey, H.H. (1978) Dual supervision: a model for counseling and supervision. *Counselor Education and Supervision* (June), 293–9.

Dawson, J.B. (1926) The case supervisor in a family agency. *Family* 6, 293–5.

DeBell, D.E. (1963) A critical digest of the literature on psychoanalytic supervision. *Journal of the American Psychoanalysis Association* 11(3), 546–75.

Delaney, D.J. (1972) A behavioural model for the practicum supervision of counselor candidates. *Counselor Education and Supervision* 21, 46–50.

Disney, M.J. and Stephens, A.M. (1994) *Legal Issues in Clinical Supervision*. Alexandria, VA: American Counseling Association.

Dixon, D.N. and Clairborn, C.D. (1987) A social influence approach to counselor supervision. In J.E. Maddux, C.D. Stoltenberg and R. Rosenwein (eds), *Social Processes in Clinical and Counseling Psychology*. New York: Springer.

Doehrman, M.J. (1976) Parallel process in supervision and psychotherapy. *Bulletin of the Menninger Clinic* 40(1), 1–104.

Dryden, W. (ed.) (1986) *Therapists' Dilemmas*. London: Harper & Row.

Dryden, W. and Thorne, B. (1991) (eds) *Training and Supervision for Counselling in Action*. London: Sage.

Eberlein, L. (1987) Introducing ethics to beginning psychologists: a problem-solving approach. *Professional Psychology: Research and Practice* 18, 353–9.

Edelstein, B.A. and Berler, E.S. (1987) *Evaluation and Accountability in Clinical Training*. New York: Plenum Press.

Edelstein, B.A. and Brasted, W.S. (1983) Clinical training. In M. Hersey, Kazdin and A.S. Dellach (eds), *The Clinical Psychology Handbook*. New York: Plenum Press.

Efstation, J.F., Patton, M.J. and Kardash, C.M. (1990) Measuring the working alliance in counselor supervision. *Journal of Counseling Psychology* 37(3), 322–9.

Egan, G. (1993) The shadow side. *Management Today*, September, 33–8.

Ekstein, R. (1964) Supervision of psychotherapy: Is it teaching? Is it administration? Or is it therapy? *Psychotherapy: Theory, Research and Practice* 1, 137–8.

Ekstein, R. and Wallerstein, R.S. (1976) *The Teaching and Learning of Psychotherapy*. New York: International.

Ellis, M.V. and Dell, D.M. (1986) Dimensionality of supervisor roles: supervisors' perceptions of supervision. *Journal of Counseling Psychology* 33(3), 282–91.

Ellis, M.V. and Douce, L.A. (1991) Group supervision of novice clinical supervisors: eight recurring issues. *Journal of Counseling and Development* 7(2), 520–25.

Estadt, J.R. (1987) The core process of supervision. In B.K. Estadt, J.R. Compton and M.C. Blancette (eds), *The Art of Clinical Supervision*. Rahway, NJ: Paulist Press.

Falvey, J. (1987) *Handbook of Administrative Supervision*. Alexandria, VA: ACES.

Faugier, J. (undated) *Clinical Supervision: A Position Paper*. Manchester: University of Manchester.

Feltham, C. and Dryden, W. (1994) *Developing Counsellor Supervision*. London: Sage.

Fine, M. and Ulrich, L. (1988) Integrating psychology and philosophy in teaching a graduate course in ethics. *Professional Psychology: Research and Practice* 19, 542–6.

Fizdale, R. (1958) Peer group supervision. *Social Casework* 39 (October), 443.

Fleming, J. and Benedek, T. (1966) *Psychoanalytic Supervision*. New York: Grune & Stratton.

Frankham, H. (1987) *Aspects of Supervision: Counsellor Satisfaction, Utility and Defensiveness and the Tasks of Supervision*. M.Sc. thesis, Roehampton Institute, London.

Freeman, R. (1985) The importance of feedback in clinical supervision: implications for direct practice. *Clinical Supervisor* 3(1), 5–26.

Friedlander, M.L. and Ward, L.G. (1984) Development and validation of the supervisory styles inventory. *Journal of Counseling Psychology* 31, 541–57.

Friedlander, M.L., Siegel, S. and Brenock, K. (1989) Parallel processes in counseling and supervision: a case study. *Journal of Counseling Psychology* 36, 149–57.

Fukuyama, M.A. (1994) Critical incidents in multicultural counseling supervision: phenomenological approach to supervision research. *Counselor Education and Supervision* 134, 142–51.

Gallessich, J.M. (1982) *The Profession and Practice of Consultation*. San Francisco: Jossey-Bass.

Gallessich, J.M. (1985) Towards a meta-theory of consultation. *Counseling Psychologist* 13(3), 335–54.

Gardiner, D. (1989) *The Anatomy of Supervision*. Milton Keynes: Open University Press.

Gardner, L.H. (1980) Racial, ethnic, and social class considerations in psychotherapy supervision. In A.K. Hess (ed.), *Psychotherapy Supervision: Theory, Research and Practice*. New York: Wiley.

Gawthrop, J.C. and M.R. Uhlemann (1992) Effects of the problem-solving approach to ethics training. *Professional Psychology: Research and Practice* 23(1), 38–42.

Gediman, H.K. and Wolkenfeld, F. (1980) The parallelism phenomenon in psychoanalysis and supervision: its reconsideration as a triadic system. *Psychoanalysis Quarterly* 49, 234–55.

Gendel, M.H. and Reiser, D.G. (1981) Institutional countertransference. *American Journal of Psychiatry* 138, 508–11.

Getzel, G.S. and Salmon, P. (1985) Group supervision: an organizational approach. *Clinical Supervisor* 3(1), 27–43.

Gilligan, C. (1982) *In a Different Voice*. Cambridge, MA: Harvard University Press.

Goldberg, C. (1981) The peer supervision group – an examination of its purpose and process. *Group* 5, 27–40.

Goldberg, D.A. (1985) Process notes, audio and videotapes: modes of presentation in psychotherapy training. *Clinical Supervisor* 3(3), 3–13.

Grann, I., Hendricks, B., Hoop, L., Jackson, G. and Traunstein, D. (1986) Competency-based evaluation: a second round. *Clinical Supervisor* 3, 81–91.

Gray, A. and Fiscalini, J. (1987) Parallel process as transference–countertransference interaction. *Psychoanalytic Psychology* 4(2), 131–44.

Gurk, M.D. and Wilas, E.A. (1979) Generic models of counseling supervision: counseling/instruction dichotomy and consultation metamodel. *Personnel and Guidance Journal* 57, 402–7.

Handelsman, M. (1986) Ethics training at the Masters level: a national survey. *Professional Psychology: Research and Practice* 17, 24–6.

Harman, R. and Tarleton, K. (1983) Gestalt therapy supervision. *Gestalt Journal* 6(1), 29–37.

Hart, G.M. (1982) *The Process of Clinical Supervision*. Baltimore: University Park Press.

Hawkins, P. (1985) Humanistic psychotherapy supervision: A conceptual framework. *Self and Society* 13(2), 69–76.

Hawkins, P. and Shohet, R. (1989) *Supervision in the Helping Professions*. Milton Keynes: Open University Press.

Hawkins, P. and Shohet, R. (1991) Approaches to the supervision of counsellors. In W. Dryden and B. Thorne (eds), *Training and Supervision for Counselling in Action*. London: Sage.

Hayman, P.M. and Covert, J.A. (1986) Ethical dilemmas in college counselling centers. *Journal of Counseling and Development* 64, 298–302.

Hays, R.L. (1989) Group supervision. In L.J. Bradley (ed.), *Counselor Supervision: Principles, Process, Practice* (2nd edn). Muncie, IN.: Accelerated Development Inc.

Heppner, P.P. and Roehlke, H.J. (1984) Differences among supervisees at different levels of training: implications for a developmental model of supervision. *Journal of Counseling Psychology* 31, 76–90.

Heron, J. (1977) *Dimensions of Facilitator Style*. University of Guildford, Surrey: Human Potential Research Project.

Hess, A.K. (1980) Training models and the nature of psychotherapy supervisior. In A.K.Hess (ed.), *Psychotherapy Supervision: Theory Research and Practice*. New York: Wiley.

Hess, A.K. (1986) Growth in supervision: stages of supervisor and supervisee .evelopment. *Clinical Supervisor* 4(2), 51–67.

Hess, A.K. (1987a) Psychotherapy supervision: stages, Buber, and a theory of relationships. *Professional Psychology* 18(3), 251–9.

Hess, A.K. (1987b) Advances in psychotherapy supervision: introduction. *Professional Psychology* 18(3), 187–8.

Hess, A.K. and Hess, K.A. (1983) Psychotherapy supervision: a survey of internship training practices. *Professional Psychology: Research and Practice* 18, 251–9.

Hilton, D.B., Russell, R.K. and Salmi, S.W. (in press) The effects of supervisor's race and level of support on perceptions of supervision. *Journal of Counseling and Development.*

Holloway, E.L. (1984) Outcome evaluation in supervision research. *Journal of Counseling Psychology* 12(4), 167–74.

Holloway, E.L. (1987) Developmental models of supervision: is it development? *Professional Psychology* 18(3), 189–208.

Holloway, E. (1992) Supervision: a way of teaching and learning. In S. Brown and R. Lent (eds), *The Handbook of Counseling Psychology* (2nd edn). New York: Wiley.

Holloway, E.L. (1995) *Clinical Supervision: A Systems Approach.* California: Sage.

Holloway, E.L. and Acker, M. (1989) *The EPICS (Engagement and Power in Clinical Supervision) Model.* (University of Oregon; private publication).

Holloway, E.L. and Johnson, R. (1985) Group supervision: widely practised but poorly understood. *Counselor Education and Supervision* 24, 332–40.

Hosford, R.E. and Barmann, B. (1983) A social learning approach to counselor supervision. *Counseling Psychologist* 11(1), 51–8.

Houston, G. (1985) Group supervision of groupwork. *Self and Society* 13(2), 64–8.

Houston, G. (1990) *Supervision and Counselling.* London: Rochester Foundation.

Inskipp, F. and Proctor, B. (1988) *Skills for Supervising and Being Supervised* (private publication).

Inskipp, F. and Proctor, B. (1993) *Making the Most of Supervision. Part 1.* Twickenham, Middlesex: Cascade Publications.

Inskipp, F. and Proctor, B. (forthcoming) *Making the Most of Supervision. Part 2: Becoming a Supervisor.* Twickenham, Middlesex: Cascade Publications.

Jenkins, P. (1992) Counselling and the law. *Counselling* 3(2), 165–7.

Jennison, M. (1982) Staff supervision in a social service department. *Contact* 4, 15–18.

Johnston, J.A. and Gysbers, N.C. (1967) Essential characteristics of a supervisory relationship in counseling practicum. *Counselor Education and Supervision* 6, 335–40.

Kaberry, S.E. (1995) *Abuse in Supervision.* M.Ed. thesis, University of Birmingham.

Kadushin, A. (1985) *Supervision in Social Work* (2nd edn). New York: Columbia University Press.

Kagan, N. (1980) Influencing human interaction – eighteen years with IPR. In A.K. Hess (ed.), *Psychotherapy Supervision: Theory, Research, and Practice.* New York: Wiley.

Karasu, T. (1981) Ethical aspects of psychotherapy. In S. Bloch and P. Chodoff (eds), *Psychiatric Ethics.* Oxford: Oxford University Press, pp. 89–116.

Kell, B.L. and Mueller, W.J. (1966) *Impact and Change: A Study of Counseling Relationships.* New York: Appleton-Century-Crofts.

Kevlin, F. (1988) *Peervision: A Comparison of Hierarchical Supervision of Counsellors with Consultation amongst Peers.* M.Sc. thesis, University of Surrey /Roehampton Institute, London.

Kinder, S. (1981) *Psychotherapy Supervision: Some Perceived Influences on Supervision Experiences.* Ph.D thesis, University of Massachusetts.

Kitchener, K.S. (1984) Intuition, critical evaluation and ethical principles: the foundation for ethical decisions in counseling psychology. *Counseling Psychologist* 12(3), 43–55.

Kitchener, K.S. (1986) Teaching applied ethics in counselor education: an integration of psychological processes and philosophical analysis. *Journal of Counseling and Development* 64, 298–302.

Kitchener, K.S. (1991) The foundations of ethical practice. *Journal of Mental Health Counseling* 13(2), 236–46.

Kolb, D.A. (1984) *Experiential Learning.* Englewood Cliffs, NJ: Prentice-Hall.

Kurpius, D.J. and Baker, R.D. (1977) The supervision process: analysis and synthesis. In D.J. Kurpius, R.D. Baker, and I.D. Thomas (eds), *Supervision of Applied Training: A Comparative Review.* Westport, CT: Greenwood.

Lambert, M.J. (1980) Research and the supervisory process. In A.K. Hess (ed.), *Psychotherapy Supervision: Theory, Research and Practice.* New York: Wiley, pp. 423–50.

Lambert, M. and Arnold, R. (1987) Research and the supervisory process. *Professional Psychology* 18(3), 217–24.

Lane, D. (1990) Counselling psychology in organizations. *Psychologist* 12, 540–44.

Langs, R. (1980) Supervision in the bipersonal field. In A.K. Hess (ed.), *Psychotherapy Supervision: Theory, Research and Practice.* New York: Wiley.

Lanning, W. (1986) Development of the supervisory rating form. *Counselor Education and Supervision* 25, 191–6.

Leddick, G.R. and Bernard, J.M. (1980) The history of supervision: a critical review. *Counselor Education and Supervision* 20, 186–96.

Leong, F.T.L. and Wagner, N.S. (1994) Supervision: What do we know? What do we need to know? *Counselor Education and Supervision* 34, 117–31.

Lesser, R.M. (1984) Supervision: illusions, anxieties and questions. In L. Caligor, P.M. Bromberg and J.D. Meltzer (eds), *Clinical Perspectives on the Supervision of Psychoanalysis and Psychotherapy.* New York: Plenum Press.

Levy, C. (1983) Evaluation of students in clinical psychology programs: a program evaluation perspective. *Professional Psychology: Research and Practice* 14, 497–503.

Lewin, B.D. (1972) Foreword. In R. Ekstein and R.S. Wallerstein, *The Teaching and Learning of Psychotherapy.* New York: International Universities Press.

Liddle, H.A. (1988) Systemic supervision: conceptual overlays and pragmatic guidelines. In H.A. Liddle, D.C. Breunlin and R.C. Schwartz (eds), *Handbook of a Family Therapy Training and Supervision.* New York: Guilford.

Linehan, M.M. (1980) Supervision of behaviour therapy. In A. Hess (ed.), *Psychotherapy Supervision: Theory, Research and Practice.* New York: Wiley.

Littrell, J.M., Lee-Borden, N.A. and Lorenz, J.R.A. (1979) Developmental framework for counseling supervision. *Counselor Education and Supervision* 19, 129–36.

Loganbill, C., Hardy, E. and Delworth, U. (1982) Supervision: a conceptual model. *Counseling Psychologist* 10, 3–46.

McCartney, J.B. and O'Mahoney, D.S. (1977) The legal responsibilities of psychologists. *Bulletin of the British Psychological Society* 30, 378–9.

McKay, A. (1986) Non-managerial supervision. In M. Marken and M. Payne (eds), *Enabling and Ensuring: Supervision in Practice.* Leicester: National Youth Bureau.

McNeil, B.W. and Worthen, V. (1989) The parallel process in psychotherapy supervision. *Professional Psychology: Research and Practice* 20, 329–33.

McRoy, R.G., Freeman, E.M., Logan, S.L., Blackmon, B. (1986) Cross-cultural field supervision: implications for social work educating. *Journal of Social Work Education* 22, 50–6.

McRoy, R.G., Freeman, E.M. and Logan, S. (1986) Strategies for teaching students about termination. *Clinical Supervisor* 4(4), 45–56.

Markowitz, M. (1958) A supervisor supervised: a subjective elective experience. *American Journal of Psychotherapy* 12, 488–92.

Mattison, J. (1975) *The Reflective Process in Casework Supervision.* London: Tavistock.

Megranahan, M. (1989) *Counselling: A Practical Guide for Employers.* London: Institute of Personnel Management.

Mearns, D. (1993a) Against indemnity insurance. In W. Dryden (ed.), *Questions and Answers on Counselling in Action.* London: Sage.

Mearns, D. (1993b) The ending phase of counselling. In W. Dryden (ed.), *Questions and Answers on Counselling in Action.* London: Sage.

Meyer, R.J., Jr (1978) Using self-supervision to maintain counselling skills: a review. *Personnel and Guidance Journal* 57, 95–8.

Mintz, E. (1983) Gestalt approaches to supervision. *Gestalt Journal* 6(1), 17–27.

Moldawsky, S. (1980) Psychoanalytic psychotherapy supervision. In A.K. Hess (ed.), *Psychotherapy Supervision: Theory, Research and Practice.* New York: Wiley.

Mueller, W.J. and Kell, B.L. (1972) *Coping with Conflict: Supervising Counselors and Psychotherapists.* New York: Appleton-Century-Crofts.

Nelson, M.L. and Holloway, E.L. (1990) Relation of gender to power and involvement in supervision. *Journal of Counseling Psychology* 37, 473–81.

Nobler, H.A. (1980) A peer group for the therapists. *International Journal of Group Psychotherapy* 30, 51–61.

Nooder, T.E. (1978) *Organization and Management Problems of National Health Hospitals.* London: DHSS/HMSO.

Orton, J.W. (1965) Areas of focus in supervising counseling practicum students in groups. *Personnel and Guidance Journal* 14, 167–70.

Paisley, P.O. (1994) Gender issues in supervision. In L.D. Borders (ed.), *Supervision: Exploring the Effective Components.* ERIC/CASS Digest: University of North Carolina.

Page, S. and Wosket, V. (1994) *Supervising the Counsellor: A Cyclical Model.* London: Routledge.

Parker, M. (1990) *Supervision Constructs and Supervisory Style as Related to Theoretical Orientation.* M.Sc. thesis, University of Surrey, Guildford.

Patterson, C.H. (1982) A client-centred approach to supervision. *Counseling Psychologist* 11, 21–6.

Peterson, F.K. (1991) *Race and Ethnicity*. New York: Haworth.

Ponterotto, J.G. and Zander, T.A. (1984) A multimodal approach to counselor supervision. *Counselor Education and Supervision* 24, 40–50.

Pope, R.S. and Vasquez, M.J.T. (1991) *Ethics in Psychotherapy and Counselling: A Practical Guide for Psychologists*. San Francisco: Jossey-Bass.

Prichard. J. (ed.) (1995) *Good Practice in Supervision*. London: Jessica Kingsley.

Priest, R. (1994) Minority supervisor and majority supervisee: another perspective of clinical reality. *Counselor Education and Supervision* 34, 152–8.

Proctor, B. (1986) Supervision: a co-operative exercise in accountability. In M. Marken and M. Payne (eds), *Enabling and Ensuring: Supervision in Practice*. Leicester: National Youth Bureau.

Pruitt, D., McColgan, E.B., Pugh, R.L. and Kiser, L.J. (1986) Approaches to psychotherapy supervision. *Journal of Psychiatric Education* 10(2), 129–47.

Pryor, R.G.L. (1989) Conflicting responsibilities: a case study of an ethical dilemma for psychologists working in organizations. *Australian Psychologist* 24, 293–305.

Randall, R., Southgate, J. and Tomlinson, F. (1980) *Cooperative and Community Group Dynamics*. Barefoot Books.

Reddy, M. (ed.) (1993) *EAPs and Counselling Provision in UK Organizations 1993*. Milton Keynes: ICAS.

Reisling, G.N. and Daniels, M.H. (1983) A study of Hogan's model of counselor development and supervision. *Journal of Counseling Psychology* 30, 235–44.

Remley, T.P., Benshoff, J.M. and Mowbray, C.A. (1987) A proposed model for peer supervision. *Counselor Education and Supervision* 27, 53–60.

Rest, J. (1984) Research on moral development: implications for training counseling psychologists. *Counseling Psychologist* 12(3), 19–29.

Rice, L.N. (1980) A client-centred approach to the supervision of psychotherapy. In A.K. Hess (ed.), *Psychotherapy Supervision: Theory, Research and Practice*. New York: Wiley.

Rioch, M.J. (1980) The dilemma of supervision in dynamic psychotherapy. In A.K. Hess (ed.), *Psychotherapy Supervision: Theory, Research and Practice*. New York: Wiley.

Robiner, W.N. and Schofield, W. (1990) References on supervision in clinical and counseling psychology. *Professional Psychology: Research and Practice* 21(4), 297–312.

Rogers, C. (1983) *Freedom to Learn for the 80s.* Columbus, OH: Charles E. Merrill.

Rosenblatt, A. and Mayer, J.E. (1975) Objectionable supervisor styles: students' views. *Social Work* 20, 184–8.

Russell, R.K., Crimmings, A.M. and Lent, R.W. (1984) Counselor training and supervision: theory and research. In S.D. Brown and R.W. Lent (eds), *Handbook of Counseling Psychology.* New York: Wiley.

Ryan, T.A. (ed.) (1978) *Systems Models for Counselor Supervision.* Washington, DC: American Personnel and Guidance Association.

Sansbury, D.L. (1982) Developmental supervision from a skills perspective. *Counseling Psychologist* 10(1), 53–7.

Schlessinger, M. (1966) Supervision of psychotherapy: a critical review of the literature. *Archives of General Psychiatry* 15, 129–34.

Schmidt, J.P. (1979) Psychotherapy supervision: a cognitive behavioural model. *Professional Psychology* 10, 278–84.

Searles, H. (1955) The informational value of the supervisor's emotional experience. *Psychiatry* 18, 135–46.

Searles, H. (1962) Problems of psychoanalytic supervision. In J. Masserman (ed.), *Science and Psychoanalysis*, Vol. 5. New York: Grune & Stratton.

Sharpe, M. (ed.) (1995) *The Third Eye: Supervision of Analytic Groups.* London: Routledge.

Shulman, L. (1982) *Skills of Supervision and Staff Management.* Itasco II: Peacock Publications.

Simms, J. (1991) *Dimensions and Differences of Supervision in a Psychiatric Setting: Supervisees' Perceptions.* M.Sc. thesis, University of Surrey, Guildford.

Skovholt, T.M. and Ronnestad, M. (1992) *The Evolving Professional Self: Stages and Themes in Therapist and Counselor Development.* New York: Wiley.

Slovenko, R. (1980) Legal issues in psychotherapy supervision. In A.K. Hess (ed.), *Psychotherapy Supervision: Theory, Research and Practice.* New York: Wiley.

Stoltenberg, C.D. and Delworth, U. (1987) *Supervision Counselors and Therapists.* London: Jossey-Bass.

Strauss, A.L. and Corbin, J. (1990) *Basics of Qualitative Research: Grounded Theory Procedures and Techniques.* Newbury Park, CA: Sage.

Tash, J. (1984) *Supervision in Youth Work* (2nd edn). London: YMCA.

Tennyson, W.W. and Strom S.M. (1986) Beyond professional standards: developing responsibleness. *Journal of Counseling and Development* 64, 298–302.

Thompson, J. (1991) *Issues of Race and Culture in Counseling Supervision Training Courses.* M.Sc. thesis, Polytechnic of East London.

Tousley, M.M. and Kobberger, K. (1984) Supervision in psychotherapy: a systems viewpoint. *International Journal of Psychiatry in Medicine* 14, 133–52.

Traux, C.B. and Carkhuff, R. (1967) *Towards Effective Counseling and Psychotherapy: Theory and Practice.* Chicago: Aldine.

Tucker, B.Z., Hart, G. and Liddle, H.A. (1976) Supervision in family therapy: a developmental perspective. *Journal of Marriage and Family Counseling* July, 269–76.

Vander Kolk, C.J. (1974) The relationship of personality, values and race to anticipation of the supervisory relationship. *Rehabilitation Counseling Bulletin* 18(1), 41–6.

Vasquez, M.J.T. and McKinley, D.L. (1982) Supervision, a conceptual model: reactions and an extension. *Counseling Psychologist* 10(1) 59–63.

Verity, M.L. (1991) *Supervision: Perceptions of Functions and the Structure of Interaction.* M.Sc. thesis, University of Surrey, Guildford.

Villas-Boas Bowen, M. (1986) Personality differences and person-centred supervision. *Person-Centred Review* 1(3), 291–309.

Virgo, L. (1982) A model of individual supervision in a group setting. *Contact* 4, 27–30.

Waite, J. (1992) *An Investigation of the Experience of Supervision in the Context of Counselling at Work.* M.Sc. thesis, University of Bristol.

Wall, J.C. (1994) Teaching termination to trainees through parallel processes in supervision. *Clinical Supervisor* 12(2), 27–37.

Ward, D.E. (1989) Termination in individual counseling: concepts and strategies. In W. Dryden (ed.), *Key Issues for Counselling in Action.* London: Sage.

Wessler, R.L. and Ellis, A. (1980) Supervision in rational-emotive therapy. In A.K. Hess (ed.), *Psychotherapy Supervision: Theory, Research and Practice.* New York: Wiley.

Williams, A. (1987) Parallel process in a course on counseling supervison. *Counselor Education and Supervison* 26, 245–54.

Wolberg, L. (1967) *The Techniques of Psychotherapy* (2nd edn). New York: Grune & Stratton.

Worthington, E.L. (1984) Empirical investigation of supervision of counselors as they gain experience. *Journal of Counseling Psychology* 31, 63–75.

Worthington, E.L. (1987) Changes in supervision as counselors and supervisors gain experience: a review. *Professional Psychology* 18(3), 189–209.

Yager, G.G. and Park, W.D. (1986) Counselor self-supervision. *Journal of Counseling and Human Service Professions* 1, 6–17.

Yalom, I. (1975) *The Theory and Practice of Group Psychotherapy* (2nd edn). New York: Basic Books.

Yogev, S. (1982) An eclectic model of supervision: a developmental sequence for beginning psychotherapy students. *Professional Psychology* 13, 236–43.

Zangwill, O. (1980) *Behaviour Modification*. London: HMSO.

Zinkin, L. (1989) The impossible profession. In *Clinical Supervision: Issues and Techniques* (papers from the public conference, April, 1988). London: Jungian Training Committee.

Name index

Subject index